D1607511

JORDAN PEELE'S *GET OUT*

NEW SUNS:

RACE, GENDER, AND SEXUALITY IN THE SPECULATIVE

Susana M. Morris and Kinitra D. Brooks, Series Editors

JORDAN PEELE'S *GET OUT*

Political Horror

Edited by Dawn Keetley

THE OHIO STATE UNIVERSITY PRESS
COLUMBUS

Library of Congress Cataloging-in-Publication Data
Names: Keetley, Dawn, 1965– editor.
Title: Jordan Peele's Get out : political horror / edited by Dawn Keetley.
Other titles: Get out | New suns: race, gender, and sexuality in the speculative.
Description: Columbus : The Ohio State University Press, [2020] | Series: New suns: race, gender, and sexuality in the speculative | Includes bibliographical references and index. | Summary: "Essays explore Get Out's cultural roots, including Shakespeare's Othello, the female gothic, Ira Levin's Rosemary's Baby, The Stepford Wives, and the zombie, rural, suburban, and body-swap subgenres of the modern horror film. Essays make connections with Nat Turner, W. E. B. Du Bois, and James Baldwin"—Provided by publisher.
Identifiers: LCCN 2019045485 | ISBN 9780814214275 (cloth) | ISBN 0814214274 (cloth) | ISBN 9780814277812 (ebook) | ISBN 0814277810 (ebook)
Subjects: LCSH: Peele, Jordan, 1979– —Criticism and interpretation. | Get out (Motion picture : 2017) | Horror films—History and criticism. | Racism in motion pictures. | United States—Race relations—21st century.
Classification: LCC PN1997.2.G46 J67 2020 | DDC 791.43/72—dc23
LC record available at https://lccn.loc.gov/2019045485

Cover design by Black Kirby
Text design by Juliet Williams
Type set in Adobe Palatino

CONTENTS

INTRODUCTION

GET OUT

Political Horror

DAWN KEETLEY

RELEASED ON February 24, 2017, Jordan Peele's *Get Out*, which he wrote and directed, was by any standards a game-changing film. It has been acclaimed by critics, accruing almost unanimously positive reviews—a virtually unheard of feat for a horror film. (It has 98% on Rotten Tomatoes, with 345 positive and only six negative reviews.)[1] Peele's film was not only a success with critics but also with audiences. Produced on a mere $4.5 million budget, *Get Out* has grossed over $255 million worldwide. It was nominated for four Academy Awards (again, unusual for a horror film)—Best Picture, Best Director, Best Actor (Daniel Kaluuya), and Best Original Screenplay. Peele won the award for best Original Screenplay, becoming the first African American writer to win in this category.[2]

Get Out centers on an African American man, Chris Washington, who takes a trip to upstate New York to visit the wealthy family of his white girlfriend, Rose Armitage. The off-putting family visit immerses Chris in a world of microaggressions that get progressively more unnerving, even sinister, culminating in the terrifying moment when he realizes he has been

1. "Get Out," Rotten Tomatoes, June 15, 2019, https://www.rottentomatoes.com/m/get_out.

2. "Get Out," Box Office Mojo, June 15, 2019, https://www.boxofficemojo.com/movies/?id=blumhouse2.htm.

seduced into a deadly trap. Knocked unconscious, Chris wakes up in the family's basement strapped to a chair and watching a video that tells him he will be undergoing an operation, the Coagula procedure, that will transplant a white man's brain into his head, divesting him of almost all consciousness and rendering him a mere passenger in his own body. Both a horror film about race and a parable about contemporary racial relations told through horror tropes, *Get Out* has been at the center of a storm of controversy over genre. It was infamously nominated as Best Picture in the Musical or Comedy category at the Golden Globe Awards in 2017, a designation that sat well with no one, including Peele himself, who publicly entered the fray by tweeting somewhat tongue-in-cheek that *Get Out* was actually a documentary.[3] *Get Out* has also—and equally controversially—been dubbed an exemplar of "elevated horror,"[4] a term at which horror fans tend to take umbrage since it presumes that any horror film with artistic and cultural merit must have a qualifier—that it can't be simply *horror.*

Get Out in the Political Horror Tradition

While virtually every interview Peele has given positions *Get Out* as a "horror film,"[5] he has self-consciously chosen to designate it a "social thriller"—a film, as Peele describes it, in which the "monster" is society itself. As Peele explains the genesis of this term, he was trying to figure out how to categorize *Get Out* and felt that neither "horror" nor "psychological thriller" captured exactly what he was doing, so he thought, "social thriller," because the "bad guy is society." Peele continued, "I coined the term *social thriller,* but I definitely didn't invent it."[6] Peele has elaborated to *Business Insider* about the central tenet of the "social thriller," which certainly defines the particular brand of horror in *Get Out*: "The best and scariest monsters in the world are

---

3. Jordan Peele, @JordanPeele, Twitter, November 15, 2017, https://twitter.com/jordanpeele/status/930796561302540288?lang=en.

4. John Krasinski dubbed *Get Out* an example of "elevated horror" as he was talking about his own *The Quiet Place* (2018). See Olsen, "How John Krasinski." See also Knight, "There's No Such Thing," for a powerful refutation of the term "elevated horror."

5. For instance, as he describes writing the screenplay for *Get Out* and then making the decision to direct it himself, Peele says, "I have seen so few horror movies where a black person has been given the director's chair that I realized, *Why not me? I know this thing.*" Yuan and Harris, "First Great Movie."

6. Yuan and Harris, "First Great Movie." On Peele's comments on the "social thriller," see also Harris, "Giant Leap," and Weinstein, "'Society.'" There is now an entire Wikipedia entry on the "Social Thriller." See Wikipedia Contributors, "Social Thriller."

human beings and what we are capable of especially when we get together. I've been working on these premises about these different social demons, these innately human monsters that are woven into the fabric of how we think and how we interact, and each one of my movies is going to be about a different one of these social demons."[7] For Peele, then, the distinctive terrain of the "social thriller" is that its monster is intractably human, the "demon" inextricably part of the very real fabric of society. Debate over the exact relation between a "social thriller" and a horror film is likely to continue, as Peele intends to direct four more social thrillers; indeed, his second feature, *Us,* released in March 2019, has been dubbed both social thriller and also "more unabashedly a horror film" than *Get Out.*[8]

Acknowledging that the social thriller has a long tradition, Peele curated a series of films for the Brooklyn Academy of Music called "The Art of the Social Thriller" to coincide with the opening of *Get Out,* and most, not surprisingly, were recognizably horror films—*Rosemary's Baby* (1968), *Night of the Living Dead* (1968), *The Shining* (1980), *Misery* (1990), *The People under the Stairs* (1991), *Silence of the Lambs* (1991), *Candyman* (1992), *Scream* (1996), and *Funny Games* (1997)—along with a few nonhorror films that amplify the "social" part of "social thriller"—*Rear Window* (1954), *Guess Who's Coming to Dinner* (1967), and *The 'Burbs* (1989).[9] Peele's insistence that the monster of the "social thriller" is unambiguously human does stand at odds, though, with some of the prevailing definitions of horror. Noël Carroll, for instance, has posited that "art-horror" is distinguished as a genre by its explicitly nonhuman and "impure" monster—"categorically interstitial, categorically contradictory, incomplete or formless" and "not classifiable according to our standing categories." Carroll has rather notoriously claimed that films with human "monsters" (including *Psycho*) are not horror.[10]

As useful as Carroll's definition is, however, it does not account for what has been the longstanding tradition of the political horror film, which is indeed driven by very human monsters. The unjustly neglected *Thirteen Women* (George Archainbaud, 1932) might be said to originate this tradition in the US: it's a proto-slasher in which an Indian-white "half-breed" (Myrna Loy) takes murderous revenge on the white sorority sisters who ostracized her for her race.[11] The tradition notably includes (along with those Peele screened in his "social thriller" series) *The Last House on the Left* (1972), *The*

7. Guerrasio, "Jordan Peele."
8. Collins, "Jordan Peele's *Us.*"
9. "Jordan Peele."
10. Carroll, *Philosophy,* 32–33, 38.
11. See Keetley and Hofmann, "*Thirteen Women.*"

Crazies (1973), *The Texas Chain Saw Massacre* (1974), *Society* (1989), *American Psycho* (2000), *Hostel* and *Hostel: Part II* (2005, 2007), *Saw VI* (2009), the *Purge* franchise (2013–18), and *Don't Breathe* (2016). *Get Out*, however, has put social and political critique, and specifically racial critique, front-and-center in a way that is new—and in a way that has given a new urgency to the subgenre of the political horror film in the early twenty-first century.

Peele has been explicit about the critical influence of three films in particular on the political trajectory of *Get Out*—*Night of the Living Dead, Rosemary's Baby,* and *The Stepford Wives* (1975). Each of these films offers a precedent for Peele's project of shaping a narrative of racial paranoia centered on the threat posed to African Americans by white people. Peele has explained that he followed the "'Rosemary's Baby'-'Stepford Wives' model of inching into this crazy situation" and "justifying how the character is rationalizing staying."[12] In both of these progenitors (as in *Get Out*), the protagonists' paranoia ends up being affirmed, as their husbands have indeed embroiled them in perilous plots: Rosemary (of *Rosemary's Baby*) becomes victim to a satanic cult, and Joanna Eberhart (of *Stepford Wives*) is replaced by her own robotic doppelgänger, manufactured by the Men's Club of Stepford. The pervasive paranoia of *Get Out* is also influenced by the estrangement of the protagonist, Ben, in *Night of the Living Dead.* Like Chris, *Night*'s Ben is trapped in a house with white people, and it's both men's "racial paranoia," as Peele puts it, that helps them survive. (A dose more of "gender paranoia" would no doubt have helped Rosemary and Joanna.) Peele addresses Ben's similarity to Chris when he says that the former is "a man living in fear every day, so this [the horde of devouring ghouls] is a challenge he is more equipped to take on" than are the other characters.[13] While *Rosemary's Baby, Stepford Wives,* and *Night of the Living Dead* feature, respectively, demonic entities, animatronic doubles, and cannibalistic ghouls, they simultaneously represent societal structures—whether it be patriarchy or racism—as the monster. Indeed, characters in *Rosemary's Baby, Stepford Wives, Night of the Living Dead,* and *Get Out* live in constant fear—and constant, vigilant watchfulness—*because of* those social structures, even as that same society tries to tell them they are paranoid for doing so.

Peele also draws on these three films to unequivocally indict white people—in the same way that *The Stepford Wives* controversially indicted men. And just as the latter attracted accusations of "man-hating,"[14] so too

12. Zinoman, "Jordan Peele."

13. Zinoman, "Jordan Peele." For another discussion of the (justified) racial paranoia in *Get Out*, see Mitchum, "Get Out."

14. See Helford, "*Stepford Wives*," 146, and Silver, "Cyborg Mystique," 109–12.

has *Get Out* been accused of sowing racial division, fostering a unilateral suspicion of white people. "It's blatantly pushing a racist agenda against white people," wrote one representative viewer.[15] In Peele's comments on *Night of the Living Dead,* he has indeed aligned the ravening horde of cannibalistic ghouls with the "normal" white characters of *Get Out,* an alignment that highlights his point that *white* society specifically is the monster: whites don't have to be undead flesh-eaters to be a threat. Indeed, *Night of the Living Dead* itself suggests that the "normal" white characters (not only the ghouls) are the "monster" when the posse of white police and national guardsmen who are "cleaning up" shoot Ben in the head at the end of the film.[16] As Peele has said, "the end of the movie, that's nothing if it's a white dude."[17] Similarly, *Get Out* is nothing without its African American protagonist and its white "monsters."

Peele's primary influences also include a tradition of body horror that emphasizes the ways in which black bodies, in particular, are not their own. Indeed, this thematic goes back farther than horror to the African American gothic tradition, which, as Maisha Wester has pointed out, often centers around a "temporal collapse" in which "traumatic and destructive aspects of the past disrupt the present"—notably slavery, which "continues even now, in modern 'progressive' America."[18] Kareem Abdul-Jabbar claimed of *Get Out* that it leverages the body-horror plot of *Invasion of the Body Snatchers* precisely to dramatize this persistence of slavery by other means. Unless the body "is free from others trying to control its actions and free from constant threat of injury or death, that body, that person, that people are still enslaved."[19] Steven Thrasher has also claimed that *Get Out* is above all "a scathing indictment of the on-going theft of the Black body" and "the best movie ever made about American slavery."[20] And Peele himself has bluntly claimed that "the real thing at hand here is slavery."[21] In *Night of the Living Dead, Rosemary's Baby, The Stepford Wives,* and *Invasion of the Body Snatchers* in particular, then, the horror film tradition gave Peele a way to represent African Americans' (justified and even life-saving) racial paranoia; the profound,

15. Stoddard, "'Get Out.'"

16. See Lightning, "Interracial Tensions," and Means Coleman, *Horror Noire,* 106–12, on the racial politics of *Night.*

17. Zinoman, "Jordan Peele."

18. Wester, *African American Gothic,* 26–27.

19. Abdul-Jabbar, "Why 'Get Out.'"

20. Thrasher, "Why *Get Out*"; see also Madison, "Get Out," on the film's message about alienated black bodies and the persistence of slavery.

21. Harris, "Giant Leap."

"monstrous" threat whites pose to African Americans; and the quite literal kidnapping of the black body in the long and tentacular reach of US slavery.

Get Out and Blackface

Get Out also draws on its horror progenitors, specifically *Invasion of the Body Snatchers* and *The Stepford Wives,* to articulate a particular form of politicized "body swap."[22] Centered on bodily transformation, both *Invasion* and *Stepford Wives* dramatize the human becoming nonhuman—alien and robot, respectively. While the bodily transformations effected by the Coagula procedure in *Get Out* appear to remain in the realm of the human, the white people who have their brains transplanted into black bodies actually do, as in *Get Out*'s antecedents, take on a form that is nonhuman *to them*—indeed, *must* be nonhuman as the very grounds of the operation. (Who would treat someone fully human as a mere corporeal vessel?) Black repositories for white minds, African Americans are explicitly conceived, then, as nonhuman by the whites in the film. Dean Armitage, for instance, aligns African Americans with deer in a clearly coded tirade: "I do not like the deer. I'm sick of it. They're taking over. They're like rats. They're destroying the ecosystem. I see a dead deer at the side of the road, I think to myself, that's a start." He also suggestively references African Americans when he notes the creeping "black mold" in the basement.[23] And every guest at the Armitages' party objectifies Chris: he is a lump of flesh to them. Nothing more. There is also, however, a very human and distinctly political transformation in *Invasion, Stepford Wives,* and *Get Out.* In *Invasion,* the individualistic American becomes either the mindless Communist drone or the equally mindless postwar conformist (depending on one's reading); in *Stepford Wives,* the independent woman becomes the vacuous suburban hausfrau; and in *Get Out,* white becomes black—surely a dramatically different lived and political reality and one that evokes, I suggest, the longstanding US institution of blackface minstrelsy.

Indeed, in its body-swap plot, *Get Out* signals the distinctively twenty-first-century politics that have circulated around "blackface." As Eric Lott has copiously detailed in *Love and Theft: Blackface Minstrelsy and the Working Class* (1995), blackface minstrelsy was a common theatrical practice among working-class whites in the antebellum urban North, embedded in the often

22. See Robyn Citizen's chapter in this collection, which reads *Get Out* in the tradition of the "body-swap" genre.

23. *Get Out.* All further references to the film are to this DVD.

violent political struggles in the 1840s and 1850s over labor, slavery, abolition, and women's rights. Blackface in the twenty-first century, however, is quite different. Most notably, while blackface certainly is something still adopted by whites as a theatrical practice (often at Halloween parties), its domain has spread, becoming less theatrical and more "natural."[24] Indeed, what drives the narrative of *Get Out*, what is revealed as the secret at its center, is the desire of whites to adopt not only "black*face*" but a blackness *in toto*. By means of the Coagula procedure, whites "black up" all over. This blackface imagery expresses Peele's desire to expose the false allyship of progressive whites, "to expose 'the lie' of a post-racial America, one that grew after the election of Mr. Obama."[25] Peele's target in *Get Out*, he said, "wasn't red state racists" but "'the liberal elite, who tend to believe that they're—we're—above this.' Liberals have learned from Trump's election," Peele continued, "that racism isn't solely the province of gap-toothed cretins who live in those other states."[26] The aim of *Get Out* is not to unmask the "gap-toothed cretins" (they are already unmasked) but those who take for themselves a kind of "blackness"—as in, to quote Dean Armitage, "I would have voted for Obama a third time." It is this postracial and admiring "liberal elite" who enact the deadly desire to appropriate the black body, to "black up" all over.

Perhaps the most visible performances of blackface in the era of *Get Out*, however, have been those purportedly enacted by African Americans themselves, expressing the apprehension that inside the black body is a white consciousness, white interests, white power. The anxieties of *Get Out*, in other words, are twofold, encompassing the appropriative desire of whites for the black body as well as the anxieties of African Americans that surviving and thriving in white society risks succumbing to white interests. As philosopher Lewis Gordon puts it, there "are some, after all, who can move through the white world so long as they offer themselves as black bodies with white consciousnesses."[27] W. E. B. Du Bois famously called this fear "double consciousness," which risks becoming outright co-option.[28] President Barack Obama, for instance, has frequently been called out for being what the African People's Socialist Party succinctly labeled "white

24. Twenty-first-century blackface manifests, for instance, in Donald Trump's ventriloquizing brown and black people at political rallies (which Patricia J. Williams deftly calls out as "blackface"). See Williams, "'White Voice.'"

25. Zinoman, "Jordan Peele."

26. Adams, "In Jordan Peele's."

27. Gordon and Chevannes, "Black Issues."

28. See Mikal Gaines's chapter in this collection on *Get Out*'s deep ties to W. E. B. Du Bois's concept of "double consciousness."

power in black face!"[29] Such proclamations have not only been issued from the political margins. TV host Byron Allen declared in 2015 that "President Obama is, at this point, a white president in blackface," adding that "Black America would have done much better with a white president."[30] And Cornel West, discussing the 2012 presidential election and spiraling economic inequality in the US, commented that, in Obama, the country has ended up with "a Rockefeller Republican in blackface."[31] What these denunciations of Obama as an incarnation of white power, a white president, and a Rockefeller Republican in blackface signify is the fear that underneath Obama's black mask, a white man is running the show.

Get Out taps into this contemporary version of blackface by providing a powerful new metaphor for it—the "sunken place," where, Derefe Kimarley Chevannes claims, we see the "imprisoning of Black consciousness."[32] After Kanye West's infamous visit with President Donald Trump in the White House in October 2018, for instance, Michael Eric Dyson spoke on MSNBC about how West exemplified "white supremacy by ventriloquism. A black mouth is speaking," he claimed, "but white racist ideas are flowing from Kanye West's mouth." He continued that West demonstrated how a "black body and brain [become] the warehouse for the articulation and expression of anti-black sentiments."[33] Others have more succinctly charged that West had fallen into the "sunken place," and not least for his expressed support of Donald Trump.[34] Eric Lott has argued that the numerous media incarnations of Obama in blackface are "consoling" in that they reassure "that a white man is inside pulling the strings" while also summoning "the seductive contours of 'blackness.'"[35] Lott's claim aptly summarizes how "blackface" works in *Get Out*. The Armitages and their allies seek not only personal benefit, although that is significant, but they also want to ensure that inside every African American a "white man" is "pulling the strings." *Get Out*, in short, is a parable of complete colonization.

---

29. O'Neal, "Barack Obama."

30. Gajewski, "TV Host."

31. "Tavis Smiley." For an extended discussion of popular media accounts of Obama in blackface, see Lott, *Black Mirror*, 1–7.

32. Gordon and Chevannes, "Black Issues."

33. Schwartz, "Michael Eric Dyson."

34. There is even a "complete timeline" of how Kanye West went from "woke" to "sunken," ending with the lament that "we may have forever lost Kanye to the sunken place." See "Complete Timeline."

35. Lott, *Black Mirror*, 5–6.

Get Out's Masks and Mirrors

Get Out evokes blackface from the beginning. Even before Chris is tied up in the Armitages' basement, prepped to become the vessel for white art dealer Jim Hudson's brain, he has himself already been in blackface: indeed, Chris wears masks, both white and black. Omar P. L. Moore points out the significance of the fact that we first see Chris shaving—looking into a mirror, his face lathered in white shaving cream. Moore asks, "Is this Chris's metaphorical white face mask? . . . Is it Chris's performance mask before his white girlfriend arrives? A mask for survival in white suburbia?" Moore continues that when Rose tells Chris to "just smile, the whole time" before they descend to her family's party, it is a moment "akin to a minstrel show."[36] Certainly, Chris is enormously forbearing as he endures a steady stream of increasingly intolerable racist behaviors; he keeps his mask intact, which perhaps inspired artist Jermaine Rogers's rendering of Chris among the Armitages—blackface mask in hand (see figure 1). At the party, and despite its psychic costs, Chris manages, for the most part, to be the black man whites want him to be. Significantly, while we first see Chris in his Brooklyn apartment looking at himself in the mirror (albeit whitened with shaving cream), once he gets to the Armitage estate, he does not, again, see himself in a mirror. In the two scenes in Rose's bedroom in which Chris starts to express his escalating unease to his girlfriend—about her mother's perhaps having hypnotized him, about Walter's and then Georgina's strange behavior—there are two mirrors prominently and almost continuously in the *mise-en-scène,* and yet Chris not only does not look at himself in them but he is reflected only once, fleetingly, as he follows Rose to the window. These prominent mirrors, and Chris's failure to see himself in them, suggest that he is already losing himself, a loss caused by the masks he is compelled to wear.[37] As Ina Diane Archer puts it, *Get Out* "suggests that black people can become buried alive in whiteness, much in the way the minstrel's blackface mask engulfs performers of color, but taken to an existential extreme."[38] In the loss of his reflection, Chris demonstrates what "whiteness does to the black mind and psyche," as Robert Jones Jr. puts it; Chris embodies, specifically, "the desire

---

36. Moore, "Do the White Thing." Mikal Gaines's chapter in this collection also reads the shaving scene as an evocation of blackface minstrelsy.

37. George Toles offers a brilliant discussion of how *Psycho* expresses its characters' loss of self through their refusal/inability to look at themselves in the mirror. See Toles, "'If Thine Eye,'" 134–35.

38. Archer, "Review."

FIGURE 1. Jermaine Rogers, art inspired by *Get Out*. Used with permission of Jermaine Rogers.

to be white and what must happen to the black parts of yourself in order to make that journey."[39]

As the metaphor of the shaving cream implies, though, and as Jermaine Rogers renders it in his art, Chris's mask is still removable; Chris's authentic self is still intact. He is still performing, still has the option to step off the stage, to look in the mirror again and see himself. He has not yet gone from looking in a mirror to becoming a "black mirror" reflecting only a white fantasy. In his most recent book, Lott describes what he calls "black mirroring"—that is, "the mechanics, dispositions, and effects of the dominant culture's looking at itself always through a fantasized black Other." Lott points out that while "Du Bois's 'double consciousness' captured the way African Americans are made to see themselves through the eyes of white dominance, black mirroring is its dialectically related but asymmetrically [*sic*] inverse, the very medium of white luxury and privilege."[40] Every white person around Chris once he arrives at the Armitage house seeks to make him into a "black mirror"; they seek to see themselves in a distorted image of blackness that they urge Chris to embody. And, in the Coagula procedure, he will be wholly and forcibly remade into a black mirror to serve the needs and desires of whites. As Lott puts it, the black mirror is the

39. Son of Baldwin, "Get the Fuck."

40. Lott, *Black Mirror*, xvii.

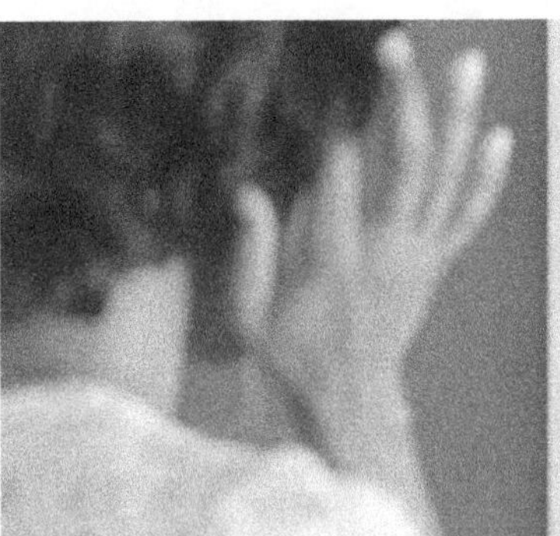

FIGURE 2. The Armitage matriarch enjoys her black body. *Get Out* (Jordan Peele, 2017).

"black mask for my white face, all the beautiful (or demonic) attractions of 'blackness' generated out of a thousand media sources and ideological state apparatuses," all of which constitute "the apparently fundamental precondition for the reproduction of national white selfhood if not dominance."[41] The Coagula procedure is designed exactly to shape a "black mask for my white face"—except it is for the entire body and it is not just a mask.

The "black mirror" logic adumbrated by *Get Out* is epitomized in the only other scene in the film (besides the scene in which Chris shaves himself) in which someone looks at their reflection. It is the uncanny moment when Chris sees Georgina looking at her reflection in the window just before Missy hypnotizes him (see figure 2). This scene is not about "Georgina" (who is she anyway?) looking at herself; it is about the Armitage matriarch looking in her personal "black mirror," seeing reflected back at her the captive black body. She preens, secure in her appropriation of the fantasized black image for herself and in the power that her appropriation secures. Her enjoyment of her reflection is less about her appearance—though she clearly enjoys that—than it is about taking pleasure in her power. She has successfully stolen the black body and (thus) secured white dominance.

The moment at which the Armitage matriarch looks at her (Georgina's) reflection in the window may be the most important moment in the film in terms of *Get Out*'s politics, marking the film's deep racial pessimism. What Georgina's smile represents is the immutability of racial power and privilege: the white woman inside her black body *has not changed*. Her smile expresses the satisfaction of existing as permanently "white" in a desired black body. In this way, *Get Out*'s representation of the immutability of race actually runs counter to the blackface tradition. Lott centrally argues

41. Ibid., 6.

that the blackface performances by antebellum, white, working-class men unsettled race in a nation that was otherwise racially divided. As he puts it, blackface performance "was based on small but significant crimes against settled ideas of racial demarcation, which indeed appear to be inevitable when white Americans enter the haunted realm of racial fantasy."[42] These "crimes" against racial demarcation were manifest in the way white men in blackface crossed racial boundaries, showed a "desire to try on" blackness and thus demonstrated "the permeability of the color line."[43] Even when Lott traces blackface into the twentieth century in his discussion of *Black Like Me,* he quotes John Griffin's experience of looking at himself (in blackface) in the mirror and feeling that "'all traces of the John Griffin I had been were wiped from existence.'" While Lott points out the obvious problems with Griffin's profound feeling of estrangement—he "imagines whiteness and blackness as insuperably distinct"[44]—Griffin's experience nonetheless keeps open the possibility of racial crossing. In becoming an "utter stranger,"[45] Griffin may indeed express racial horror, but he also embodies a dissolution of the racial divide. Indeed, he has crossed that divide, which is why he experiences the vanishing of "the John Griffin I had been." The experience of the Armitage matriarch in the mirror contains no vestige of John Griffin's loss of (white) self. She remains wholly herself in black skin. Here are none of Lott's "crimes against settled ideas of racial demarcation" but instead a settled inevitability. There is only a profound crime against a person, not a crime against the fixity of race.

Georgina will later manifest evidence of an internal struggle, as Chris confronts her in Rose's bedroom about her having unplugged his phone; even here, though, there is no dissolution of racial boundaries. In this moment, we do become palpably aware that Georgina wears a mask: we recognize the body as "blackface," see evidence of both the Armitage matriarch and the vestigial consciousness of the black woman whose body she hijacked.[46] This scene is like the mirror scene, however, in that while

42. Lott, *Love and Theft,* 4.

43. Ibid.

44. Lott, *Black Mirror,* 8.

45. Ibid.

46. Although it is beyond the scope of this argument, Georgina functions as what Kinitra Brooks, by means of bell hooks, calls an "'absent presence,'" the excluded black woman who nonetheless refuses to be erased. Indeed, Chris's mother seems even more perfectly to embody the central character in Brooks's argument about contemporary horror—Sycorax, the absent black woman/witch in Shakespeare's *The Tempest,* who, according to Brooks, haunts subsequent horror texts. As Brooks writes, "Yet Sycorax refuses to be excluded, as her absence in erasure is subverted by her presence as an idea that produces fear and suspicion." Sycorax, Brooks continues, is a "hant—or ghost—that remains spiritually and psychologically present and powerful." Brooks, *Searching,* 7–8.

it (unlike the mirror scene) offers evidence of two (differently racialized) consciousnesses, it still fails to offer Lott's "crimes against settled ideas of racial demarcation."[47] Watching Georgina's tortured face as she attempts to speak to Chris is akin to when Logan lunges at Chris screaming at him to "Get out!" and to the moment when Walter takes Rose's gun and turns it on her and then himself. They are moments when the hijacked black body and mind assert themselves. But there is no crumbling of racial boundaries; instead, there is all out war played out across an immutable border. The Coagula procedure both presumes and continues the idea that there is no racial destabilization, no racial rapprochement, only a war of one race against the other: whites seek only to colonize around fixed and settled boundaries, leaving blacks no choice but to exert the most violent of resistance. It is this violent resistance that Chris and Walter are finally forced to enact against the Armitages in order to liberate themselves. They learn they are playing a zero sum game of racial dominance.

Repression and Body Horror

It is in its view of the seeming immutability of racial difference and dominance that *Get Out* embodies a rather pessimistic strand of the horror film tradition. On the one hand, Peele's film seems perfectly to embody Robin Wood's well-known articulation of the political nature of horror. According to Wood, the horror film "is the struggle for recognition of all that our civilization represses or oppresses," and the monster is the embodiment of what is repressed and oppressed.[48] To the extent that *Get Out* is, as Peele has said, "about the lack of acknowledgment that racism exists,"[49] it represents, in the monstrous Armitage family, the very visible resurgence of what has been denied. The unleashing of repressed racism plays out spectacularly on the screen, as the Armitages are unveiled, one by one, for what they really are, and the viewer is confronted with the knowledge that even Rod's seemingly extravagant paranoid proclamations about the dangers of white girlfriends and sex slavery are in fact true. What is disavowed and denied (white racism) is brought to light.

The Coagula procedure has revealed, though, that while white racists may be spectacularly unveiled and killed, racism itself has a tenacious hold, seemingly entrenched in corporeal matter. The Coagula procedure implies that when a white brain is implanted in a black body, it brings with it,

47. Lott, *Love and Theft*, 4.
48. Wood, *Hollywood*, 75.
49. Zinoman, "Jordan Peele."

despite its new material condition, a fixed racial identity and racial beliefs that remain unwavering across the decades and that will not succumb to remediation, only to violent destruction. This horror is hard-wired. *Get Out* thus evokes (in addition to the repressive mechanisms of Wood's psychoanalytic thesis about horror) the new cognitive unconscious, which has burgeoned in the last twenty-five years or so and which supports the view that, in the words of Mahzarin Banaji and Anthony Greenwald, "much of human judgment and behavior is produced with little conscious thought."[50] Banaji and Greenwald show how intractable racial bias is in the "blindspots" of human brains.[51] *Get Out* in this way finds its roots, I suggest, in some of the very earliest of American horror films that themselves dramatized how intransigently identity was rooted in body and brain.

Indeed, *Get Out*'s antecedents extend to one of the very first US horror films, James Whale's *Frankenstein* (1931), which centrally involves a brain transplant. Procuring a brain for his master, Henry Frankenstein's assistant drops the jar containing a "normal" brain and grabs the "abnormal brain"—the brain of a criminal—dooming the scientist's innocent creature (see figure 3). In the end, though, *Frankenstein* is not wholly deterministic, as the creature's hard-wired criminality remains at war with its innocence and goodness. Another early horror film is perhaps a closer analogue to *Get Out*: Karl Freund's *Mad Love* (1935). In this film, based on the French story *Les Mains d'Orlac* (1920), a brilliant surgeon grafts the hands of an executed murderer onto a pianist after his hands are destroyed in a train accident. The pianist finds himself driven to throw knives at people, exactly like the murderer whose hands he now possesses. His transplanted body parts, in short, still embody the identity of their former owner—just as the brains of white people, transplanted into black bodies in *Get Out*, retain their white tribal identity and persistent racism. Racial identity and racism, *Get Out* proposes, are not easily dislodged—remaining mired in flesh and blood, entrenched in the very substance of the brain. *Get Out* leverages the body horror tradition, then, not only to dramatize the persistence of slavery in the ongoing theft of black bodies but also the disturbing immutability of race and racial dominance.

WHILE THE horror film and the horrors of the real world have always been thoroughly interwoven, and certainly are in *Get Out*, the two sections of this book mark different emphases in this relationship. The first section consid-

---

50. Banaji and Greenwald, *Blindspot*, xiv.

51. Ibid., especially 3–20.

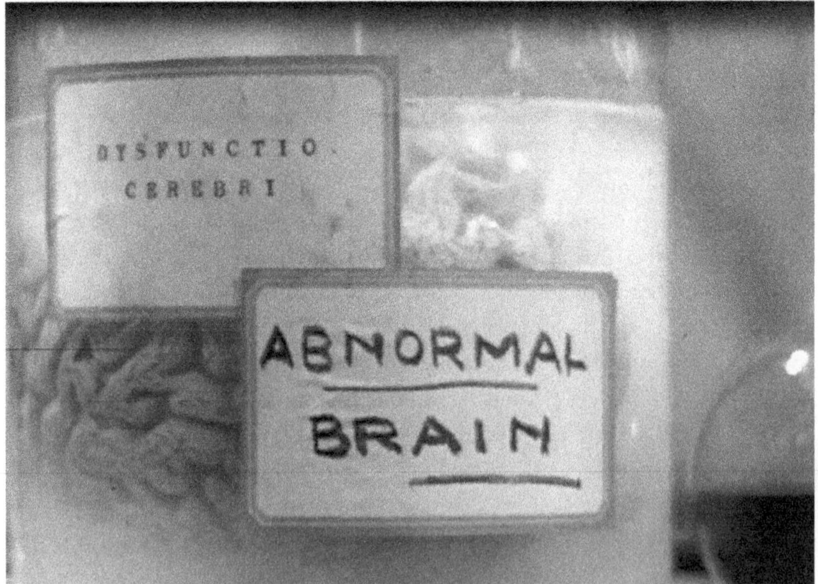

FIGURE 3. The abnormal brain transplanted in Henry Frankenstein's creature. (James Whale, *Frankenstein*, 1931.)

ers Peele's film within the horror tradition, exploring how *Get Out* employs the conventions of both gothic and horror to shape its (political) meanings. Looking back to the beginning of the seventeenth century, Jonathan Byron and Tony Perrello read *Get Out* through Shakespeare's *Othello* (including suggestively positing Missy Armitage as Iago), arguing that the psychological suffering in tragedy becomes the bodily destruction of horror. Linnie Blake then takes up the Female Gothic tradition, with its origin in eighteenth-century British literature, provocatively exploring how Chris "signifies" on the classic gothic heroine. Robin R. Means Coleman and Novotny Lawrence position *Get Out* within the black horror film tradition, going back to 1915's *The Birth of a Nation*. They argue that *Get Out* inverts the notion of the "whitopia" as safe, reclaiming the black urban space after decades of its vilification as a place of crime and danger. Taking up a particular subgenre of the horror tradition, the zombie film, Erin Casey-Williams traces *Get Out*'s roots to Victor Halperin's *White Zombie* (1932), with its central plot of stolen consciousness and appropriated will; she then goes on to position Peele's film alongside the modern zombie narrative. Bernice M. Murphy locates Peele's film within two other horror subgenres, the suburban and the rural horror film. She argues that *Get Out* emphasizes the violence lurking under suburban life not least by portraying the Armitage family as a version of the "bad white trash" clan of backwoods horror. Robyn Citizen then reads *Get*

Out in light of yet another horror subgenre, the "body swap" film, arguing that *Get Out* finds an unexplored predecessor in John Frankenheimer's *Seconds* (1966), as it explores the inevitably racialized concept of Cartesian dualism. Adam Lowenstein takes up two specific horror antecedents of *Get Out*, *Rosemary's Baby* and *The Stepford Wives*, in order to offer a distinctive argument about the horror genre more broadly. Levin's novels and Peele's film, Lowenstein claims, embody horror's ability to express the experience, specifically the real pain, of social minorities (in this case both Jews and African Americans) as opposed to merely transforming that experience into monstrosity. Finally, Sarah Ilott argues that *Get Out* exemplifies the way in which contemporary gothic functions as systemic critique, specifically a critique of neoliberal capitalism as it shapes racialized hierarchy and inequality.

The second section takes up the politics of *Get Out* more directly, exploring the film's sustained critique of racist institutions and practices. Peele's progenitors in this section are traced to the real world rather than the literary and filmic traditions. Setting up the section's political readings, the first chapter, by Todd K. Platts and David L. Brunsma, explores the racial divide in twenty-six early reviews of *Get Out*, a divide that emerges around the deeper political commitments of reviewers of color. Sarah Juliet Lauro then reads *Get Out* as a film about slave revolt, with a focus on Nat Turner's infamous 1831 insurrection. Lauro traces how the film is shaped specifically by the tropes of the slave revolt narrative: migration, plantation, rebellion, and storytelling. (Indeed, many of the chapters in this section identify how *Get Out* illuminates the persistence of slavery-by-other-means in the twenty-first-century United States.) The next set of chapters takes up how *Get Out* articulates specific racial identity formations. Mikal Gaines shows how *Get Out* extends W. E. B. Du Bois's notion of "double consciousness," making clear, through Chris, the catastrophic costs of a lifetime spent with a divided sense of self, specifically the "crippling immobility" that it induces. Robert LaRue then reads the "teacup scene," in which Missy Armitage sends Chris to the sunken place, in order to argue that *Get Out* brilliantly dramatizes the ways in which the black male psyche has been injured when men are interpellated as boys and boys are interpellated as men—an injury spectacularly on display in white police officer Darren Wilson's explanation of his fatal 2014 encounter with Michael Brown in Ferguson, Missouri. Kyle Brett continues the discussion of the sunken place and shows how Chris's underexplored occupation as professional photographer actually implicates him in the "assaultive gaze" of the sunken place, as he seeks to capture especially black bodies (Georgina and Logan) with his camera. The end of the film, however, with Chris's spontaneous shot of Walter's face, offers a more liberating kind of photography, one aligned, for instance, with street documentation of police violence against black bodies. Shifting the focus from black to white identity formation, Laura Thorp argues that Peele's film, like James Baldwin's 1965 short story "Going to Meet the Man," takes up the ways in which white identity is predicated on the violent colonization of the black body, which represents both sexual desire and a fearful finitude. Cayla McNally also explores how white racial formations have been dependent on the colonizing of the black body—specifically through an ostensibly "objective" science. She then argues, in a slight divergence from Kyle Brett's argument, that Chris's "gaze," in part through his camera eye, is ultimately a means of liberation from the grasp of a racist science. Finally, Alex Svensson's chapter moves from *Get Out*'s textual politics to the real-world political implications of the film's paratexts, specifically the "Do You Belong in This Neighborhood?" billboard ad. Like Jordan Peele's film itself, advertisements for *Get Out*, as Svensson shows, have generated a multiplicity of meanings, intervening specifically in political fights over housing in California.

Taken together, the essays in this collection explore the ways in which Jordan Peele's *Get Out* revolutionizes the gothic and horror tradition at the same time that it unmasks the particular politics of race in the early twenty-first-century United States. Among the many things for which *Get Out* became known in 2017 was the way in which it began conversations—and so, in the spirit of the film to which this book is dedicated, we hope that these essays continue the conversations, popular and academic, that have already begun. We are confident that there are still more gothic fictions and horror films that *Get Out* echoes, still more political implications to discern. Jordan Peele is now established, moreover, as one of the preeminent filmmakers of the twenty-first century, and this book is no doubt only one of many that will explore his particular brand of horror, his unfolding series of "social thrillers." After the release of his second feature, *Us*, Peele rather cryptically claimed that *Us* "proves a very valid and different point than *Get Out*, which is, not everything is about race. *Get Out* proved that everything *is* about race. I've proved both points!"[52] Peele's work—both *Get Out* and *Us*—is indeed a profound exploration of race, but it is an equally profound exploration of human nature. *Get Out* is about the human condition as well as about race, just as *Us* is about race as well as about the human condition. We hope this book proves useful in both conversations.

52. Hiatt, "All-American."

Bibliography

Abdul-Jabbar, Kareem. "Why 'Get Out' Is 'Invasion of the Body Snatchers' for the Trump Era." *Hollywood Reporter,* March 17, 2017. https://www.hollywoodreporter.com/news/kareem-abdul-jabbar-why-get-is-invasion-black-body-snatchers-trump-985449.

Adams, Sam. "In Jordan Peele's Horror Movie, *Get Out,* the 'Monster' Is Liberal Racism." *Slate,* January 25, 2017. http://www.slate.com/blogs/browbeat/2017/01/25/at_sundance_jordan_peele_explains_how_obama_s_election_inspired_his_horror.html?via=gdpr-consent.

Archer, Ina Diane. "Review: Get Out." *Film Comment,* March 3, 2017. https://www.filmcomment.com/blog/review-get-out/.

Banaji, Mahzarin R., and Anthony G. Greenwald. *Blindspot: Hidden Biases of Good People.* New York: Delacorte, 2013.

Brooks, Kinitra D. *Searching for Sycorax: Black Women's Hauntings of Contemporary Horror.* New Brunswick, NJ: Rutgers University Press, 2018.

Carroll, Noël. *The Philosophy of Horror; or, Paradoxes of the Heart.* New York: Routledge, 1990.

Collins, K. Austin. "Jordan Peele's *Us* Is Just a Horror Movie, and That's a Good Thing." *Vanity Fair,* March 22, 2019. https://www.vanityfair.com/hollywood/2019/03/jordan-peeles-us-dont-overthink-it.

"A Complete Timeline of How Kanye West Went from Woke to Sunken." *NewsOne,* October 12, 2018. https://newsone.com/3796246/kanye-west-complete-timeline-woke-sunken/.

Gajewski, Ryan. "TV Host Byron Allen Slams Obama: 'A White President in Blackface.'" *Hollywood Reporter,* May 24, 2015. https://www.hollywoodreporter.com/news/tv-host-byron-allen-slams-797804.

Get Out. Directed by Jordan Peele. USA: Universal Pictures, 2017. DVD.

Gordon, Lewis, and Derefe Kimarley Chevannes. "Black Issues in Philosophy: A Conversation on *Get Out.*" Blog of the American Philosophical Association, April 3, 2018. https://blog.apaonline.org/2018/04/03/black-issues-in-philosophy-a-conversation-on-get-out/?fbclid=IwAR3_EIsHKsNZOptM8Wi8gorl1PBopIov2b8jilc9No5nzlPCwSInNywZADs.

Guerrasio, Jason. "Jordan Peele Plans to Direct a Whole Series of Horror Movies about 'Social Demons.'" *Business Insider,* February 17, 2017. https://www.businessinsider.com/get-out-jordan-peele-horror-movie-series-social-demons-2017-2.

Harris, Brandon. "The Giant Leap Forward of Jordan Peele's 'Get Out.'" *New Yorker,* March 4, 2017. https://www.newyorker.com/culture/culture-desk/review-the-giant-leap-forward-of-jordan-peeles-get-out.

Helford, Elyce Rae. "*The Stepford Wives* and the Gaze: Envisioning Feminism in 1975." *Feminist Media Studies* 6, no. 2 (2006): 145–56.

Hiatt, Brian. "The All-American Nightmares of Jordan Peele." *Rolling Stone,* January 29, 2019. https://www.rollingstone.com/movies/movie-features/director-jordan-peele-new-movie-cover-story-782743/.

"Jordan Peele: The Art of the Social Thriller." Art Exhibition, Brooklyn Academy of Music, February 17–March 1, 2017. https://www.bam.org/film/2017/jordan-peele.

Keetley, Dawn, and Gwen Hofmann. "*Thirteen Women* (1932): An Unacknowledged Horror Classic." *Journal of Film and Video* 68, no. 1 (2016): 31–47.

Knight, Jacob. "There's No Such Thing As an 'Elevated' Horror Movie." *Slash Film*, June 8, 2018. https://www.slashfilm.com/elevated-horror/.

Lightning, Robert K. "Interracial Tensions in *Night of the Living Dead*." *CineAction* 53 (2000): 22–29.

Lott, Eric. *Black Mirror: The Cultural Contradictions of American Racism*. Cambridge, MA: Belknap Press of Harvard University Press, 2017.

———. *Love and Theft: Blackface Minstrelsy and the American Working Class*. New York: Oxford University Press, 1993.

Madison, Ira III. "*Get Out* Understands the Black Body." *MTV.com*, February 24, 2017. http://www.mtv.com/news/2986793/get-out-understands-the-black-body/.

Means Coleman, Robin R. *Horror Noire: Blacks in American Horror Films from the 1890s to Present*. New York: Routledge, 2011.

Mitchum, Preston. "Get Out Proves That 'Nice Racism' and White Liberalism Are Never to Be Trusted." *Root*, March 4, 2017. https://www.theroot.com/get-out-proves-that-nice-racism-and-white-liberalism-1792955235.

Moore, Omar P. L. "Do the White Thing." *Popcorn Reel*, March 7, 2017. http://www.popcornreel.com/htm/getoutessay.html.

Olsen, Mark. "How John Krasinski's Newfound Love for Horror Led to Defying Expectations with 'A Quiet Place.'" *Los Angeles Times*, April 8, 2018. http://www.latimes.com/entertainment/movies/la-et-mn-a-quiet-place-john-krasinski-emily-blunt-20180408-story.html#.

O'Neal, Aaron. "Barack Obama, 8 Years of White Power in Black Face!" *Burning Spear*, October 26, 2016. http://www.theburningspear.com/2016/10/Barack-Obama-8-years-of-white-power-in-black-face.

Schwartz, Ian. "Michael Eric Dyson: Blacks Can Not Stand by Kanye West." *Real Clear Politics*, October 12, 2018. https://www.realclearpolitics.com/video/2018/10/12/michael_eric_dyson_to_kanye_blacks_can_not_stand_by_you_trump_cares_less_about_black_people_than_bush.html.

Silver, Anna Krugovoy. "The Cyborg Mystique: *The Stepford Wives* and Second Wave Feminism." *Arizona Quarterly* 58, no. 1 (2002): 109–26.

Son of Baldwin. "Get the Fuck Outta Here: A Dialogue on Jordan Peele's Get Out." *Medium*, February 27, 2017. https://medium.com/@SonofBaldwin/get-the-fuck-outta-here-a-dialogue-on-jordan-peeles-get-out-831fef18b2b3.

Stoddard, Christine. "'Get Out' Movie Controversy? Film Called 'Anti-White' and 'Racist' by Some Viewers." *Mic.com*, February 24, 2017. https://mic.com/articles/169514/get-out-movie-controversy-film-called-anti-white-and-racist-by-some-viewers#.9v3nSa6mc.

"Tavis Smiley, Cornel West on the 2012 Election and Why Calling Obama 'Progressive' Ignores His Record." *Democracy Now!*, November 9, 2012. https://www.democracynow.org/2012/11/9/tavis_smiley_cornel_west_on_the.

Thrasher, Steven. "Why *Get Out* Is the Best Movie Ever Made about American Slavery." *Esquire,* March 1, 2017. https://www.esquire.com/entertainment/movies/a53515/get-out-jordan-peele-slavery/.

Toles, George. "'If Thine Eye Offend Thee . . .': *Psycho* and the Art of Infection." In *Alfred Hitchcock's* Psycho*: A Casebook,* edited by Robert Kolker, 120–45. New York: Oxford University Press, 2004.

Weinstein, Max. "'Society Is the Monster': Jordan Peele on Racism as Horror." *MovieMaker,* October 31, 2017. https://www.moviemaker.com/archives/moviemaking/directing/society-is-the-monster-film-independent-forum-2017-jordan-peele/.

Wester, Maisha L. *African American Gothic: Screams from Shadowed Places.* New York: Palgrave Macmillan, 2012.

Wikipedia Contributors. "Social Thriller." *Wikipedia, The Free Encyclopedia,* last updated December 25, 2018. https://en.wikipedia.org/wiki/Social_thriller.

Williams, Patricia J. "'White Voice,' Blackface, and the Ethics of Representation." *Nation,* August 17, 2018. https://www.thenation.com/article/white-voice-blackface-and-the-ethics-of-representation/.

Wood, Robin. *Hollywood from Vietnam to Reagan.* New York: Columbia University Press, 1986.

Yuan, Jada, and Hunter Harris. "The First Great Movie of the Trump Era." *Vulture,* February 2018. http://www.vulture.com/2018/02/making-get-out-jordan-peele.html.

Zinoman, Jason. "Jordan Peele on a Truly Terrifying Monster: Racism." *New York Times,* February 16, 2017. https://www.nytimes.com/2017/02/16/movies/jordan-peele-interview-get-out.html.

PART 1

The Politics of Horror

CHAPTER 1

FROM TRAGEDY TO HORROR

Othello and *Get Out*

JONATHAN BYRON AND TONY PERRELLO

IN A *Time Magazine* profile coinciding with the release of his 2017 horror film *Get Out,* Jordan Peele explained that one of his motivations behind the film was to expose the "postracial lie" that had been perpetuated in the eight years of Barack Obama's presidency: "If we were in a postracial society . . . I would not feel like the token black guy in a room full of white people trying to connect with me about basketball."[1] The horrifying events that beset Chris when he spends the weekend with the wealthy family of his white girlfriend puncture the narrative of racial progress and invite comparison to another text regarding an interracial romance gone wrong, Shakespeare's *Othello.* Both narratives involve accomplished black men navigating in racial isolation a white society that professes to be enlightened, a society these heroes are tied to through the white women they love. On the surface, it may seem that the similarities end there, as Othello's wife Desdemona is innocent of the suspected promiscuity that motivates him to kill her, while Chris's girlfriend Rose turns out to be a sociopath who sexually lures black men and women to a fate worse than death. A comparative analysis of the two, however, reveals that both texts explore how the nefarious forces within the dominant white society use stereotypes to manipulate and appropri-

1. Berman, "Jordan Peele," 108.

ate the black mind and body, engaging the two isolated black protagonists in a battle to retain their own agency. Furthermore, this juxtaposition of a Renaissance tragedy and a twenty-first-century horror film illuminates the relationship between tragedy and horror, as the false messages, misreadings, and imagined evils that drive the tragic hero in *Othello* become actual, violent realities in the modern horror of *Get Out.* The horror genre becomes, then, a medium in which the internal psychological suffering inherent in tragedy becomes externalized as the physical destruction of the body.

When Shakespeare wrote *Othello* in 1603, the play's audience already had well-established preconceived notions about the black Moors in their predominantly white society—notions that Shakespeare himself had perpetuated in his earlier tragedy, *Titus Andronicus* (c. 1590), in which he depicts Aaron the Moor as a scheming, violent murderer who revels in the evil acts he orchestrates.[2] In 1578, explorer George Best anticipates such racist sentiments in *A True Discourse of the Late Voyages of Discoverie,* in which he attributes the dark skin of African residents to the Curse of Ham, a Biblical damnation caused by a lineage with Noah's youngest son, an "infection of bloud" that was later used to justify slavery.[3] Xenophobia is also apparent in Queen Elizabeth's letters regarding the deportation of "Blackmoores." First, on July 11, 1596, Elizabeth argues for the deportation of ten Moors on the grounds "that there are of late divers Blackmoores brought into the Realme, of which kinde of people there are all ready here to manie."[4] In a later letter, Elizabeth declares that good Christian Englishmen should be served by their white countrymen, rather than "those kynde of people."[5] While economic and political factors likely influenced Elizabeth's decisions, these letters still reveal a prejudicial categorization that separates the white majority from England's black population.

Perhaps the most influential source of black stereotypes in Renaissance England is *A Geographical Historie of Africa.* Written in 1550 by the Moorish Leo Africanus, the book was translated into English in 1600 and is widely considered a source text for Shakespeare's depiction of race in *Othello.* For

2. Recent scholarly studies of Shakespeare and race include Emily Bartels, *Speaking of the Moor: From Alcazar to Othello* (University of Pennsylvania Press, 2009); Ania Loomba, *Shakespeare, Race, and Colonialism* (Oxford University Press, 2002); Kim Hall, *Things of Darkness: Economies of Race and Gender in Early Modern England* (Cornell University Press, 1995); Jonathan Burton and Ania Loomba, *Race in Early Modern England, A Documentary Companion* (Palgrave, 2007); and Ayanna Thompson, *Passing Strange: Shakespeare, Race, and Contemporary America* (Oxford University Press, 2011).

3. Best, *True Discourse,* 31–32.

4. Elizabeth I, "Open Letter."

5. Elizabeth I, "Those kinde of people."

example, Africanus remarks of the Moors that "no nation in the world is so subject to jealousie,"[6] that they are "abounding exceedingly with choler" and "addicted unto wrath,"[7] and that "their young men may goe a wooing to divers maides, till such time as they have sped a wife."[8] This image of a volatile, jealous, and sexually promiscuous people is clearly perpetuated by Shakespeare's Iago, who, presuming he has been cuckolded by the Moor, seeks to conjure the "green-eyed monster" of jealousy within Othello.[9] Furthermore, Iago's plan to destroy "the Moor" hinges on what he refers to as Othello's "free and open nature / That thinks men honest that but seem to be so."[10] Iago's conclusion that Othello can be "as tenderly led by th' nose / As asses are"[11] recalls another of Africanus's observations regarding Moors: "they are so credulous, that they will believe matters impossible, which are told them."[12] Clearly, Iago's very perceptions of Othello are defined by his adherence to these racial stereotypes. Thus, while Iago claims to hate Othello because he did not promote him and because he fears Othello may have cuckolded him, Iago's hatred is built upon a foundation of racial prejudice.

Nor is this prejudice unique to Iago; several Venetians refer to Othello with the contempt born of racial stereotypes associated with the inhabitants of the Mediterranean Basin. These stereotypes flourished in early modern writing, which often depicted Venice as an enlightened, civilized country that, because of its geographical location and free intercourse with foreigners, enjoyed prosperity while courting danger. Gaspar Contarini, in his 1543 book *The Commonwealth and Government of Venice,* praised the Venetian practice of integrating foreigners into their government and military. Interracial romance, however, remained taboo, leading to a general "ban on marrying foreigners."[13] This ban on miscegenation characterizes the ideal Venetian in opposition to racial others, which means that Othello's reputation for nobility and devotion to heroic ideals, which elevates his status in Venice, is as flimsy as a spider web. As soon as this older, respected black war hero, a recent Muslim convert to Christianity, dares marry a young, aristocratic, white Venetian, he is transformed into a monster, "the thick-lips," "a lascivious Moor," and a devilish "old black ram . . . tupping" the

6. Africanus, *Geographical Historie,* 40.
7. Ibid., 41.
8. Ibid., 41–42.
9. Shakespeare, *Othello,* 3.3.196.
10. Ibid., 1.3.442–43.
11. Ibid., 1.3.444–45.
12. Africanus, *Geographical Historie,* 41.
13. Draper, *Shakespeare's Audience,* 28–29.

pure white ewes of Venice.[14] According to Ania Loomba, Renaissance England "equated blackness with lechery" and "fornication"[15]—an association tied to G. K. Hunter's observation that for Elizabethans "there seems to be a considerable confusion whether the Moor is a human being or a monster."[16] Even Othello partly attributes Desdemona's attraction to him to his travels amongst the monsters of Africa, "the cannibals that each other eat, / The Anthropophagi, and men whose heads / Do grow beneath their shoulders."[17] Othello ultimately internalizes these stereotypical associations, resulting in his self-destruction.

The gradual manipulation through stereotypes that Othello experiences as a black minority is also evident in Jordan Peele's *Get Out.* Similar to Othello's conditional acceptance in the refined Venetian society, Chris's introduction into the white, upper-class world of his girlfriend is undermined by a history of racial conflict and stereotypes simmering beneath the surface of the liberal, postracial façade. Initially, Rose assures Chris that this history of racial conflict and the fear of miscegenation is a relic of the past, that her parents, Dean and Missy Armitage, are not prejudiced at all. But visually, Peele juxtaposes such reassuring language with the foreboding image of the Armitage estate, a plantation-style home isolated in a forest that recalls the environment through which escaping slaves ran 150 years ago. When Dean sees Chris noticing the family's black maid and black groundskeeper, he apologetically explains, "I know what you're thinking. . . . I hate the way it looks," attempting to influence any initial judgment Chris might make.[18] With each passing moment, though, the stereotypes of racial difference that have supposedly been left in the past become increasingly apparent, beginning with Dean's awkwardly engaging Chris with his attempts at black lingo, greeting him as "my man" and referring to Chris and Rose's relationship as "this *thang.*" Soon, these seemingly innocuous faux pas escalate into a dinner conversation in which Rose's brother Jeremy says of Chris's potential success in mixed martial arts, "With your frame and your genetic makeup . . . you'd be a fucking beast." Not only does this recall the Renaissance association of the black body with something animalistic and less than human (as when Iago calls Othello "a Barbary horse" or Othello in sexual congress as part of "the beast with two backs"[19]), it also embod-

14. Shakespeare, *Othello,* 1.1.72, 141, 97–98.

15. Loomba, *Shakespeare,* 49–50.

16. Hunter, "Elizabethans," 56.

17. Shakespeare, *Othello,* 1.3.166–68.

18. *Get Out.* All further references to the film are to this DVD.

19. Shakespeare, *Othello,* 1.1.125, 130.

ies the white culture's disproportionate value of black physicality. Just as Venetian society values "valiant Othello" for his ability to fight and win wars,[20] the Armitages assume that Chris's value lies in his physical proficiency in fighting and sports. This stereotype emerges again at a party filled with the Armitages' elderly friends who are obsessed with his physical body. As Chris is paraded around, they ask him about his golf swing, comment on his grip strength, and remark that "black is in fashion." At one point, a woman with a wheelchair-bound husband squeezes Chris's bicep, saying, "Not bad," before asking Rose, "So, is it true? Is it better?" This allusion to the stereotype—present since before the Renaissance—that black men possess enormous penises (and therefore are excellent lovers) unites the two predominant strains of prejudice seen in both *Othello* and *Get Out*: the monstrous status of the black body and the unnatural power of black sexuality over perverted white women.

Iago's sustained influence over Othello in particular builds upon these stereotypes of unnatural and monstrous black sexuality. Repeatedly, Othello hears that Desdemona's attraction to him is "against all rules of nature."[21] When Brabantio argues that their marriage is the result of witchcraft, he says, "And [Desdemona], in spite of nature, / Of years, of country, credit, everything, / To fall in love with what she feared to look on!"[22] Later, Iago disparages Desdemona to Othello, pointing out the perversion of her choice to decline the "many proposed matches / Of her own clime, complexion, and degree, / Whereto we see in all things nature tends."[23] By casting Desdemona as abnormal for her attraction to Othello, Iago, Brabantio, and others reinforce the stereotype that Othello himself is an unworthy monster. Initially, this racist conception manifests in Othello's self-deprecating comment attesting to the strength of Desdemona's love and faithfulness, that "she had eyes, and chose me" despite "mine own weak merits."[24] But after Iago continually reiterates the deceptive nature of Venetian women (especially one attracted to a black man), Othello himself voices the stereotype of unnatural interracial love, acknowledging, "And yet, how nature erring from itself—."[25] By the midpoint of the conversation, Othello has fully internalized his supposed inferiority as a black man and assumes, therefore, that Desdemona cannot be faithful to him: "Haply, for I am black / And have not

20. Ibid., 1.3.56.
21. Ibid., 1.3.119.
22. Ibid., 1.3.114–16.
23. Ibid., 3.3.269–71.
24. Ibid., 3.3.218–20.
25. Ibid., 3.3.267.

those soft parts of conversation / That chamberers have. . . . She's gone. I am abused, and my relief / Must be to loathe her."[26] When Othello states that Desdemona's once pure name "is now begrimed and black / As mine own face,"[27] he reveals his own self-loathing, created by the stereotypes of the world around him. He becomes what Janet Adelman describes as "the victim of the racist ideology everywhere visible in Venice, an ideology to which he is relentlessly subjected and which increasingly comes to define him as he internalizes it."[28] Thus, by causing Othello to internalize the prejudiced beliefs of the society around him, Iago and the white power structure exert control over his self-perception, dictating his actions through psychological manipulation, ultimately removing his agency so that he perceives his murder of Desdemona—his "black vengeance"[29]—as an inevitable consequence of his racial status.

As in *Othello,* stereotypes of racial difference are weaponized in *Get Out* by those who seek influence over Chris's body and mind. In fact, if Iago employs stereotypes to undermine Othello's faith in Desdemona and destroy his marriage, Chris's friend, Rod, might appear at first to be a surprising version of Iago, forcing Chris to question his relationship with Rose. Although Peele uses Rod's attempts at influence via cell phone as comic relief, his warnings to Chris nevertheless accentuate his racial difference. For instance, while Rose is driving Chris to her house, Rod tells Chris over the phone, "You're just nervous 'cause you didn't take my advice. . . . Don't go to a white girl's parents' house." Rod's insinuation is clear: any attempt at interracial romance is dangerous, and Chris will never be accepted into white society. Moments later, just as Iago does with Desdemona, Rod accuses Rose of a perverted sexuality that is dictating Chris's actions: "What she doin'? Lickin' your balls?" Again, the implication is that Rose might possess an unnatural sexuality herself that she is using to control her boyfriend.[30] Throughout the film, Rod reiterates his distrust in interracial romance and his fear of white sexual perversion, warning Chris that "white people love making people sex slaves and shit." Nor do Rod's concerns exist in a vacuum; rather, they are a reflexive response to a general and persistent ideology of anti-miscegenation in America, just as Iago's accusations reflect the

26. Ibid., 3.3.304–9.

27. Ibid., 3.3.442–43.

28. Adelman, "Iago's Alter Ego," 125.

29. Shakespeare, *Othello,* 3.3.507.

30. Othello voices a fear of white female influence over the black body when, after Desdemona argues for Cassio's reinstatement as lieutenant, he states, "I will deny thee nothing. . . . Perdition catch my soul / But I do love thee!" See Shakespeare, *Othello,* 3.3.93, 100–101.

racist attitudes of early modern Venice. In the end, though, Rod emerges not as a malicious Iago, attempting to destroy his friend's happiness, but rather as an embodiment of Chris's (and the audience's) own anxieties regarding the taboo of interracial romance. Not surprisingly, the Armitages strive to cut off communication between Rod and Chris once he arrives at their house, maintaining unopposed the lie that there is nothing for Chris to fear, a lie that will allow them to control him entirely. Rod, then, becomes a voice for African Americans' cultural history: he speaks out against what the Armitages' plantation-style home communicates visually, expressing a discourse the postracial society attempts to suppress.

The battle for influence over Chris's mind and body becomes clear once Missy Armitage begins the process of hypnotizing him. In this sense, Missy the hypnotherapist becomes the film's actual embodiment of Iago, brazenly using the spoken word and the audio cue of a spoon scraping and tapping a teacup to reprogram Chris's mind so that his agency is removed and the rightful control of his own body can be usurped by a white pilot. Just as Iago fills Othello's head with white society's stereotypes of black men, and so dictates Othello's actions, so does Missy's hypnotism and the Coagula cult's brain transplant procedure seek to fill Chris's black body with the thoughts of a white man, locking Chris's consciousness in "the sunken place," where he would become a prisoner in his own body. When Missy first administers hypnotherapy to a reluctant Chris, his consciousness descends into darkness while his physical body in the chair goes rigid and silently convulses. Othello experiences a similar loss of speech and motor control when Iago drives him into an epileptic seizure by using sly verbal cues regarding Desdemona's alleged promiscuity. As Othello "falls in a trance," Iago casts himself as psychiatrist, proclaiming, "Work on, / My medicine, work!"[31] Interestingly, multiple critics of Shakespeare's play link Iago's power over Othello with hypnotism and mind control. Paul Cefalu argues that "Iago's evil seems to lie in his talent for what cognitive theorists would describe as mind reading, the relative ability to access imaginatively another's mental world and, in Iago's case, to manipulate cruelly that world."[32] Likewise, Haim Omer and Marcello Da Verona call Iago "a therapist from hell" who tries to destroy his client rather than help cure him,[33] who "acts like a hypnotist . . . [and] leads the subject to doubt his own eyes and then view the illusion as possible, probable and, finally, certain."[34] Without doing more than

31. Shakespeare, *Othello*, 4.1.53–54.

32. Cefalu, "Burdens," 265.

33. Omer and Da Verona, "Doctor Iago's," 99.

34. Ibid., 106.

altering the pronouns, these descriptions could apply to *Get Out*'s Missy, who places Chris in a stage of "heightened suggestibility" by pretending to help cure his past traumas, just as a therapist would. And as Iago's suggestions embed themselves within Othello's psyche, so does Missy's hypnotherapy unearth inescapable thoughts within Chris, who tries to explain to Rose, "She got in my head. And now I'm thinking all this fucked up shit that I don't want to think about"—specifically, the implication that Chris's inaction as a boy was somehow responsible for his mother's death. Missy uses this idea to paralyze Chris, to convince him that he, because of his past trauma, has already given up his ability to act, metaphorically preparing him for the literal removal of agency that the Coagula procedure represents.

Of course, in the film's third act, the audience learns that Rose, too, has been using the spoken word to control Chris, not via hypnosis, but through subtle manipulation, coercing him to stay at her parents' house despite his (and Rod's and the audience's) better judgment. During these scenes of ostensible emotional connection between the two leads, Peele uses a tender, romantic musical theme to heighten the impression of affection and intimacy. As Rose appears disgusted by her family's prejudices, Peele encourages the audience to worry not just for the safety of Chris, but for the safety of their authentic interracial romance as well. This desire for healing through interracial unification is visually expressed in the wardrobes of Chris and Rose during a private, lakeside debate about whether or not to leave the increasingly uncomfortable weekend at the Armitage house. Chris wears a blue shirt, and Rose wears a red and white striped sweater, so that when they lean against one another, they approximate a unified American flag—visually embodying the healing of America through interracial love. Unfortunately, though, Rose is no innocent Desdemona; she is just as manipulative and evil as her mother. Indeed, she practices exactly the sexual manipulation that Rod had accused her of earlier in the film. When Chris finds a private box of pictures—too late—he flips through images of Rose's multiple black boyfriends, all lured to her house, until he sees the final picture of Rose romantically hugging the black woman whose body became the vessel for her grandmother, known to Chris as Georgina the housekeeper. Rose represents, it turns out, the promiscuous and exotic sexuality of the white woman attracted to black men—the very stereotype that Iago falsely attributes to Desdemona. Thus, while Dean and Jeremy Armitage pose physical threats to the body of Chris, the white women ultimately manipulate and control the black mind.

Chris's realization about the true nature of Rose marks one of the defining differences between *Othello* as a tragedy and *Get Out* as a horror film.

According to Leon Golden, *Othello* is the rare post-Classical tragedy that follows the ideal Aristotelian tragic format: "the fall from happiness to misery, caused by a serious intellectual error, on the part of a hero who is worthy of respect and whose fate consequently evokes pity and fear as appropriate audience responses."[35] Indeed, Shakespeare initially depicts "brave Othello" as heroic and admirable,[36] both for his military accomplishments and for what Iago admits is his "constant, loving, and noble nature."[37] Even in the prejudiced Venetian rhetoric, Othello "is far more fair than black."[38] *Get Out*'s Chris also appears to possess heroic attributes: he is a successful photographer able to capture profound images of beauty in ordinary, urban settings; he is affectionate and caring with Rose; and he is patient in the face of the seemingly innocuous racism he encounters at the beginning of the film. But while Othello certainly makes a "serious intellectual error" (his *hamartia*) in listening to "Honest Iago" and believing that his wife is unfaithful,[39] Chris is immediately suspicious of Missy's practice of hypnosis. Whereas Othello's tragic journey involves trusting more and more in Iago's lies, Chris's horrific journey involves trusting everyone around him less and less. If he makes an intellectual error at all, it occurs before the film begins, when he ignores Rod's advice and agrees to meet Rose's parents in the first place. The tragedy of *Othello*, therefore, is one based on misreadings, suspicions that are wrong but nevertheless acted upon, causing unnecessary suffering and death. The horror of *Get Out*, on the other hand, is based on suspicions that are correct—the racial anxieties voiced by Rod—but not acted upon quickly enough, leading to physical pain and death. It is fitting, then, that in *Get Out*, Chris's Rose is exactly the deceptive devil that Othello incorrectly fears his Desdemona to be.[40]

If horror represents the actualization of fears that the tragic hero imagines and misinterprets, it is logical that the suffering of the genres' respective protagonists would be of different natures. Othello's suffering is psychological, born from his doubts about Desdemona: "Farewell the tranquil mind! Farewell content!" he cries upon first considering Desdemona's

35. Golden, "*Othello*," 142, 150.

36. Shakespeare, *Othello*, 2.1.42.

37. Ibid., 2.1.311.

38. Ibid., 1.3.331.

39. Ibid., 1.3.336.

40. Chris's desperate near-strangulation of Rose reverses Othello's tragically mistaken strangulation of Desdemona. Othello uncannily foreshadows the murder with the phrase, "When I have plucked the rose, / I cannot give it vital growth again" (5.2.13–15)—perhaps inspiring the name of Peele's evil Desdemona.

infidelity.[41] Meanwhile, the pity and fear that the audience experiences is based on dreading the character's psychological suffering, linked to the terrible actions the tragic hero might take as a result of his *hamartia*; the audience fears that they, too, may psychologically suffer should they make the same tragic mistake. Chris's suffering, on the other hand, is experienced through his body as the result of very real, external threats; he is strangled, stabbed through the hand, tied to a chair, and forced to await his looming lobotomy. The audience's fear is caused by dreading the physical torture inflicted upon the hero, not the mistaken actions the hero might inflict upon others. Indeed, according to Carol J. Clover, horror films both create and require in their audience the "masochistic pleasure" of victim identification, the empathetic association with the "fear and pain" of the horror protagonist.[42] The genre overcomes what Elaine Scarry calls the "unsharability" of pain[43] by transcending the limitations of language, not just through depictions of violence and gore, but through formal techniques such as claustrophobic camera framing, smash cuts in the editing, and stingers in the musical score—assaulting the viewer's physical senses just as the villains assault the hero's physical body. Thus, the juxtaposition of *Othello* and *Get Out* shows how the internal, psychological suffering of tragedy, caused by abstract threats, becomes the external, physical suffering of horror caused by tangible objects. The threat to Othello's agency represented by Iago and his manipulative stereotypes is a predominantly psychological threat, without tangible form, while the threat to Chris's agency is predominantly physical: the Armitages intend to literally remove his brain and take control of his body using a hypnotic technique reliant on a very real teacup.[44]

Not surprisingly, Chris's final escape from this horrific scenario induces a different type of catharsis than what is typically associated with tragedy. Golden argues that the Aristotelian concept of catharsis in *Othello* represents an "ultimate clarification of the events presented in the *mimesis*" of the play, framing the entire tragedy as a learning experience for the audience.[45] As

41. Shakespeare, *Othello*, 3.3.400.

42. Clover, *Men, Women*, xii, 5.

43. Scarry, *Body in Pain*, 4.

44. Othello's downfall hinges on Iago's manipulation of a physical object, Desdemona's handkerchief. The handkerchief's power, however, is purely symbolic; Iago conjures from it proof of Desdemona's infidelity, casting it as a symbol for "her honor . . . an essence that's not seen" (4.1.19). Missy's teacup, conversely, is physically necessary to her process of hypnosis; its power resides in its function as a tangible mechanism, not in any symbolic meanings attached to it. For more on the handkerchief as a symbol, see Smith, "Othello's Black Handkerchief."

45. Golden, "*Othello*," 143.

Othello finally understands the schemes that led to his demise, he proves his noble nature and can rationally explain what had before seemed irrational. The catharsis present in the climax of *Get Out,* however, shares more with the modern psychoanalytic concept of the term as a purgative experience that frees one from past trauma. Chris's escape is dependent on the reclamation of both the personal trauma that Missy uses to enslave him and the collective cultural trauma of African Americans' enslavement. Chris reclaims both traumas at once: while forced through hypnosis to relive his memories of the night his mother died, Chris begins scratching the arms of the chair to which Missy's hypnosis binds him; it is an automatic, unconscious, nervous response, a physical manifestation of posttraumatic stress. Later, when he is literally bound to a chair awaiting his lobotomy, hypnosis is used again, causing the same scratching of his fingers against the leather arms of the chair. This phantom reflex from his past trauma leads to his freedom, as his scratching reveals cotton within the chair; by picking this cotton—by appropriating this symbol of African Americans' collective enslavement—Chris is able to fashion ear plugs that protect him from the next wave of hypnosis. Fittingly, just as Othello's demise comes as the result of succumbing to the influence of Iago's words, Chris's salvation is accomplished by removing external influences, momentarily making himself deaf through the recovery of African Americans' past commodification, discovered through his own personal trauma.

Paradoxically, in order to complete his cathartic escape, Chris also appropriates some of the very stereotypes that white society has used to judge and control him. Although he earlier told Jeremy that MMA was "too brutal" for him, by the end of the film, Chris seems to have turned into the physical "beast" Jeremy believed he could be, smashing heads with bocce balls, impaling necks with antlers,[46] and stomping on heads. Ironically, these stereotypes of Chris's animalistic physical ability and superior genetic makeup fill the white power structure with the desire to own his body; the very existence of the stereotypes themselves creates the threat to his agency. Thus, in order to escape the racist society that wants to control the same black body it stereotypes, Chris must become a version of those stereotypes. Unlike

46. Not only does this represent a moment in which Chris truly identifies as a beast by charging toward Dean with the stuffed bust of a stag, but it also provides poetic justice based on Dean's earlier comment that he would kill all the deer in the woods if he could, since they are invading the Armitages' land and supposedly ruining the ecosystem. Dean's rationale, of course, is reminiscent of arguments used by xenophobic Americans against minorities and immigrants. Thus, the prejudiced parallel between wild animals and minorities hinted at by Dean is appropriated by Chris to earn his freedom, killing Dean in the process.

Othello, whose coerced transition into the image of the violent and jealous Moor represents the culmination of his tragic journey, Chris's transformation into a physically dominant presence is what frees him. By willfully appropriating both his past traumas as well as the stereotypes that white society perpetuates to condemn black men to a tragic fate—the very stereotypes that lead to Othello's downfall—Chris wields the tools of tragedy for his own cathartic healing and salvation, a feat only possible because the threats he faces are not strictly psychological, but external, physical dangers. Therefore, because Jordan Peele confronts the tragic, psychological suffering caused by racial stereotypes and cultural appropriation by repositioning it as an attack on the physical body, Chris's escape in *Get Out* depicts the ultimate triumph over tragedy through horror. By externalizing fears and threats, modern horror provides its protagonists the chance to elude the ultimate suffering of death, to outwit fate and the forces that would make a tragedy of their lives, to purge the psychological suffering of tragedy through overcoming physical pain.

Bibliography

Adelman, Janet. "Iago's Alter Ego: Race as Projection in *Othello*." *Shakespeare Quarterly* 48, no. 2 (1997): 125–44.

Africanus, John Leo. *A Geographical Historie of Africa*. Translated by John Pory. London: George Bishop, 1600. https://www.bl.uk/collection-items/leo-africanuss-geographical-history-of-africa.

Berman, Eliza. "Jordan Peele Made Us Seriously Laugh. Now He's Going to Scare Us Silly." *Time*, February 27–March 6, 2017.

Best, George. *A True Discourse of the late voyages of discoverie, for the finding of a passage to Cathaya, by the Northweast, under the conduct of Martin Frobisher Gernerall: Devided into three Bookes*. London: Henry Bynnyman, 1578. https://quod.lib.umich.edu/e/eebo/A09429.0001.001?rgn=main;view=fulltext.

Cefalu, Paul. "The Burdens of Mind Reading in Shakespeare's *Othello*: A Cognitive and Psychoanalytic Approach to Iago's Theory of Mind." *Shakespeare Quarterly* 64, no. 3 (2013): 265–94.

Clover, Carol J. *Men, Women, and Chain Saws: Gender in the Modern Horror Film*. Princeton, NJ: Princeton University Press, 2015. First published 1992.

Contarini, Gaspar. *The Commonwealth and Government of Venice*. Translated by Lewes Lewkenor. London: John Windet for Edmund Mattes, 1599. *Early English Books Online*. http://gateway.proquest.com.libproxy.csustan.edu/openurl?ctx_ver=Z39.88-2003&res_id=xri:eebo&rft_id=xri:eebo:citation:99844276.

Draper, John W. *The* Othello *of Shakespeare's Audience*. New York: Octagon Books, 1978. First published 1952.

Elizabeth I, Queen of England. "An Open Letter about 'Negroes' Brought Home." July 11, 1596. PC 2/21, f. 304. *Black Presence: Asian and Black History in Britain, 1500–1850.* The National Archives, Richmond, Surrey, England. http://www.nationalarchives.gov.uk/pathways/blackhistory/early_times/transcripts/privy_council.htm.

———. "Those kinde of people may be well spared." July 18, 1596. PC 2/21, f. 306. *Black Presence: Asian and Black History in Britain, 1500–1850.* The National Archives, Richmond, Surrey, England. http://www.nationalarchives.gov.uk/pathways/blackhistory/early_times/transcripts/privy_van_senden.htm.

Get Out. Directed by Jordan Peele. USA: Universal Pictures, 2017. DVD.

Golden, Leon. "*Othello, Hamlet,* and Aristotelian Tragedy." *Shakespeare Quarterly* 35, no. 2 (1984): 142–56.

Hunter, G. K. "Elizabethans and Foreigners." In *Shakespeare and Race,* edited by Catherine M. S. Alexander and Stanley Wells, 37–63. Cambridge: Cambridge University Press, 2000.

Loomba, Ania. *Shakespeare, Race, and Colonialism.* Oxford: Oxford University Press, 2002.

Omer, Haim, and Marcello Da Verona. "Doctor Iago's Treatment of Othello." *American Journal of Psychotherapy* 45, no. 1 (1991): 99–112.

Scarry, Elaine. *The Body in Pain: The Making and Unmaking of the World.* New York: Oxford University Press, 1985.

Shakespeare, William. *Othello.* Ed. Barbara A. Mowat and Paul Werstine. New York: Simon & Schuster, 1993. First Published 1603.

Smith, Ian. "Othello's Black Handkerchief." *Shakespeare Quarterly* 64, no. 1 (2013): 1–25.

CHAPTER 2

BURNING DOWN THE HOUSE

Get Out and the Female Gothic

LINNIE BLAKE

WITH ITS blighted landscapes, cruel patriarchs, etiolated bloodlines, inescapable haunted houses, and terrified victims, the Gothic mode is an ideal means by which to represent the horrors of African American life. Certainly, black American author Richard Wright believed this—asserting that "the oppression of the Negro" had cast "a shadow athwart our national life dense and heavy enough to satisfy even the gloomy brooding of a Hawthorne."[1] Were Edgar Allan Poe alive in the American 1940s, Wright observed, "he would not have to invent horror," as the horrors of contemporary inequalities would, in effect, "invent him."[2] Some eighty years on, Jordan Peele's award-winning *Get Out* is a filmic actualization of Wright's observations: it deftly adopts a range of Gothic narrative and stylistic strategies—most notably those of the Female Gothic—and adapts them to the purpose of African American representation, most specifically black inequality under the law. Peele thus repudiates the depiction of African Americans as passive victims of white violence, a trope that has beleaguered black representation in America since J. Hector St. John de Crèvecoeur first symbolized the horror of racial injustice in his eighteenth-century depiction of a caged slave left to die in an otherwise idyl-

1. Wright, "How Bigger," xxxiv.
2. Ibid., xxvii.

lic forest.[3] In the cinematically released version of the film at least, *Get Out*'s protagonist Chris Washington resists his victimization at every turn; Peele's film eschews the appeal to the sympathies of the white middle classes such as was practiced by Crèvecoeur and is familiar from abolitionist novels of the nineteenth century like Harriet Beecher Stowe's *Uncle Tom's Cabin* (1852). While Peele situates his narrative firmly within the Female Gothic tradition, he refuses to feminize his protagonist or to make him passive in the face of overwhelming oppression. In this, he draws upon the Female Gothic's ability to capture the emotional impact of white patriarchal violence while charting the voyage undertaken by the Female Gothic's protagonist toward empowered self-actualization and delightfully ironic revenge.

The Female Gothic, critic Ellen Moers claims, is "easily defined as the work that women writers have done in the literary mode that, since the eighteenth century, we have called the Gothic."[4] Its progenitor was the English novelist Ann Radcliffe, whose work pioneered much of the sub-mode's narrative and symbolic machinery. Commonly, an orphaned young woman, haunted by the absence of her mother, would find herself imprisoned within an uncanny domestic setting in which she was pursued or persecuted by a feudal patriarch seeking to curtail her independence and bend her to his will. Thus, Moers argues, it was terror and not explicit horror that characterized the mode: Female Gothic texts were infused with a palpable sense of dread, manifesting as an atmosphere of uncanny and supernaturally inflected secrecy that frequently would be explained away at the end. Enacting a proto-feminist consciousness, early Female Gothic texts linked ostensibly supernatural events to the buried secrets of the patriarchy. These secrets were embodied in the patriarchal family and often led to the violation of the protagonist, the expropriation of her resources, or her punishment for real or fabricated crimes.

In time, the Female Gothic sub-mode would become a staple of cinematic culture. It blossomed in the 1940s, for example, when the emotional dislocations of the decade were captured in films such as Alfred Hitchcock's *Rebecca* (1940), Joseph Mankiewitz's *Dragonwyck* (1946), and Lewis Allen's *The Uninvited* (1944). In each, a young woman took up residence in a remotely located Gothic house where, oppressed by an atmosphere of conspiracy and secrecy, she would come to discover the terrible history of the house and its nefarious inhabitants. Only by doing so, this film cycle argued, might the protagonists gain a knowledge of themselves and the strength to break free

3. Crèvecoeur, *Letters*, 163.

4. Moers, *Literary Women*, 90.

of the forces that oppressed them. More recently, films like Joseph Ruben's *Sleeping With the Enemy* (1990), Damian Harris's *Deceived* (1991), and Robert Zemekis's *What Lies Beneath* (1991) have returned to the domestic space as a means of engaging with contemporary women's fears—of male infidelity, duplicity, cupidity, and murderous violence. They are themes that have survived into the present, of course; Cary Fukunaga's adaptation of *Jane Eyre* (2011) and Guillermo del Toro's *Crimson Peak* (2015) return us to sinister houses, dangerous patriarchs, and the ongoing repudiation of victim status by women who have come to understand just how strong they are. Across centuries, national borders, and media representations, the Female Gothic has remained a means of capturing not only the despotic cruelties of patriarchy but also the emotional impact of power unjustly wielded, all while propounding the necessity of resisting such injustice by whatever means necessary.

Peele's decision to adopt the Female Gothic in service of African American representation is potentially problematic, however. For, as Donald Bogle has argued, while American society initially deemed African Americans subhuman property, and later depicted them as comical children, rapists, murderers, and thieves, it has also undertaken a rather troubling conflation of black men and white women—positioning both, in Maisha Wester's words, as "Other, commodity, and monster."[5] *Get Out* challenges this conflation at every turn, though, in part by emphasizing Chris's youthful masculinity and in part by foregrounding the African American linguistic and cultural practice of "signifying." As defined by Henry Louis Gates Jr. in his groundbreaking study *The Signifying Monkey: A Theory of African American Literary Criticism*, signifying is a linguistic practice drawn from West African storytelling traditions and made manifest in black American vernacular speech, literature, and culture. Operating, in part, as a "mode of encoding for self-preservation,"[6] signifying is also a "mode of linguistic circumnavigation"[7] that parodies white racism, cultural forms, and the state institutions that embody it, mounting in the process what Ralph Ellison would term "a technical assault on the styles which have gone before."[8] Acting as counterpoint to the Female Gothic tropes and practices of *Get Out*, then, it is signifying that furnishes much of the film's bleak humor—Rod's telephone conversations, with their playful sexual innuendo, wordplay, and ostensibly ridiculous (yet entirely accurate) talk of white body snatchers and sex slavery

5. Wester, *African American Gothic*, 27.
6. Gates, *Signifying*, 67.
7. Ibid., 76.
8. Ellison, *Shadow*, 137.

being a case in point. Thus, signifying practice refashions Female Gothic conventions in service of black representation by signifying on bourgeois American culture and white social practices, proffering a powerful indictment of a white privilege rooted in the intergenerational transfer of both financial assets and racist ideology. In its signifying practice, *Get Out* fosters affective identification with the black male protagonist: Chris emerges as a resourceful survivor whose ultimate escape from murderous white oppression occurs both as a product of his own abilities and of solidarity with other black men.

Early in the film, Chris travels from the urban America of his youth to a terrifying place in which he is not only geographically isolated but is culturally distanced from what Ralph Ellison called the "Negro American . . . concord of sensibilities . . . which . . . has come to constitute a subdivision of the larger American Culture."[9] Here Chris encounters other black people, but when he attempts to address them in ways that are both culturally and historically situated, he is met with blank incomprehension. Walter's mechanical midnight running and Georgina's mirror-gazing, wig-adjusting, kitchen-polishing passivity become doubly uncanny, therefore, when the characters fail to recognize Chris's signifying practices. Chris's "Workin' you good?" to a wood-chopping Walter is met with an incongruously defensive "Nothing I don't want to be doing" that is evocative of the myth of the contented slave.[10] Georgina fails to recognize Chris's use of the terms "snitch" and "rat you out" and suggests "tattle tale" instead. And both these instances are echoed by the handshake with which Logan King returns Chris's proffered fist bump. Peele is clearly adopting here the Female Gothic trope of the sinister servant—that uncanny figure possessed by the spirit of the past, familiar from Jack Clayton's *The Innocents* (1961) and, more recently, Alejandro Amenábar's *The Others* (2001). But its adoption here is highly sophisticated: the servants quite literally embody the disjunction between black and white perception, social interaction, and cultural experience that

9. Ibid., 131.

10. It was a myth Frederick Douglass challenged passionately in 1848. He not only denied that slaves ever could be happy but also argued that even "if slaves were contented and happy, that fact alone should be the everlasting condemnation of slavery, and hunt the monster from human society with curses on its head. What! does it so paralyze the soul, subvert its instincts, blot out its reason, crush its upward tendings, and murder its higher nature, that a man can become 'contented and happy,' though robbed of his body, mind, free choice, liberty, time, earnings, and all his rights, and while his life, limbs, health, conscience, food, raiment, sleep, wife and children, have no protection, but are subject every moment to the whims and passion-gusts of an owner, a manstealer?" See Douglass, "Happy Slaves."

is played upon in the act of signifying. Peele's cinematography heightens the effect; innumerable close ups of Chris's raised eyebrow, half smiles, knowing nods, and decisions to remain silent simultaneously make the audience complicit with his ironic commentary on the Armitage circle's disguised yet palpable racism whilst heightening the utter incongruity of Walter and Georgina. These servants are sinister, in other words, because they actualize a commonly used metaphor for black people whose values, allegiances, and cultural practices make them "white on the inside." In an intriguing act of Gothic doubling, moreover, Peele links Walter, Georgina, and Logan to the three cops to whom Rod presents his admittedly rather outlandish claims that white people are kidnapping black people for their own nefarious ends. In laughing uproariously at Rod while refusing to investigate his claims, the police officers not only humiliate him personally but underscore the fact that African Americans are seldom equal to whites under the law,[11] and police officers of color are not, necessarily, black all the way through. The melding of the Female Gothic's "sinister servant" and "double" conventions with Chris's signifying speech effectively tempers terror with humor while intimating that African Americans need, in Rod's words, to "handle shit" for themselves in the absence of judicial protection.[12]

In undertaking his perilous journey, then, Chris is reminded of a distinctively African American truth—not only is the countryside no safer than the city for a black man but US race relations are themselves haunted by the past, including slavery and ongoing failures to make good on the demands of the Civil Rights Movement. This paradigm is a further instance of doubled signification. It overturns the historic depiction of the city as *the* place of danger, repository of "a myriad of social ills that disproportionately affected Blacks—such as poverty, crime, drug abuse, high unemployment, and welfare abuse."[13] It then also recasts the white suburbs in this role—the film opening with the abduction of Andre Hayworth on an affluent leafy street and moving to an upstate community of ostensibly postracial liberals. For how can the terrors of black oppression exist in an affluent postracial world where golf-fanatic Gordon "loves Tiger" and patriarch Dean Armitage "would have voted for Obama a third time"? Peele shows us how, the historic mansion of the Female Gothic having transmuted into a new site

11. It is a paradigm explored at length in the superlative documentary *13th* by Ava DuVernay, which examines the interrelation of ethnicity and justice in the United States to indict the prison-industrial complex, especially the enormous corporate profits garnered by mass incarceration of people of color.

12. *Get Out.* All further references to the film are to this DVD.

13. Means Coleman, *Horror Noire,* 145.

of distinctively African American terror. On first sight, in other words, the Armitage home may appear to be a comfortable bourgeois utopia, replete with tolerant attitudes and good-humored camaraderie. But on closer inspection (close inspection being, after all, a function of the entrapped protagonist of the Female Gothic), it is revealed as a plantation-encoded site of murderous conspiracy, medical experimentation, enslavement, and death.

Thus Peele critiques the ideology of place that is promulgated by popular culture and encapsulated in numerous cinematic offerings, of which the Female Gothic-inflected *Candyman* (1992) is but one example. Representations are dangerous, he warns, particularly when one is habitually represented by those outside one's class and race. They are even more dangerous when those representations are internalized. Rod knows this—repeatedly warning Chris against travelling to a white girl's parents' house—and insisting that it is a potentially lethal undertaking to allow a white person to penetrate one's consciousness. For this is precisely the means by which Rose's mother pacifies Chris—hypnosis itself being a strongly Gothic trope since Ann Radcliffe inaugurated a tradition of piercing-eyed villains (Montoni of *The Mysteries of Udolpho* and Schedoni of *The Italian*) who used their mesmerizing gifts to seduce or otherwise endanger the heroine. *Get Out*'s hypnotism scene thus serves to consolidate Chris's status as Female Gothic protagonist, particularly given that it cuts between extreme close-ups of his weeping face in the present and a flashback childhood point-of-view sequence of the night his mother died. The orphaned protagonist, traumatized by his childhood loss, is thus catapulted down to the "sunken place" in which he is unable to move, speak, or act as he gazes helplessly upward at his captor from the dungeon of his own psyche. It is a quintessentially Female Gothic vision, particularly in the interjection here of the African American past. Sunk down to the dark place, Chris becomes the captive of US history—particularly the history of slavery indicted so forcibly in the speech "I Have a Nightmare (I Charge the White Man)," reproduced by Spike Lee as soundtrack to the opening credits of his biopic *Malcolm X* (1992). For the white man, Brother Malcolm observed, did not say to black people, "Black man, Black woman, come on over and help me build America." He said, instead, "Nigger, get down in the bottom of that boat and I'm taking you over there to help me build America."[14] Hurled to the bottom of his own psychic boat by Missy Armitage's hypnotic instruction prior to the expropriation of his body by the white upper-middle classes, Chris becomes a powerful warning against acceptance of white power and

14. *Malcolm X.*

white control. For acceptance leads to a Female Gothic encoded entrapment from which it is impossible to escape alone.

As a photographer, though, Chris is well positioned to see things differently and to challenge, in his work, what David Marriott has termed the violent "racial scopophilia"[15] that has been historically actualized in the United States as pictures of murderous violence done to black bodies by whites.[16] He does this in taking pictures of his own community—monochrome renderings of urban America that impart a sense of value to the quotidian world of Chris's urban childhood, a value the assembled party guests at the Armitage estate would be unable to perceive. Chris's depictions of urban American life appear to be a further act of signification on Peele's part, evoking the double consciousness of a young black man whose photographic renderings of his home are purchased by white Americans in much the same way black areas have been bought up by white speculators seeking to gentrify the neighborhood. The blind art dealer Jim Hudson sees Chris's work as "brutal," "melancholic," and "powerful," focusing on its sublime qualities in much the same way as a Gothic novelist might focus on a dread-imbued landscape. Hudson's perspective, though, is that of the affluent outsider entirely disengaged from the ebullient humanity of Chris's photographic subjects and the emotional realities of their lives. The culture of the Armitage circle, after all, can be seen to prize the black celebrity as "some kind of house pet one lets roam all through the house,"[17] but its perspective on black people in general is that of the slave auction. Black people may be star athletes and may even rise to the status of president, but mostly they are denizens of the ghetto, intrinsically frightening and valuable only as potential host bodies. Chris's "great eye" sees this. Hudson's never will, even if he comes to inhabit Chris's body.

Other photographs in *Get Out*, specifically the family portraits of the Armitage clan, usher in a buried history of eugenic science that, like Gothic mode and racial theory itself, emerged from the revolutionary turbulence of

15. Marriott, *On Black Men*, 32.

16. David Marriott explores the phenomenon of lynching photography at length. Five thousand people died by lynching between 1882 and 1946, many of them forming a horrifying postmortem centerpiece to commemorative photographs that not only captured the glee with which white communities came together to celebrate such events but which frequently echoed contemporaneous pictures of hunters commemorating their animal kills.

17. Samad, "O. J. Did It!"

the eighteenth century and survives to the present day.[18] The Gothic has long deployed the trope of the family portrait as a means of exploring the ways in which ancient families transfer both material assets and ideologies of identity from generation to generation. The first Gothic novel, Horace Walpole's *The Castle of Otranto* (1764), has Manfred, the novel's villain, terrified when his grandfather Ricardo steps out of a family portrait, spelling the end of his blood line. In the nineteenth-century United States, Nathaniel Hawthorne's *The House of the Seven Gables* (1854) featured a portrait of Judge Pynchon whose greedy expropriation of another man's land has cursed his successors and led to a marked decline in the family fortunes. In the twentieth century, the Female Gothic film cycle of the 1940s would undertake a similar deployment: *Rebecca, Dragonwyck,* and George Cukor's *Gaslight* (1944) foreground portraits of female ancestors or predecessors to point to the heroine's entrapment within both the patriarch's ancestral home and contemporary ideologies of gender.

Peele makes similar use of the portrait in *Get Out*—the photograph of Rose's grandparents, parents, and brother assembled before their colonial-era home serving as a visual encapsulation of their history, their class position, and their ethnicity, all of which position them as inheritors of the Declaration's discourse of natural rights and beneficiaries of capitalist economics. This portrait comes to life, moreover, when Chris is strapped to a chair in the family's subterranean laboratory awaiting the expropriation of his body. The portrait is revealed as a still from a video made by Roman Armitage to explain the "Coagula" process to its victims. The Gothic trope of the animated portrait is given a new and sinister twist, in other words,

18. The appeal to an ancestry distinct from and yet tragically entwined with that of the white patriarch is further encapsulated in the protagonist's name—Chris Washington's surname, as the journalist Jesse Washington has written, being widely acknowledged as the "blackest" of all patronymics following the Census of 2000 in which only 5.2% of Americans bearing the name were discovered to be white. Dating to the antebellum period, the popularity of the name is attributed to public knowledge, even among former slaves, of the first president's deathbed emancipation of his human property. Thus adopting the name in recognition of their own emancipation, African Americans would so make it their own that *all* "Washingtons" recorded between 1880 and 1930 were black. The irony is not lost on Peele. Chris's name reminds us that the enslavement of African Americans was practiced at the very heart of democratic governance. But also, as ostensible beneficiary of postracial American opportunity, Chris continues to carry his ancestors' history with him. Chris's name, then, signals not only his distant ancestors' antebellum dispossession of their African identities but his Reconstruction descendants' attempts to enter American civic life—ironically, by adopting the name of a democracy-touting slave owner. See Washington, "Washington."

as Roman outlines his projected appropriation of "the physical advantage" imparted by Chris's "genes." It has now become imperative that Chris pays heed to the Swahili-language title song "Sikiliza Kwa Wahenga," that was first heard when he left the city and secondly when the momentarily revived Andre Heyworth warned him to "Get out." Its warning is familiar from the Female Gothic, too. Chris must "Listen to the Ancestors" and "Run!"[19]

Chris's flight from the Armitage mansion is neither surreptitious, as in the Female Gothic mode, or without cost to those who have sought to reinstate a new form of enslavement of African American people. He first stuffs his ears with padding pulled from his chair in a manner designed to delight anyone even vaguely familiar with the cotton-picking history of the southern US. He then bludgeons the son and heir Jeremy Armitage to unconsciousness with a yellow boule—an act that not only offers an ironic comment on the way sports in the US is encoded by class and ethnicity but further signifies on Jeremy's earlier characterization of Chris as a potential "beast" in the wrestling arena. That Chris then looks to the mounted head of a deer hanging on the wall is the final irony, our hero reclaiming for his own purposes the role of "buck"—a slavery-era term for a powerful black man, often characterized by a rapacious sexuality and a penchant for terrifying violence. Chris is no trophy, this sequence veritably shouts. He will survive. The motif is hammered home in his killing of the patriarch himself: the man who affirmed that deer "are takin' over . . . like rats" is impaled on a set of mounted antlers. Chris has indeed listened to the ancestors and to the historic conventions of the Female Gothic and worked to escape his entrapment. But to do so, he has been forced to become all that white masculinity fears in the black man. He has become stronger, quicker, and smarter. And, in so becoming, he snuffs out the Armitage line. The role of victim enshrined in the American imagination by generations of lynching photographs, which Marriott has linked iconographically to pictures of slaughtered deer, is here rejected. Chris leaves the Armitage house ablaze. It is a trope familiar from the Female Gothic—Bertha Mason burning down Thornfield Hall in *Jane Eyre* and Mrs. Danvers burning down Manderley in *Rebecca,* for example. But it is also familiar from both sporadic slave revolts and General Sherman's 1864 March to the Sea, which destroyed the infrastructure of the Civil War South's plantation-based economy. "You ruined my house," the Armitage matriarch screams. And Chris is nearly free.

It is entirely appropriate that in the cinematic release of the film, Chris is rescued not by a love interest, as was so frequently the case in Radcliffe's novels, but by two black men: the unnamed individual whose body was

19. Pulliam-Moore, "Hidden Swahili."

expropriated by Roman Armitage and Chris's best friend Rod. This conforms to the traditionally happy ending of the Female Gothic mode while refashioning its heteronormative romance convention—rescue coming as an act of friendship and ethnic solidarity and not as a precursor to marriage between a man and a woman.

The alternate ending, however, is an entirely different proposition—Chris strangling Rose, being arrested by two white policemen and incarcerated, presumably, for life. In this horrifying alternative world, Rod visits Chris in prison, where the Gothic trope of portraiture is revisited for a final time: three black prisoners are framed within the glass partition panels between the visit cubicles. The film's critique of the criminal justice system is concluded in a highly Gothic manner, an orange jumpsuit-clad Chris walking back to his cell down a stark, white corridor as a series of massive internal gates slide closed behind him. The title song swells on the soundtrack. The penalty for failing to listen to the ancestors when there was time, it seems, is a new mode of entrapment in another kind of big house. If the cinematic release melded the conventions of the Female Gothic with signifying practices to present the protagonist as a wily trickster who survives all that class and racial privilege can visit upon him, then the alternate ending presents him as a defeated man who takes comfort only from the fact that he put an end to the activities of the Armitage family and their circle. Only in the film's alternate ending, in other words, does Chris become a Crèvecoeurian victim—of racist science, economic disadvantage, and the utter failure of the criminal justice system to ensure the equality of black people under the law. If the Female Gothic, as Mary Wollstonecraft's *Maria; or, the Wrongs of Women* (1798) put it, had encapsulated all the "misery and oppression, peculiar to women, that arise out of the partial laws and customs of society,"[20] then Jordan Peele's alternative ending accomplishes much the same for contemporary African American men.

With the alternative ending, I think there is little doubt that *Get Out* would have failed to win the Academy Award for Best Original Screenplay. But it is in this version that the Female Gothic and signifying practices that structure the film come to their fullest and most searing realization; the themes of entrapment, bodily appropriation, photographic representation, and victimhood also find resolution here. The result is a powerful indictment of the US judicial system that is insistently Female Gothic. We leave Chris trapped behind innumerable sets of bars, no longer the subject of photography but its shuffling object. For such, as Richard Wright once argued, is African American life: nightmarish, horrifying, and unjust at every turn.

---

20. Wollstonecraft, *Maria*, 7.

Bibliography

Bogle, Thomas. *Toms, Coons, Mulattos, Mammies and Bucks: An Interpretive History of Blacks in American Films*. New York: Continuum International, 2001.

Crèvecoeur, Hector St. John. *Letters from an American Farmer*, edited by Susan Manning. Oxford: Oxford University Press, 1997. First published 1782.

Douglass, Frederick. "The Myth of the Happy Slaves." *North Star*, April 28, 1848. http://www.accessible-archives.com/2012/04/the-myth-of-the-happy-slaves-in-the-north-star/.

Ellison, Ralph. *Shadow and Act*. New York: Vintage, 1964.

Gates, Henry Louis Jr. *The Signifying Monkey: A Theory of African American Literature*. Oxford: Oxford University Press, 1988.

Get Out. Directed by Jordan Peele. USA: Universal Pictures, 2017. DVD.

Malcolm X. Directed by Spike Lee. 1992. USA: Warner Home Video, 2000. DVD.

Marriott, David. *On Black Men*. Edinburgh: Edinburgh University Press, 2000.

Means Coleman, Robin R. *Horror Noire: Blacks in American Horror Films from the 1890s to Present*. New York: Routledge, 2011.

Moers, Ellen. *Literary Women*. London: Women's Press, 1978.

Pulliam-Moore, Charles. "The Hidden Swahili Message in *Get Out* the Country Needs to Hear." *Splinter*, March 1, 2017. https://splinternews.com/the-hidden-swahili-message-in-get-out-the-country-needs-1793858917.

Samad, Anthony Asadullah. "O. J. Did It! (to Himself)." *Black Commentator*, no. 303, December 11, 2008. http://www.blackcommentator.com/303/303_btl_oj_did_it_printer_friendly.pdf.

Walpole, Horace. *The Castle of Otranto*, edited by W. S. Lewis. Oxford: Oxford University Press, 2008. First published 1764.

Washington, Jesse. "Washington: The 'Blackest Name' in America." *Seattle Times*, February 20, 2011. https://www.seattletimes.com/nation-world/washington-the-blackest-name-in-america/.

Wester, Maisha. *African American Gothic: Screams from Shadowed Places*. New York: Palgrave Macmillan, 2012.

Wollstonecraft, Mary. *Maria: or the Wrongs of Women*. New York: Norton, 1975. First published 1798.

Wright, Richard. "How Bigger Was Born." Introduction to *Native Son*. New York: Harper and Row, 2001. First published 1940.

CHAPTER 3

A PEACEFUL PLACE DENIED

Horror Film's "Whitopias"

ROBIN R. MEANS COLEMAN AND NOVOTNY LAWRENCE

The Birth of a Segregated Nation

Journalist and political commentator Rich Benjamin calls them "Whitopias." They are those defiant communities that, in spite of the fact that the United States is transforming into an increasingly racially and ethnically diverse nation, remain willfully less multicultural.[1] Sociologist and media scholar Isabel Pinedo defines horror, in part, as: (1) that which disrupts the everyday world; (2) that which violates boundaries; and (3) that which evokes fear.[2] Taking up these definitions, we assert that the horror genre upsets the purported rationality of "White," turning the Whitopia—often prized for its segregation and homogeneity (marketed as "exclusivity")—into something monstrous. Horror works to *evoke fear* by turning on Whitopias, just as it has turned on the urban, casting it as a dangerous social, political, and racialized space. Ever adept at exposing our cultural anxieties, horror simultaneously marks Whitopias as the quintessential *"everyday"* as well as a terrifying *violation of cultural and economic boundaries.*

In the US popular imagination, the monstrous has often been synonymous with the urban, envisaged as a gritty, criminally rife landscape due

1. Benjamin, *Searching*, 2–6.
2. Pinedo, *Recreational Terror*, 4.

to the supposed sociocultural deficiencies of the predominantly Black and Brown inhabitants who reside there. As Adilifu Nama explains, beginning in the 1980s, the urban became Reagan-era political shorthand for all manner of social ills that people of color were held accountable for, such as crime, illegal drugs, poverty, and fractured families.[3] In many instances, these deviance-based narratives amounted to victim-blaming in which political exploitation and neglect, judicial abuses, over-policing, and the absence of social programs were absolved of their roles in urban degradation.[4]

Within the horror genre, films advanced storylines of White preservation through segregation as Whites and even White monsters fled to Whitopias (e.g., *A Nightmare on Elm Street,* 1984), thereby freeing themselves from the dangers of the urban. All of this racialized spatial angst finds its origins in D. W. Griffith's 1915 horror film (yes, it is a horror film) *The Birth of a Nation. Nation* has fueled White racism for over a century by depicting northern Blacks (portrayed by Whites in blackface) as trampling upon and destroying Whites' Southern homeland and cultural traditions. Importantly, *Nation*'s presentation of an innocent, genteel Southern lifestyle and space desecrated by Blacks is a product of the Lost Cause tradition, which has informed the US's collective memory of the antebellum period, the Civil War, and Reconstruction. In explaining the emergence of this influential mythology, Gary Gallagher asserts, "Former Confederates confronted the postwar world as a people thoroughly beaten on the battlefield, but defiantly unapologetic about their attempts to establish a slaveholding republic."[5] Though disinterested in making amends for engaging in a struggle fueled by White supremacy, those invested in this mythology fully understood that "slavery posed the greatest obstacle to their constructing a version of secession and war that would position them favorably before the bar of history."[6] With that in mind, Lost Cause writers downplayed or ignored slavery, instead positioning states' rights as the catalyst for the Civil War, and focusing on Confederate soldiers' bravery on the battlefield. By engaging in an historic sleight of hand, the perpetrators of Lost Cause lore "hoped to provide their children and ensuing generations of Southerners with what they contended was the 'correct' narrative of the war."[7]

Audiences attending *The Birth of a Nation*'s debut, and subsequent screenings of the film in the White House and in theaters across the US, bore witness to one of cinema's first Whitopias in the form of the Cameron

---

3. Nama, *Black Space,* 137.
4. For more, see Means Coleman, *Horror Noire.*
5. Gallagher, *Causes Won,* 19.
6. Ibid., 19.
7. Ibid., 17.

family's Piedmont, South Carolina slave plantation. The film opens during the antebellum era with the Stoneman family, who hail from the North, visiting the Camerons at their home. In true Lost Cause fashion, Griffith puts on full display the family's beautiful property—a space characterized by an immaculate two-story mansion, surrounded by lush acreage and, significantly, happy, contented slaves. Blacks enjoy their time picking cotton in the fields, and singing and dancing for the Stoneman and Cameron families when the latter deign to descend from the big house to visit them in their derelict slave quarters. These scenes mask the atrocities of chattel slavery and make Griffith's perspective on the type of Blackness that is appropriate for "inclusion" in Whitopias clear: as long as Blacks revel in their inferior status, happily provide free labor, and entertain upon request, they are not a threat to the dominant social order.

Notably, Griffith further emphasizes his and other White racists' ideologies by setting up a harrowing vision of what a Black homeland lacking White oversight would look like, leaving us with images of Black violence and ineptitude. While rife with examples of how freedom transforms happy slaves into beasts, one characterization in particular clearly constructs Blacks as monstrous threats to seemingly quaint Southern Whitopias. It is the oft-discussed renegade soldier Gus (Walter Long), whose uncontrollable lust for the virginal Flora Cameron (Mae Marsh) leads to the infamous chase scene that ends with her leaping to her death from the top of a cliff. As Gus pursues her, he is wide-eyed and enraged, traits that in conjunction with the unconvincing blackface makeup, make him appear animalistic. Hence as Means Coleman asserts, Griffith used Gus "to solidify the idea that Black is horrifying."[8]

Nation constructs Blacks as the ultimate threat to White civility, and as such, we argue these are the representations that influenced constructions of Blackness and Black places in ensuing horror films. This is clear when examining select films from the horror genre. Importantly, while we only discuss a small sampling of horror movies, the titles on which we focus provide telling insight as they represent the predominant manner in which the genre has historically constructed Blacks.

Chocolate Cities

In the decades since *The Birth of a Nation*, the themes of cultured, advanced Whitopias and deviant, roguish Black communities have broken out of the

8. Means Coleman, *Horror Noire*, 22.

confines of the antebellum South and into the horror film. For example, there is the horror film *Ingagi* (1930) about White research scientists attempting to bring White enlightenment to the Congo only to discover that Blacks there are too aberrant to be socialized. In *Ingagi,* which was marketed as "reality" and presenting "amazing facts," Blacks are depicted as having sex with apes. The "gorilla sex picture" broke box office records.[9] Black places and culture saw similar attacks in horror movies such as *Black Moon* (1934), which cast the inhabitants of a Caribbean island as malevolent. The 1943 horror movie, *I Walked with a Zombie,* similarly denigrated Blackness and the inhabitants of the Caribbean as wicked. Then there was *The Alligator People* (1959) set in a predominately Black "primitive, savage" Louisiana. The message was clear: Blacks are deficient. White colonization of Black spaces could help. If Blacks were too far gone, however, then Whites should flee, leaving Blacks and their evil behind.

However, in the 1970s, there was a critical cinematic intervention that cut against stereotyped notions of Black communities as monstrous. The Black Exploitation (Blaxploitation) movement—or "movies made between 1970 and 1975, by both Black and White filmmakers alike, to exploit the Black film audience"—gave rise to a small selection of Black-themed horror films that countered the genre's historic presentation of Black inferiority.[10] Conceived during a period of struggle, resistance, and pride, Blaxploitation films presented a number of characters that reflected Black audiences' dissatisfaction with the White status quo, and they thus served as a release of sorts for people tired of the systemic degradation of Black life, culture, and identity in the US. In stark contrast to the majority of films featuring Blacks prior to the 1970s, Blaxploitation films often featured proud, assertive Black heroes, predominantly Black urban settings, Black supporting characters, White villains, plot themes relating to the Black experience, strong displays of Black sexuality, and funky, rhythm and blues soundtracks.[11]

The majority of the aforementioned characteristics were prominently displayed in the pioneer Blaxploitation film, Ossie Davis's action-comedy, *Cotton Comes to Harlem* (1970). Shot on location in the title city, the film follows African American police detectives Grave Digger Jones (Godfrey Cambridge) and Coffin Ed Johnson (Raymond St. Jacques), as they work to discover the culprits responsible for stealing $87,000 in passages from a Back to Africa Rally. Davis effectively brought to the screen two well-dressed, hip, street-savvy detectives who balance the difficult task of enforcing law

9. Ibid., 39.
10. Lawrence, *Blaxploitation,* 18.
11. Ibid., 18–20.

and order in Harlem while also remaining true to their racial and cultural identities. As they do so, Harlem is also showcased as a result of what Paula Massood deems "an almost obligatory walk down, or at least a shot of, well-known Harlem landmarks such as 125th Street, the Apollo Theater, Small's Paradise, or The Cotton Club."[12] This previously unmatched presentation of Black life and space resonated with Black moviegoers who flocked to theaters to view *Cotton*. Shot on a budget of $1.2 million, the film grossed over $8 million in its theatrical run, an estimated 70% of which came from Black moviegoers.[13]

Cotton's box-office success served as the catalyst for a host of ensuing Blaxploitation films highlighting Black culture and places, including American International Pictures' (AIP) *Blacula* (1972), the first of a small number of classic horror films adapted for Black audiences. Though AIP was a B-movie studio that had a reputation for making exploitation movies on the cheap, *Blacula* serves as a prime example of the value of Black input in the filmmaking process. The film was directed by African American director William Crain and stars William Marshall, who managed to change elements of the film's script to inject the title character with a level of dignity. For example, Blacula's straight name was originally "Andrew Brown," the same as the character in *Amos 'n' Andy*, a popular radio show centering on the exploits of two buffoonish Black men performed by White men using blackvoice. Marshall forced producers to change the character's name to Mamuwalde and created a backstory in which the character was formerly an African prince working to end the slave trade. As Marshall explained, "I wanted the picture to have a new framing story. A frame that would remove it completely from the stereotype of ignorant, conniving stupidity that evolved in the United States to justify slavery."[14]

Marshall's input helped transform *Blacula* from a simple tale of a Black vampire stalking Los Angeles into a careful study of histories of home that shattered the binary demarcating Whitopia as good and predominantly Black urban space as bad. The film begins in 1780 when Mamuwalde, an African prince, leaves his rich, cultured Black home and winds up in the dark depravity of White Transylvania. There, he encounters Dracula, a virulent racist, who is stealing Blacks from their homes to sell them into the slave trade. Angered by the African Prince's attempts to end the inhumane practice, Dracula bites Mamuwalde and entombs him in Transylvania, ensuring that he will never see his homeland again. Centuries later, Mamuwalde

12. Massood, *Black City Cinema*, 85.

13. Gold, "Director Dared," 1.

14. Martinez, Martinez, and Chavez, *What It Is*, 42.

makes a belated trek through the Middle Passage when his coffin is auctioned off and sent to the US. In his new anti-home he awakens to see firsthand the enduring legacies of slavery, Jim Crow, and White sociopolitical contempt. Even worse, Mamuwalde is now part of the systemic problem as the curse of vampirism, or perhaps more appropriately the infection of White racism, leads him to prey upon the Black descendants of the African peoples that he once worked to free from chattel slavery.

In recounting its story, *Blacula* features an urban setting where its Black residents' lives unfold in a manner comparable to their Whitopia counterparts. As Lawrence explains, Crain uses cues in *Blacula*'s diegesis to demonstrate that the space inhabited by the title character and the supporting cast members is occupied primarily by people of color. For instance, a nightclub that the characters frequent codes the environment as a thriving predominately Black urban locale. This scene is significant because it provides a glimpse into the diversity of Black residents who inhabit the space, a point that refutes dominant ideologies that position such urban communities as lawless and dangerous. Thus, like canonical Blaxploitation films, *Blacula*'s setting offered its spectators "undeniable voyeuristic (fetishistic and narcissistic) pleasure, either acting as anthropological documents for audiences unfamiliar with the ghetto or as sources of identification for those who were familiar with it."[15] *Blacula* proved lucrative at the box office and gave rise to other Black-themed, albeit derivative and uninspired, horror films, among them, *Blackenstein* (1973), *Abby* (1974), and *Dr. Black and Mr. Hyde* (1976).

Importantly, an original entry on the Blaxploitation horror landscape, *Soul Vengeance* (1975), emerged as a treatise on what Michelle Alexander calls the New Jim Crow: "Rather than rely on race, we use our criminal justice system to . . . engage in all the practices we supposedly left behind. Today it is perfectly legal to discriminate against criminals in nearly all the ways that it was once legal to discriminate against African Americans."[16] Spectators see this play out in *Soul Vengeance* when the lead character Charles (Marlo Monte) is harassed and picked up by two White LAPD officers who resort to horrific brutality. While Charles is handcuffed in the back of their squad car, the policemen sever his penis with a straight razor before housing him in prison where he has a mental breakdown. When Charles is freed and returns to his real home, he has lost his sense of belonging. Unemployable, physically and mentally damaged by the prison industrial complex, and without social support, Charles is unable to "go home" again, opting instead for a

15. Massood, *Black City Cinema*, 85.
16. Alexander, *New Jim Crow*, 2.

final, perhaps more peaceful resting place in death. His experiences are significant in that they give a face and a name to those in urban communities all too easily destroyed by the system. Consequently, *Soul Vengeance* sheds light on how the power structure creates impoverished urban spaces and then leaves them to fester and die.

Unfortunately, the demise of Blaxploitation cinema in 1975 halted the burgeoning trend of featuring the Black urban in the horror genre. Unsurprisingly, ensuing 1970s horror films were set primarily in Whitopias. For example, the events in *Halloween* (1978) unfold in the lily-White town of Haddonfield, Illinois, while *The Amityville Horror* (1979) takes place in the predominantly White Suffolk County, New York. In both films, Whiteness—its people, experiences, values, and culture—prevail ever so briefly, only to be compromised by Whites' own missteps in their quest for a peaceful place. In *Halloween*, Michael Myers's parents unintentionally gave birth to a murderous child who, out of an insatiable and inexplicable bloodlust, slaughters the community's denizens. The White family in *The Amityville Horror* accidently moves into a haunted house, but the movie made certain to blame people of color for the fact that they succumb to the dark side. According to the film, it was the evil First Nations residents from centuries earlier who lived in Amityville and who ruined Suffolk County's Whitopia charm. As the Whites featured in both films dealt with the consequences of their mistakes, they did so primarily in the absence of Blacks. This reinforced the purity of Whitopias—hence elevating the shock and alarm when things went awry in those spaces. *Halloween* and *The Amityville Horror* thus also relegated Blacks to purportedly vile urban spaces that would become all too familiar in the ensuing decades.

Menaces to Society—Again

> What does it mean when the genre violates conventions by locating violence in the city, where it is most expected, and furthermore plays openly on prevailing cultural anxieties by marking the monster as a racial Other?[17]

The 1980s brought a swift end to entertainment's interrogations of the systemic exploitation of Blacks, and CBS helped. In 1986, *CBS Reports* (1959–present) aired, "The Vanishing Black Family," placing social ills at the feet of Black teenagers. Featured was an anonymous young parent—a mother

17. Pinedo, *Recreational Terror*, 112–13.

of two children, expecting her third—who is quoted as saying, "I don't think I would have had the second two children if I didn't think welfare was there. I don't like welfare because it makes me lazy."[18] In addition, a father of six children by four different women says he does not support his children because, "What I'm not doing, the Government does."[19] And, with that, Reaganomics—freezing the minimum wage at $3.35 an hour, cutting the budget for public housing and Section 8 rent subsidies in half, and eliminating antipoverty programs—was given a pass.

The Reagan-era ideology regarding race and class was pervasive in horror cinema, which featured blade-wielding killers like Jason Voorhees and Freddy Krueger in largely segregated worlds wreaking havoc on teens at summer camps and others living in the suburbs. Aside from a few token characters who were generally the first to die, Blacks did not occupy a prominent space in those worlds. When filmmakers did approach Black-themed subject matter, they took aim at people of color and their communities. The 1988 film *The Serpent and the Rainbow* continued to perpetuate the clichéd Black-Haiti-as-horrifying theme featured in earlier movies, marking the country as a dangerous place that is appalling to Whites while being life as usual for Blacks. Like *The Alligator People* before it, 1987's *Angel Heart* argued that a predominately Black New Orleans serves as home to depraved Blacks and their wicked voodoo. Indeed, so evil is Black New Orleans that (White) Lucifer (Robert De Niro) decides to make it his home.

The 1990s were hardly different. For example, the horror film *Candyman* (1992), set in the predominantly Black high-rise low-income housing project Cabrini Green (Chicago), and juxtaposed against the project's twin high-rise-turned-predominately White and costly condominium, continues the assertion that urban Black spaces are rife with monsters. These monsters include violent gang members, negligent fathers, and an utterly confused Black spirit who haunts and murders Black people instead of walking a few blocks over to the condominiums to exact revenge on the descendants of the White people who lynched him a century earlier.

Means Coleman attends to the theme of race, racism, and home in *Candyman,* arguing that, with little self-reflection, the film depicts the lead character, a White woman named Helen (Virginia Madsen), as far more prized than Chicago's Black citizenry. In Helen's attempt to interrogate ghost-story lore for her thesis, she visits Cabrini Green to investigate stories of the Candyman—a free Black man and artist named Daniel Robitaille (Tony

18. Streeter, "Vanishing Family."

19. Ibid.

Todd) who lived during the late nineteenth century. When he fell in love with a White woman, Robitaille was lynched for his "sins," but not before the White lynch mob sawed off his hand with a rusty blade and smeared him with honey (hence, his moniker "Candyman") to be stung by bees. Still, the lynch mob is not the monster in the *Candyman* tale. It is Blackness: Robitaille-turned-Candyman, Cabrini Green's gangs, and the project's grim and dangerous physical structure.

Further, Means Coleman asserts that the film assigns value to home spaces along racial lines, with Blacks and their homes deemed expendable. "Though Cabrini residents call for police protection [and are ignored]," Means Coleman writes, "the film makes explicit that when Helen [calls], the police rush to her rescue because she is White."[20] Candyman haunts Cabrini Green, beheads a resident's dog, and kidnaps and attempts to burn a Black infant alive. But, he does not dare to trouble White homes—that is, until he briefly ventures into the condos to kill Helen's visiting Black friend, Bernadette. Then, he promptly leaves. Candyman, then, can only be monstrous to Black people in Black spaces.

Get Out of the Vanilla "Burbs"

As the discussions of *The Serpent and the Rainbow, Angel Heart,* and *Candyman* illustrate, the horror genre has long relied on narratives of Black home as despicable. Notably, it is home that takes center stage in Jordan Peele's *Get Out,* functioning to expose Whitopias, recuperate the urban, and tacitly reject Reagan-era, "The-Vanishing-of-the-Black-Family" claims. Instead, forty-five years after *Blacula, Get Out* appears to return to the theme of the enduring value of Black home spaces as sites of multidimensional cultural belonging, sociopolitical savvy, and love and loyalty.

Certainly, in telling the story of Chris, a Black photographer who finds himself in peril when he travels with his White girlfriend, Rose, to visit her "liberal" parents at their secluded country estate, Peele challenges the ludicrous postracial American ideology. As Peele noted, "It was very important to me to just get the entire audience in touch in some way with the fears inherent [in] being black in this country. Part of being black in this country, and I presume being any minority, is constantly being told that . . . we're seeing racism where there just isn't racism."[21] We contend that *Get Out* also

20. Means Coleman, *Horror Noire,* 189.
21. "'Get Out.'"

represents, however, an important intervention in disrupting the persistent narrative that stable Black home life is vanishing. Instead, the film extends our conception of "home" using Chris's relationship with and feelings about his deceased mother and the bond that he shares with his friends—his surrogate family. These relationships are emblematic of the love, concern, and loyalty that exists in Black Brooklyn and similar urban spaces, more broadly.

Get Out begins with Andre Hayworth, outside of his Black urban home of Brooklyn, talking to a friend on his mobile phone while walking through an unspecified neighborhood, or perhaps more appropriately, any Whitopia, USA. He feels out of place in this environment, as is evidenced when he complains to his friend (read "fam") on the other end of the line: "They got me out here in this creepy ass suburb. . . . I stick out like a sore thumb."[22] So tranquil-turned-creepy is this environment that Andre's voice functions as the only aural signifier of life and, as such, it calls even more attention to his Black body.

This introductory scene does two things. First, it establishes the Black urban as nonthreatening; it is unambiguously not "creepy ass." Second, the urban becomes home to the kindred among whom one does not "stick out like a sore thumb." A product of that environment, Andre senses potential danger in what is commonly understood as a safe space. Peele reinforces this, turning dread into violence when the driver of a white car slows upon seeing Andre walking down the street, turns around, and begins following him. Though he attempts to flee from the vehicle, Andre is eventually grabbed from behind and rendered unconscious by the masked driver who then places his catch in the trunk of the car and drives away. The scene is disturbing as it brings the threat posed to Black urbanites to fruition, instantly constructing the well-manicured, sterile Whitopia as monstrous.

Peele further illustrates the danger posed by Whitopias in *Get Out*'s opening credits, which appear immediately after the kidnapping sequence. They roll over a tracking shot of a forest, a shot that appears to originate from the inside of Rose Armitage's car as she drives toward Chris's apartment in the city. The credits are set to "Sikiliza Kwa Wahenga," a Swahili song that, when translated to English, forewarns of the danger to come:

> Brother,
> Listen to the ancestors,
> Run!
> You need to run far! (Listen to the truth)

22. *Get Out.* All further references to the film are to this DVD.

Brother,
Listen to the ancestors,
Run! Run!
To save yourself
Listen to the ancestors.[23]

Peele explains the use of the song:

> I was into this idea of distinctly black voices and black musical references. . . . I wanted Michael Abels, who did the score, to create something that felt like it lived in this absence of hope but still had [black roots]. And I said to him, "You have to avoid voodoo sounds, too." That something ended up being the song that begins and ends the film, "Sikiliza Kwa Wahenga," a Swahili phrase that translates to "listen to (your) ancestors" and the song's lyrics loosely mean "something bad is coming. Run."[24]

Hence the song and forest image work to code the car's driver, Rose, a product of the tranquil, wooded Whitopia as monstrous; yet it is important to note that this is not immediately apparent in the narrative precisely because of how race and space intermesh. On arriving in the city, Rose visits a bakery in Chris's neighborhood—a stop that comments on her White privilege, as the color of her skin affords her access to and comfort across environments. That very privilege allows her to infiltrate Chris's world, making her an imminent threat to him and, by extension, to the Black urban.

Importantly, in *Get Out* the Black urban home is understood as sanctuary, an association that Peele further emphasizes when he introduces Chris after the opening credits. An abrupt cut in the image and sound transports viewers from the inside of Rose's vehicle into his small, yet charming, city apartment. Spectators first see a series of Chris's photographs depicting a range of Black folk, including a man carrying a large bundle of helium-filled balloons, a close-up of a pregnant woman's exposed stomach, and an image of an unidentifiable person walking a pit bull. The montage is set to singer Childish Gambino's "Redbone," a smooth and soulful track about desire that serves as a gentle, sultry aural accompaniment to the images. This brief portrait of Black life via Chris's photography echoes the "walks" featured in Blaxploitation films such as *Shaft* and *Super Fly*. Much like Gordon Parks and his son Gordon Parks Jr. showed their protagonists, John Shaft and Young-

23. Pulliam-Moore, "Hidden Swahili."
24. Ibid.

blood Priest, navigating predominantly Black communities to cool tracks such as "Theme from Shaft" and "Freddy's Dead," Peele showcases the beauty and diversity of Black life as seen through Chris's eyes, set to a beat of desirability (rather than soundscapes of menace).

When Chris finally graces the screen, he is completely at ease in his apartment as he prepares for the trip to Rose's parents' home. He greets her when she arrives, and as they talk she senses that something is bothering him. Chris eventually asks if her parents know that he is Black, a painful question that she responds to by ensuring him that his race will not matter to them. This exchange is critically important as it demonstrates that Chris feels safe in his urban environ, while the very thought of Whitopias, and those who inhabit them, makes him uneasy. As a result of having witnessed Andre's abduction from the "creepy ass suburb," the film's viewers have the benefit of knowing that Chris's concerns are warranted and, as such, recognize that he will need to "get out" of the Whitopia and back to the safety of the Black urban.

If Andre's fateful foray into the "creepy ass suburb" was not enough of a clue of the coming dangers that Chris is to encounter in Rose's Whitopia home, there are other more pointed signals. *Get Out*'s taglines—"Do you belong in this neighborhood?" and "Just because you're invited, doesn't mean you're welcome"—provide a clearer picture of the risk to Blacks in White spaces. In the case of the former, there is a reminder of the segregationist impulses gripping the Armitages' Whitopia. In the case of the latter tagline, there is an echoing of Lost Cause narrative as witnessed in *The Birth of a Nation,* in which Whites are understood to (barely) tolerate Blacks, and only while Blacks are in service to them.

And then there is Chris's best friend, TSA Agent Rod. Not one for subtleties, Rod is someone who is depicted as skeptical of Whites' motives when it comes to their interest in Blacks and who is fearsome of Whitopias. Over the course of the film, Rod makes his concerns about White suburban homes clear.[25] He warns Chris "Don't go to a white girl's parents' house," and "I mean, I told you not to go in that house." Indeed, Rod's fears center on what happens when one goes "in that house." His terror is rooted in the presumption that Whites buy into a long circulated myth of Black sexual superiority, according to which, "as long ago as the sixteenth century Englishmen were imputing to Africans an unrestrained lustfulness and describing them as 'large' propagators."[26] Blacks, then, were understood to be well endowed

25. See Bernice M. Murphy's chapter in this collection on suburban and rural spaces.
26. Qtd. in Staples, "Myth," 16.

and also to enjoy a sexual ethos that, for Whites, was either taboo or physically unobtainable. Hence, Blacks were simultaneously deemed repulsive but also secretly enviable.

These stereotypes of Black sexual prowess are played upon in *Soul Vengeance* when Charles, upon release from prison, wills his envied penis (as evidenced by the police's decision to savage it) to grow to an impossible length and strength to seduce and literally have Whites "choke on it." It is this secret envy—behind closed Whitopia doors—that is Rod's horror. He warns: "Sex slave! Oh, shit! Chris, you gotta get the fuck up outta there, man! You in some 'Eyes Wide Shut' situation." And, "I don't know if you know this. But, white people love making people sex slaves and shit." Of course, *Get Out* is about a new twist on enslaved auctioned-off Blacks: Whites not only enjoy Black bodies but literally inhabit them, sans Black culture, of course.

When Chris and Rose finally arrive at her parents' home, his race does not at first seem to be a problem, even though the family is far from colorblind. In fact, Rose's father, Dean Armitage, uses slang while adopting a stereotypical Black affect, and he proclaims his love for former President Barack Obama in an attempt to connect with Chris (later we learn these are early tactics to disarm him). Aside from being slightly annoyed that Chris smokes, Rose's mother, Missy, is also warm and welcoming. However, in a twist that reverses longstanding myths about the danger that Black men pose to White women, Peele positions Missy as a quintessential threat to Black masculinity. A skilled psychiatrist, she uses hypnosis to enter Chris's mind without his permission. Having infiltrated his psyche, Missy forces Chris to relive the night that his mother died—a scene that further illustrates the mother-son connection and how he came to view their home in the Black urban as sanctuary. Chris relates at the onset of his hypnosis that he was at home watching TV when his mother, who was at work, was killed: "She was coming home," he explains with grief. He finally realized something was wrong when, as he agonizes, "she wasn't home." It is Chris's innocence, denial, and comfort inside his home that led him to continue watching television instead of stepping outside of his sanctuary to search for his mother. When asked why he did not leave his home, he elucidates, "I don't know. I thought if I did it would make it real." In this moment Chris's actions, or lack thereof, reinforce the importance of the Black home. In such spaces, Black families are generally safe, shielded from the dangers associated with simply existing while Black (as witnessed through the assault on Andre Hayworth).

Unfortunately, choosing to stay inside his home could not shield Chris from the reality of his mother's death, and it is apparent at different moments throughout *Get Out* that he remains haunted by his loss. The notion of the safety of Black families is illustrated through Chris's relationship with his mother: his memorialization of her cuts against predominant cinematic constructions of Black women in urban spaces as matriarchs and welfare mothers. Through the *absence* of a stereotypical portrayal of Chris's mother, specifically as toxic Black urban mother—think Mary in *Precious* (2009), Wanda in *Holiday Heart* (2000), Ms. Baker in *Boyz in the Hood* (1991)—what does exist is an understanding of her and Chris's strong relationship and the emotional scarring left by her death. This is readily apparent in the scene in which Rose hits a deer. When Chris gets out of the vehicle to investigate, he discovers the badly injured animal lying in the woods alongside the road. As the deer moans in pain, Chris looks at it slightly glassy-eyed, as if he is finally seeing what his mother must have looked like lying in the street after being struck by the car that ended her life. While a sad moment, it demonstrates Chris's deep connection to his mother and further positions Black homes as sites of Black love and caring, attributes rarely associated with such environs.

Chris's love for his mother, and the comfort of the space in which he grew up, makes more significant Rose's false promise to flee the Whitopia and go back home. After Chris demands to leave her parents' home due to the odd behavior of the guests at their party, Rose eventually agrees saying, "Let's go home; this sucks. I'll make something up." However, it is Rose as trickster that ultimately gets Chris to a place where his home will be forever inaccessible. She is actually forcing Chris into something more insidious than a Whitopia; it is the sunken place, or Blackness forever recessed into Whiteness, ironically, to further advance Whiteness and Whitopias. Consider for example that if Chris undergoes the Coagula procedure, giving Jim Hudson, the White man who purchased him, access to his body and mind, the Black urban will be destroyed as a result. Hudson will be able to utilize Chris's photography skills, moreover, while making certain that his Black body will act in a manner that is "acceptable" in Whitopias.

What makes *Get Out* extraordinary, then, is threefold. First, Peele, as writer and director, opts for an ending that lifts Chris out of the sunken place, or, as he described it, "the dark hole we throw black people in."[27] As such, Chris beats the inhabitants of that "creepy ass suburb." Second, when Rod pulls up in his TSA cruiser at the end, Chris defeats the New Jim

27. Lopez, "Jordan Peele."

Crow-ism of the prison industrial complex. And he is spared the fate of Ben (Duane Jones) from the horror classic *Night of the Living Dead* (1968), who survives the zombie horrors away from his home only to be shot down and burned (read, lynched) by police. When audiences cheer at Rod's arrival, it is because Chris will not become 2017's 1,148th police killing.[28] Third and finally, we are assured that Rod, as his "fam," will return Chris to the safety of his Brooklyn home with the closing line—"consider this shit handled."

Horror does not provide us with a safe cover from our social world. Instead, it assaults us with the horrendous realities of how homelessness truly disrupts the everyday. The genre assaults us with the horrifying reality that what most provokes fear is what scholar Colin Dickey in the *New Republic* argues is a "latent anxiety Americans have about the land they 'own.'"[29] We would add, ours are anxieties about the people who "own" the land. For they are the ones who enslaved, brutalized, and exploited Blacks (and other people of color) with the distinct goal of profiting off of the crops produced on "their" property. Using space—Whitopias and the urban—Peele's *Get Out* comments on such histories, shedding important light on overt and covert racism in the US, and the very prominent role that land plays in our understandings of the world. That is to say, in trading in land, we are also offering up histories, cultures, and bodies—dead and alive—to the highest bidder. And that notion of ownership—this is what haunts us.

Bibliography

Alexander, Michelle. *The New Jim Crow: Mass Incarceration in the Age of Colorblindness.* New York: New Press, 2010.

Benjamin, Rich. *Searching for Whitopia: An Improbable Journey to the Heart of White America.* New York: Hyperion, 2009.

Dickey, Colin. "The Suburban Horror of the Indian Burial Ground." *New Republic,* October 19, 2016. https://newrepublic.com/article/137856/suburban-horror-indian-burial-ground.

D'Onofrio, Kaitlyn. "The Data Is In: Police Disproportionately Killed Black People in 2017." *DiversityInc,* January 3, 2018. https://www.diversityinc.com/news/data-police-disproportionately-killed-black-people-2017.

Gallagher, Gary W. *Causes Won, Lost and Forgotten: How Hollywood & Popular Art Shape What We Know about the Civil War.* Chapel Hill: University of North Carolina Press, 2008.

Get Out. Directed by Jordan Peele. USA: Universal Pictures, 2017. DVD.

28. 2017 Police Violence Report, https://policeviolencereport.org/, accessed July 31, 2018. See also D'Onofrio, "Data."

29. Dickey, "Suburban Horror."

"'Get Out' Sprang from an Effort to Master Fear, Says Director, Jordan Peele." Interview by Dave Davies. *Fresh Air*, NPR Radio, January 5, 2018. https://www.npr.org/2018/01/05/575843147/get-out-sprang-from-an-effort-to-master-fear-says-director-jordan-peele.

Gold, Ronald. "Director Dared Use Race Humor: Soul as Lure for Cotton's B. O. Bale." *Variety*, September 30, 1970, 1, 62.

Lawrence, Novotny. *Blaxploitation Films of the 1970s: Blackness and Genre*. New York: Routledge, 2008.

Lopez, Ricardo. "Jordan Peele Explains How He Tackled Systemic Racism as Horror in 'Get Out.'" *Variety*, November 1, 2017. https://variety.com/2017/film/news/jordan-peele-get-out-systemic-racism-1202604824/.

Martinez, Gerald, Diana Martinez, and Andres Chavez. *What It Is . . . What It Was: The Black Film Explosion of the '70s in Words and Pictures*. New York: Hyperion, 1998.

Massood, Paula J. *Black City Cinema: African American Urban Experiences in Film*. Philadelphia: Temple University Press, 2003.

Means Coleman, Robin. *Horror Noire: Blacks in American Horror Films from the 1890s to Present*. New York: Routledge, 2011.

Nama, Adilifu. *Black Space: Imagining Race in Science Fiction in Film*. Austin: University of Texas Press, 2008.

Pinedo, Isabel Christina. *Recreational Terror: Women and the Pleasure of Horror Film Viewing*. Albany: State University of New York Press, 1997.

Pulliam-Moore, Charles. "The Hidden Swahili Message in *Get Out* the Country Needs to Hear." *Splinter*, March 1, 2017. https://splinternews.com/the-hidden-swahili-message-in-get-out-the-country-needs-1793858917.

Staples, Robert. "The Myth of Black Sexual Superiority: A Reexamination." *Black Scholar* 9, no. 7 (April 1978): 16–23.

Streeter, Ruth C. "The Vanishing Family—Crisis in Black America." *CBS Reports*. Aired January 25, 1986.

CHAPTER 4

GET OUT AND THE ZOMBIE FILM

ERIN CASEY-WILLIAMS

IN THE 2012 SKIT "White Zombies," a terrified Keegan-Michael Key and Jordan Peele confront a horde of undead. Their white defender (Kevin Sorbo) is almost immediately eaten in a scene that references *The Walking Dead*, which was at peak viewership at the time.[1] As they dash through the throng of monsters, Key and Peele notice that no zombies are pursuing them; not only that, but when they reach out, the zombies actively dodge away. Just as they realize that "these are some racist motherfuckin' zombies," another black man strolls up carrying a case of beer. "Hey guys," he calls, "isn't this great? These racist zombies are leaving us alone!"[2] Rather than going to the sheriff's office—the physical manifestation of white, patriarchal power—Key and Peele party in a backyard with other people of color. While Kyle Bishop and others have pointed out that most zombie films demonstrate Sigmund Freud's notion of the uncanny—spaces and people that were once familiar are now strange—"White Zombies" demonstrates a double uncan-

1. Key and Peele are obliquely critiquing the fact that most individuals of color in *The Walking Dead* live barely long enough to be introduced, and the "hero" remains a Kevin Sorbo-like white dude with long hair, muscles, and violent tendencies (aka, Rick Grimes played by Andrew Lincoln). For more on the racial politics of *The Walking Dead*, see Sugg, "The *Walking Dead*." For more on the portrayal of men and heroes in zombie cinema in general, see Cady and Oates, "Family Splatters."

2. Peele and Key, "White Zombies."

niness.[3] Even in a world that was once familiar and is now strange, there are certain elements that persist, like an older zombie couple locking their car door when Key and Peele walk by, even though there is no glass left in the window and the couple themselves have become the "super[natural] predators."[4]

Although *Get Out* is classified as a horror film, its links to zombie horror conventions are less obvious. Unlike Peele's earlier skit, there are no hordes of undead shuffling through the 2017 film. And yet *Get Out* draws upon and redeploys classic zombie cinematic tropes associated with personal agency, loss of identity, and racialized power. Peele thus elucidates the new kinds of racism at work in the twenty-first century—racism that is familiar and yet strange, that has evolved from the traditional into something newly monstrous. In the film's climactic scenes, Peele challenges the structures of power underpinning patriarchy and white supremacy by featuring the triumph of a historically disempowered black male hero.

Get Out features a protagonist who has obtained personal and economic success through his artistic talent. After Chris accompanies his white girlfriend Rose to her parents' remote estate for a weekend house party, he learns that her family performs brain transplants that allow aging white people to take over the bodies of kidnapped black men and women. While the premise of brain surgery and mad scientists does not initially suggest zombification, the fear that permeates the film is one that was endemic to the early examples of this genre: "not of being harmed by zombies [. . . but] of becoming one."[5] The first night that Chris stays at the Armitages' house, Rose's psychiatrist mother hypnotizes him, ostensibly to cure his smoking addiction. The hypnosis paralyzes Chris's body and traps his consciousness in dark, empty space where he is unable to be heard, seen, or acknowledged. Chris's powerlessness while in this "sunken place"[6] echoes "the supplanted, stolen, or effaced consciousness . . . the appropriation of one person's will

3. For a discussion of Mashahiro Mori's "uncanny valley" and the *unheimlich* elements of Romero's *Night of the Living Dead,* see Bishop, *American Zombie Gothic,* 94–128; for the uncanniness of zombie physiology, see McFarland, "Philosophy."

4. John J. DiIulio Jr. is credited with coining the term "superpredator" to describe youths (usually black or brown men) raised in poverty without parental figures who commit violent crimes without conscience or remorse. See Bennett, DiIulio, and Walters, *Body Count.* "Superpredator" was used by the Clintons in their 1996 tough-on-crime political campaigns and has since been exposed as a racist fiction. See Robinson, *Superpredator.*

5. Davis, *Serpent,* 187.

6. *Get Out.* All further references to the film are to this DVD.

by that of another" that Peter Dendle articulates as the defining feature of the zombie.[7]

More specifically, *Get Out*'s portrayal of physical helplessness and psychological horror appropriates elements from Victor Halperin's *White Zombie* (1932)—a film that informs, and is no less racially charged than, Peele's 2012 skit. In this film, an American couple traveling to Haiti encounters the menacing Murder Legendre (Bela Lugosi), a voodoo priest. Legendre kidnaps and hypnotizes the young woman, turning her into a white zombie that will bring him social advancement and sexual gratification.[8] The parallels between *White Zombie* and *Get Out*, made eighty-five years apart, are striking: both feature a character of color pursuing an intimate relationship with a white woman and a loss of agency through hypnosis. In *White Zombie*, however, it is the woman who is subjugated by a black-coded male; the relationship is involuntary, and the horror comes from white people becoming infected by black culture and enslaved to black individuals. Dendle writes, "The zombie, a soul-less hulk mindlessly working at the bidding of another, thus records a residual communal memory of slavery: of living a life without dignity and meaning, of going through the motions."[9] The early film capitalizes on the horror of zombified slavery only as it is visited upon whites. Peele's film represents the opposite: *Get Out* features a white woman subjugating and controlling a young black man, highlighting the more historically grounded fear of black individuals being subjected to, and controlled by, whites. Like Murder's zombies, Chris would become, after the surgery to implant a white consciousness into his brain, a "body without a soul,"[10] or at least a body disassociated from his soul. He would be enslaved without hope of escape or rebellion in a way that recalls a history of racialized oppression that reaches its epitome in zombified slavery.

Chris directly encounters three "zombified" individuals during his time at the Armitages' house: the groundskeeper, Walter; the maid, Georgina; and a party guest, Logan King. These characters are not traditional zombies, however; instead, their uncanniness—the horror of their existence—is revealed when they are unable to connect to Chris's racial experiences. Walter creepily congratulates Chris on his relationship with Rose; Logan

7. Dendle, "Zombie," 47.

8. Lugosi is white, but Bishop, in *American Zombie Gothic*, and Gary Rhodes, in *White Zombie*, point out his association with Haitian blackness: he uses the local religion to enslave people, runs a sugar mill, and is generally exoticized in his appearance and accent. He is additionally dressed in black clothing throughout the film, contrasted sharply with the white costumes of the middle-class American romantic leads.

9. Dendle, "Zombie," 46.

10. Cohen, "Undead," 398.

attempts to shake Chris's hand rather than bump fists. And when Chris says to Georgina, "All I know is . . . if there's too many white people, I get nervous," a tear rolls down her face as she chuckles and denies the legitimacy of his experience. The other black people in the Armitage household do not talk, dress, or act like Chris and cannot understand him: Walter, Georgina, and Logan are racially uncanny. While Logan is *literally* familiar (Chris knew Logan as Andre), all three characters are repressed—enslaved and marginalized within their own bodies by a white consciousness. They are zombified in their strange behaviors and their exaggerated and mask-like facial expressions, but also in that they are people of color whose bodies have been literally and psychologically enslaved by white masters.

And yet, if white individuals are being inserted into black bodies because those bodies are somehow more desirable, this is a break from traditional forms of racism, which sees blackness—and black bodies—as inferior. Peele elucidates a new and more subtle form of racism in Chris's interactions with the Armitages' guests: a former professional golfer discusses how much he loves Tiger Woods and asks to see Chris's swing; an aging trophy wife discusses how handsome Chris is before feeling his bicep and asking Rose "Is it true? Is it better?"; a middle-aged couple discusses how "fairer skin" has been popular for the last several centuries, but now "Black is in fashion." As the audience soon realizes, these are not mundane microaggressions: the golfer wants to see Chris's swing in order to appropriate it; the aging trophy wife asks Rose about a potential new body for her decrepit husband; the couple wants to be fashionable. Whites still want the bodies of African Americans, not to work the sugar fields or plantations but rather to bring whites the pleasure, achievement, and renown of African American athletic, sexual, artistic, or cultural accomplishments.

Get Out draws on and inverts not only century-old zombie cinematic traditions but also current and problematic zombie tropes. Numerous scholars have demonstrated that, "regardless of skin color, we speak of the undead in terms inherited from racialist discourse."[11] Chris's comment to Georgina that "too many white people" make him nervous would ring true to most people of color in zombie cinematic universes, perhaps most strikingly to Ben (Duane Jones) from George A. Romero's *Night of the Living Dead* (1968). Robert K. Lightning points out that the white characters in the film are ineffectual against the (white) zombies; their violence is more consistently directed toward Ben, who alone can physically stave off the white undead.[12]

11. Cohen, "Undead," 404.
12. Lightning, "Interracial Tensions," 24.

Such heroism cannot save him, however, and he is gunned down by white vigilantes who seem unable to distinguish between a black man and a zombie in the film's climax. The ending is elucidated by Jon Stratton's insights that zombies are mimetic of those who occupy "half-lives" or what Giorgio Agamben calls "bare life."[13] Anthony Downey expands on the contingent nature of those who occupy such a position: "on the margins of social, political, cultural and economic borders," disposable people are "denied access to legal, economic, and political redress."[14] Historically, those living "half-lives" have included African Americans, Muslims, refugees, and more. Zombies become metaphors for any population marginalized and dispossessed by neoliberal, capitalist culture, and this is why *Night*'s vigilantes cannot distinguish between Ben and the zombies he has survived. Like Ben, Chris's identity is always already disposable to the white people he encounters, discarded to allow their appropriation of those elements deemed desirable in neoliberal culture. The echoes of such racialized thinking—and the willingness to coopt the bodies of people of color, erasing their agency, identity, and desires—resonate throughout *Get Out* and the horror in which it traffics.

People of color, interchangeable with zombies, are sacrificed in most zombie cinematic universes to make room for what Sarah Trimble calls "patriarchal survivalist" societies, where the law is both created and policed by white, cis-gendered, heterosexual male protagonists.[15] Such individuals commit the worst forms of violence against zombies/minorities/dispossessed peoples without guilt or consequence in the name of safety, convenience, and/or preservation of the nation-state. *Get Out* demonstrates that the new "zombie" state emerges when black bodies are coopted by neoliberal market ideologies, which is enabled by white supremacist ideology; the new zombie condition is marked by the removal of black identity from blackness, as is the case for Georgina, Logan, and Walter. Peele's film forces viewers to acknowledge a form of racism that allows privileged individuals to appropriate the parts of blackness that are advantageous (athleticism, sexuality, cultural fashionableness) while retaining white consciousness, power, and control. The horrifying perversion committed by the neoliberal state is the division of people into parts, which enables precisely this commodification of blackness and the psychological imperialism of white patriarchy. *Get Out* perfectly illustrates Trimble's "patriarchal survivalist fantasy," then, in that patriarchs (like Roman Armitage) ensure their own survival in the best body possible but retain the mind, priorities, and privileges of affluent

13. Stratton, "Trouble," 188.
14. Downey, "Zones," 109.
15. Trimble, "(White) Rage," 295. See also Williams, "Birthing."

whites. People of color in the Armitage household may as well be the zombies of *Warm Bodies* (2013) as described by Chera Kee: "an Other that has the benefit of a living white male's brain."[16]

And yet, as the slasher-film/zombie-cinematic "final girl," Chris ultimately escapes this appropriation and defeats the racist, neoliberal, patriarchal system.[17] He impales Rose's father on a taxidermied deer head, stabs her mother, and bludgeons her brother (twice) to escape into the night. He is aided in these endeavors by the other men of color who momentarily escape the dominance of the white patriarchs squatting in their brains. Chris snaps a photo of Logan at the party, and as the flash of light fades from his eyes, Andre fleetingly surfaces and warns Chris to "Get out." After Chris has defeated the family and escaped from the house, Roman Armitage follows him in the body of Walter; again, Chris snaps a flash, and Walter surfaces long enough to shoot Rose and then himself, allowing Chris to escape. The black male bodies that the patriarchs occupy prove unruly and disobedient. After Chris escapes the house and survives his final confrontation with a shotgun-toting Rose, his best friend Rod arrives in what initially appears to be a police car. Rod reminds Chris, "I told you not to go in that house," and the two drive away, leaving Rose to bleed to death. Black men aid Chris in not only his escape but also his elimination of the system of domination and subjugation perpetuated by the patriarchy—they help him literally and symbolically burn the house down and rescue him from the scene of (what some might perceive as) the crime. In this way, *Get Out* suggests that white supremacy, neoliberal society, and heteronormative patriarchy *can* be defeated by the right hero, and by the solidarity of black men resisting appropriation and working together—even those who have been enslaved by the culture they seek to overthrow.

And yet, such solidarity is not unproblematic, especially in that it seems to omit both white women (Rose, who seemed like a staunch ally yet turns out to be the monster of the film) and women of color (Georgina). Initially, Georgina seems the most rebellious of the zombified characters: she momentarily breaks out of her hypnosis with the clinking of a spoon against glass (the sound Rose's mother later uses to paralyze Chris), spilling the iced tea she is serving. The tears that roll down her face as Chris admits his discom-

16. Kee, "Good Girls," 182.

17. Peele labels Chris the "final girl" of *Get Out*. See Izadi, "*Get Out*." Carol J. Clover defines the "final girl" of slasher horror films as a figure of "abject terror personified" who "looks death in the face," yet "finds strength either to stay the killer long enough to be rescued . . . or to kill him herself." See Clover, *Men, Women*, 35. Erika Cornelius Smith and I analyze the similarity of slasher and zombie films, and the absence of the final girl trope in the latter. See Casey-Williams and Smith, "Twice Dead."

fort seems like an attempt to warn him of the horrors that await. And yet, such breaks are momentary and incomplete; Chris is unable to read them as warnings and instead concludes "this bitch is crazy." Georgina impedes his escape rather than aiding him: when Chris takes her with him from the burning estate, the Armitage matriarch surfaces and attacks him. Unlike Walter and Logan, Georgina is never wholly released from her psychological imprisonment.

The gender dynamics of Chris's triumph are even more problematic in his final interactions with Rose. In the film's theatrical ending, Chris attempts to strangle her but is prevented by his emotional response; she is not similarly affected. This reinforces the idea that white women's loyalty will always lie with the white patriarchy, and that any healthy relationship between black men and white women is doomed.[18] In the film's original ending (included on the DVD as the alternate ending), such a division is only widened when Chris successfully kills Rose; she smirks as she dies, seeming to indicate that by forcing him to violence, she has won after all. Chris is then arrested by white police officers who arrive and witness her final breaths. This scene critiques white America's assumptions about black men as violent, especially against (white) women, but does not challenge the idea that white women cannot be trusted, especially by vulnerable black men.[19] The last scenes show Chris in jail; Rod asks him about what happened that night, but Chris won't look at him and keeps woodenly repeating "I don't remember."[20] No story of his will negate the fact that white officers witnessed him killing a white woman, rendering him guilty and a criminal in the eyes of society.

In this original ending, discarded by Peele, Chris's victory is shown to be hollow. He is in jail and physically limited if not enslaved; perhaps he has beat the new uncanny neoliberal racism that attempts to suppress his mind, but his body is still controlled by the familiar racisms and disenfranchisement of the prison industrial complex and a corrupt criminal justice system.[21] In this way, he is very much like Ben at the end of *Night*, who has survived only to become an erased and unrecognized martyr to the true

18. More work remains to be done on how the film portrays interracial relationships and, specifically, how it reproduces their foreclosure, like most of traditional zombie cinema. For a discussion of zombie cinema's failures to imagine black male heroes with white female leads, see Kee, "Good Girls," and Ponder, "Dawn."

19. Welch, "Black Criminal," 278, and Russell, "Racial Hoax," 354.

20. *Get Out*, "Alternate Ending."

21. I am thinking here of the insights afforded by the award-winning documentary *13th* (Ava DuVernay, 2016), which argues that the Constitution's Thirteenth Amendment abolishes slavery "except as a punishment for crime" and discusses the overrepresentation of black men in America's criminal justice system. See also Alexander, *New Jim Crow*.

monsters. Peele claims in the video commentary that "even though [Chris] is in prison, like many black men unjustly [are], his soul is free."[22] Chris might escape the literal zombification that the Armitages planned for him, but in the original ending, he continues to exist in an alternative living death, a slave to the neoliberal system. Perhaps the hollowness of this victory is caused by his inability to save or connect to the women in the film, as he saved and drew upon his relationships with men. Although *Get Out* elucidates and begins to imagine alternatives to neoliberal, patriarchal racism, it stops short of envisioning the solidarity of all dispossessed or marginalized individuals in the triumph over this system—women as well as men.

Bibliography

13th. Directed by Ava DuVernay. USA: Netflix, 2016. Film.

Alexander, Michelle. *The New Jim Crow: Mass Incarceration in the Age of Colorblindness.* New York: New Press, 2010.

Bennett, William J., John J. DiIulio Jr., and John P. Walters. *Body Count: Moral Poverty . . . And How to Win America's War against Crime and Drugs.* New York: Simon & Schuster, 1996.

Bishop, Kyle William. *American Zombie Gothic: The Rise and Fall (and Rise) of the Walking Dead in Popular Culture.* Jefferson, NC: McFarland, 2010.

Cady, Kathryn A., and Thomas Oates. "Family Splatters: Rescuing Heteronormativity from the Zombie Apocalypse." *Women's Studies in Communication* 39, no. 3 (2016): 308–23.

Casey-Williams, Erin, and Erika Cornelius Smith. "Twice Dead: Gender, Class, and Crisis in *Pride and Prejudice + Zombies* (2016)." In *Monsters and Monstrosity in 21st-Century Film and Television,* edited by Cristina Artenie and Ashley Szanter, 39–58. Montreal: Universitas, 2017.

Clover, Carol J. *Men, Women, and Chain Saws: Gender in the Modern Horror Film.* Princeton, NJ: Princeton University Press, 1992.

Cohen, Jeffery Jerome. "Undead (A Zombie Oriented Ontology)." *Journal of the Fantastic in the Arts* 23, no. 3 (2012): 397–412.

Davis, Wade. *The Serpent and the Rainbow: A Harvard Scientist's Astonishing Journey into the Secret Societies of Haitian Voodoo, Zombis, and Magic.* New York: Touchstone, 1997.

Dendle, Peter. "The Zombie as Barometer of Cultural Anxiety." In *Monsters and the Monstrous: Myths and Metaphors of Enduring Evil,* edited by Niall Scott, 45–58. New York: Rodopi, 2007.

Downey, Anthony. "Zones of Indistinction: Giorgio Agamben's 'Bare Life' and the Politics of Aesthetics." *Third Text* 23, no. 2 (2009): 109–25.

Get Out. Directed by Jordan Peele. USA: Universal Pictures, 2017. DVD.

22. *Get Out,* "Director's Commentary."

Izadi, Elahe. "*Get Out* was a Genre-bending Hit. Here's Why It's a Remarkable Oscar Contender." *Washington Post*, January 23, 2018. https://www.washingtonpost.com/news/arts-and-entertainment/wp/2018/01/23/get-out-was-a-genre-bending-hit-heres-why-its-a-remarkable-oscar-contender/?utm_term=.4365747d6747.

Kee, Chera. "Good Girls Don't Date Dead Boys: Toying with Miscegenation in Zombie Films." *Journal of Popular Film and Television* 42, no. 4 (2014): 176–85.

Lightning, Robert K. "Interracial Tensions in *Night of the Living Dead*." *CineAction* 53 (2000): 22–29.

McFarland, James. "Philosophy of the Living Dead: At the Origin of the Zombie Image." *Cultural Critique* 90 (2015): 22–63.

Night of the Living Dead. Directed by George A. Romero. 1968. USA: Elite Entertainment, 2002. DVD.

Peele, Jordan, and Keegan-Michael Key. "White Zombies." Comedy Central. Uploaded October 24, 2012. https://www.youtube.com/watch?v=4xyhVO-SWfM.

Ponder, Justin. "Dawn of the Different: The Mulatto Zombie in Zack Snyder's *Dawn of the Dead*." *Journal of Popular Culture* 45, no. 3 (2012): 551–71.

Rhodes, Gary D. *White Zombie: Anatomy of a Horror Film*. Jefferson, NC: McFarland, 2006.

Robinson, Nathan J. *Superpredator: Bill Clinton's Use and Abuse of Black America*. Somerville, MA: Demilune Press, 2016.

Russell, Katheryn. "The Racial Hoax as Crime: The Law as Affirmation." In *African American Classics in Criminology and Criminal Justice*, edited by Shaun Gabbidon, Helen Greene, and Vernetta Young, 349–76. Thousand Oaks, CA: Sage, 2002.

Stratton, Jon. "The Trouble with Zombies: Bare Life, *Muselmänner*, and Displaced People." *Somatechnics* 1, no. 1 (2011): 188–208.

Sugg, Katherine. "*The Walking Dead*: Late Liberalism and Masculine Subjection in Apocalypse Fictions." *Journal of American Studies* 49, no. 4 (2015): 793–811.

Trimble, Sarah. "(White) Rage: Affect, Neoliberalism, and the Family in *28 Days Later* and *28 Weeks Later*." *Review of Education, Pedagogy, and Cultural Studies* 32 (2010): 295–322.

Welch, Kelly. "Black Criminal Stereotypes and Racial Profiling." *Journal of Contemporary Criminal Justice* 23, no. 3 (2007): 276–88.

White Zombie. Directed by Victor Halperin. 1932. USA: The Film Detective, 2015. DVD.

Williams, G. Christopher. "Birthing an Undead Family: Reification of the Mother's Role in the Gothic Landscape of *28 Days Later*." *Gothic Studies* 9, no. 2 (2007): 33–44.

CHAPTER 5

PLACE, SPACE, AND THE RECONFIGURATION OF "WHITE TRASH" MONSTROSITY

BERNICE M. MURPHY

THE RELATIONSHIP between place and race represents one of *Get Out*'s most notable thematic concerns. The ways in which it reconfigures key elements from the backwoods horror and suburban gothic subgenres significantly underlines the film's scathing depiction of white arrogance and entitlement. Crucially, the film's white characters have the freedom to move from one locale to another with a sense of security and ease denied to black characters. Indeed, it is made clear from the film's opening moments that spatial freedom is one of the most striking, yet most overlooked, forms of white privilege there can be.

Fittingly, *Get Out* begins in a liminal space—"Evergreen Way," the suburban neighborhood in which Andre gets lost on the way to a friend's house. Jordan Peele's staging of the quiet, tree-lined, bucolic neighborhood evokes John Carpenter's representation of the streets of Haddonfield in his 1978 suburban horror classic *Halloween*. Like Carpenter's famous "final girl" Laurie Strode (Jamie Lee Curtis), Andre is being stalked by an unseen predator. However, Laurie is a middle-class white girl who, like her nemesis Michael Myers, is a native of that social and spatial milieu. The same cannot be said for Andre, for whom the locale is, as he puts it, the "creepy confusing-ass suburbs," in which he feels that as a black man he sticks out like "a sore thumb."[1] Andre's unease is lent further resonance by the fact that these opening moments subtly evoke a real-life tragedy: the circumstances surrounding the 2012 death of unarmed black teenager Trayvon Martin, gunned down on the streets of a Florida gated community by a member of the local neighborhood watch who was subsequently, controversially, absolved of any legal wrongdoing.[2] As J. Hoberman notes, the film "opens with a familiar horror-movie trope. Someone walking down a dark street stalked by a mysterious force." The fact that "the someone is a young, increasingly panicked black man, and the predator is driving a white car gives the scenario an unmistakable reality. . . . That the black youth is not shot but rather abducted is a dreamlike condensation of the movie to come."[3]

This opening scene is the only one set in the suburbs. Nevertheless, the thematic resonances of this milieu resonate throughout the rest of the narrative. As a subgenre of the wider American gothic tradition, the suburban gothic has always been concerned with articulating middle-class white anxiety.[4] Racial disquiet (in particular the fear that the majority white neighborhood will be invaded by the wrong kind of "outside" element) represents one of the major thematic underpinnings of the subgenre, expressed most openly in postwar texts such as Richard Matheson's *I Am Legend* (1954) and Shirley Jackson's 1948 novel *The Road Through the Wall.* In many of these texts, including Matheson's postapocalyptic classic, racial and class anxieties are deflected onto an overtly supernatural "Other." Like their generic predecessors, even recent suburban-set horror movies such as *It Follows* (2014) and *Don't Breathe* (2016) center on white characters and exclude nonwhite characters, an omission that is particularly noticeable in these films because both are set in the decaying suburbs of "post-industrial" Detroit—a city that has had a majority black population for decades.[5]

Significantly, then, *Get Out* begins by dramatizing suburban racial anxieties from the perspective of the nonwhite "outsider," who is more usually seen as a potential threat than a victim. But *Get Out*'s debt to the suburban gothic tradition also has an even more direct provenance. As acknowledged by writer/director Peele, the film owes a substantial debt to one of the most famous suburban horror narratives of the 1970s, the 1975 film adaptation

---

1. *Get Out.* All further references to the film are to this DVD.
2. Blow, "Curious Case."
3. Hoberman, "Real American."
4. For a discussion of suburban racial anxieties in Matheson's *I Am Legend,* see Murphy, *Suburban Gothic,* 32–33.
5. Aguilar and MacDonald, "Detroit's White Population."

of Ira Levin's satirical thriller *The Stepford Wives* (1972).[6] Levin's novel, like Bryan Forbes's movie, chronicles the growing paranoia of a middle-class housewife and mother Joanna Eberhart (Katharine Ross), who initially seems reconciled to a family move from New York City to the upscale WASP neighborhood of Stepford, Connecticut. Soon after the family's arrival, however, Joanna and her friend Bobbie Markowe (Paula Prentiss), another newcomer, notice that many of the other women in Stepford are of a very specific physical and sartorial "type." They are also bizarrely fixated on their household chores. It eventually transpires that Joanna, like many local women before her, has been set up by her seemingly devoted husband to be "replaced" by a submissive robot double. Although she makes a valiant effort to escape, Joanna is ultimately murdered, her place within both home and community now filled by her dead-eyed duplicate.

The similarities between this premise and the basic plot of *Get Out* are obvious. Chris, like Joanna, has been set up by a trusted loved one—his white girlfriend Rose. Like Joanna's husband Walter, who feigns support for the women's movement, Rose falsely espouses principles of equality and respect in which she clearly does not believe. Like Chris, Joanna is a talented photographer who has had some professional success (although her ambitions have been put on hold by marriage and motherhood). And also like Chris, Joanna tries to exert some control over her new environment by capturing it on film. In many respects then, Chris is essentially an updated version of Levin's doomed heroine, although race has replaced gender as the principal locus of anxiety.

The form of technological/scientific abuse found in Stepford—the creation of uncannily lifelike robotic duplicates—is paralleled in *Get Out* by the "Coagula Procedure," which is arguably even more dreadful because the victim remains alive and dimly aware of the fact that they have become a prisoner (or "passenger") in their own body, trapped in the endlessly plunging "sunken place." However, both developments still result in the elimination of the victim's independent personhood and their reduction to a physical shell. Just as Andre becomes a pliable doll to be dressed up in the incongruous looking duds of his elderly white "controller" Logan King, all that remains of the original Joanna by the end of *The Stepford Wives* is her animatronic duplicate, whose ultra-feminine attire represents a pointed rebuke to the boyishly casual dress sense of the real-life woman who has been murdered and "replaced."

---

6. For a discussion of the relation of *Get Out* to Levin's *Stepford Wives* and *Rosemary's Baby*, see Adam Lowenstein's chapter in this collection.

Another parallel between the two films lies in the fact that the protagonists first detect the profound *wrongness* of their new surroundings during social occasions. In *The Stepford Wives,* it is as Joanna and Bobbie visit friends in their well-appointed homes, attend dinner parties, and try to set up a women's group that they come to understand that something is very off indeed about most of the women of Stepford. Furthermore, Joanna's fruitless attempts to make a personal connection with the community's detergent-fixated hausfraus are obviously reminiscent of Chris's effort to find common ground with eerily compliant housekeeper Georgina, groundskeeper Walter, and Logan (Andre). Just as one Stepford housewife's dramatic malfunction at a social gathering significantly heightens Joanna's suspicions, so too does Logan's unexpectedly frantic response to Chris's camera flash alert Chris to the fact that something is very wrong. In both films, it is also during social gatherings from which our trusting protagonist is excluded that the conspiracy to rob them of their personhood is advanced. The "boys only" Stepford Men's Club is where the plans to replace the pesky real women of the suburb are hatched. Similarly, the "Bingo" game in *Get Out* is really a modern-day slave auction, and the entire garden party has been staged to show off the merchandise—Chris—to potential buyers.

Although racial contexts are barely mentioned in the novel or film, in the final pages of Levin's *Stepford Wives,* it is implied that a black newcomer to the community, Ruthanne, will be the next victim. Tellingly, she attributes her almost subconscious disquiet about the behavior of the eerily "languid" women of Stepford to their race, ruefully thinking, "How white could you get? Even filling their *carts* just so!"[7] Like Andre in the opening moments of *Get Out,* and Chris throughout much of rest of the film, Ruthanne attributes her feeling of unease about this new environment to the fact that it is a specifically *white* space. These are understandable (and accurate) responses given that both Stepford and the Armitage estate are presented as unambiguously *white* spaces. But what neither Chris nor (perhaps) Ruthanne realizes—but Chris's best friend Rod instinctively articulates (albeit in a manner that is initially easy for Chris to dismiss because it is expressed in comedic fashion)—is that the danger here involves much more than the more nebulous feeling of being "out of place" they have presumably often experienced in a white-dominated society. Both Chris and Andre's hyper-awareness of their position as young black men in an inherently racist society—individuals who can be unfairly perceived as a supposed threat if they do not "behave" in a certain manner—arguably distracts them from the reality of the horrific

7. Levin, *Stepford Wives,* 120.

trap they have unwittingly fallen into. Like Ruthanne in Levin's novel, they are already on the alert, but the microagressions and exclusion they experience on an everyday basis at least initially obscures the very specific (and extreme) nature of this even more pronounced threat to their personhood.

As well as reflecting many of the most important thematic concerns of the suburban gothic (particularly in relation to Peele's use of *The Stepford Wives*), *Get Out* also incorporates a savvy and politically charged take on another landscape-specific subgenre, that of the backwoods horror movie. As Carol J. Clover has observed, "An enormous proportion of horror takes as its starting point the visit or move of (sub)urban people to the country."[8] Such texts presume that any trip a city dweller takes into the more uncharted regions of the American landscape will end in disaster, a premise grounded in the assumption that people from the city "are people like us." People from the country, on the other hand, "are people not like us."[9] The fact that the countryside of upstate New York is indeed where Chris will encounter people who are most definitely *not* like him is emphasized during the atmospheric opening credits, which depict a passenger's-eye view of a forest—a conceit possibly intended to depict Andre's journey from the suburbs to the rural seat of the Armitage family.

The sense of "urbanoia" that Clover identified in American horror cinema takes on an even more pronounced aspect when the naïve city folks venturing into backwoods territory are black. As Robin R. Means Coleman notes, "Blacks were nowhere to be found in popular horror films [of the 1980s] set outside of the urban"; they are absent, then, from such important late 1970s and 1980s horror films as *The Amityville Horror* (1979), *Friday the 13th* (1980), *The Evil Dead* (1981), and *Poltergeist* (1982).[10] Instead, she argues, black characters, then as now, are overwhelmingly associated with the inner city, which is often depicted as "savage, lawless terrains to which the most irredeemable in our society—the underclass and people of color, two groups often understood to be one and the same—should be consigned."[11] With a few minor exceptions, black (and nonwhite characters generally) are also absent from almost every major (and minor) backwoods horror movie released since the subgenre emerged with the release of *Two Thousand Maniacs!* back in 1964.[12] The backwoods are virtually always seen as a white

8. Clover, *Men, Women,* 124.

9. Ibid.

10. Means Coleman, *Horror Noire,* 146.

11. Ibid., 145.

12. For a more detailed discussion of race in the backwoods horror movie, see Murphy, *Rural Gothic,* 133–77.

space, in which both those who pose a threat, and the clear majority of their victims, are white.

Get Out resembles American horror cinema more generally, then, in that it also associates its black protagonist with the city. However, here the urban space is associated with warmth and safety. Chris's apartment is cozy and well-appointed, decorated with his own black-and-white photographs, which represent inner-city life and its black inhabitants in an empathetic manner.[13] Although we see very little of the city, it is clearly a place where Chris is safe and at ease. This changes the moment he begins his journey. During the couple's drive to Lake Pontaco, Rose occupies the driver's seat. This detail takes on an even more sinister resonance when we find out that the Coagula procedure literally renders its victims "passengers" in their own bodies. Even before the couple arrives at the Armitage family home, Chris has already ceded a degree of spatial and bodily autonomy. These ominous signs are further enhanced when Rod calls him during the drive and jokingly says, "Don't go to a white girl's parent's house." Although the comment is clearly meant to be humorous, Rod's words are also a warning. Once Chris crosses the threshold of the Armitage home, he will have entered spatial, cultural, and emotional territory that he may not be able to traverse safely.

The fact that Rod works as an agent for the Transportation Security Administration (TSA), and has federally mandated spatial and legal authority over airline passengers of all races, colors, and creeds, may mean that his caution carries extra weight—and that he is able to navigate multiple spaces. Fittingly, it is he who rescues Chris in the final moments of the film. Not only have Rod's most outrageous conspiracy theories about the nefarious injustices white people inflict upon African Americans been vindicated by the horrific reality of his friend's ordeal, but his job as a TSA agent means that he works for an organization that is, according to their mission statement, dedicated to protecting "the nation's transportation systems to ensure freedom of movement for people and commerce."[14] This professional status (underlined by the fact that he comes blazing to the rescue in an official TSA vehicle, complete with police-style livery and flashing lights), when combined with his instinctive (and historically justified) suspicion of whites, means that although he too is an African American urban outsider like Chris and Andre, Rod *can*, unlike them, travel from the safety of the city to the

13. For a different reading of these photographs, see Kyle Brett's chapter in this collection.

14. Transportation Safety Administration, "Mission."

sinister backwoods with a sense of confidence and control the other men were denied.

Backwoods horror films often feature early scenes involving either road kill, as in the opening moments of *The Texas Chain Saw Massacre* (1974), and/or deer hunting, as in *Deliverance* (1972), which serve to prepare us for the fact that the line between the human and the nonhuman animal is going to be violently blurred in the movie that follows. The fact that Chris and Rose's drive is joltingly interrupted by their collision with a panicked deer, therefore, represents another obvious nod to the subgenre's thematic conventions. Furthermore, the reaction of Rose's father, Dean, to this incident provides us with an important early indication of his eugenicist beliefs: he declares that deer are "like rats" and should be eliminated to preserve the ecosystem. It's little wonder then, when Chris is later hypnotized and confined to the games room, that a stuffed deer head is mounted on the wall behind him. As in many backwoods horror narratives before it, *Get Out* underlines the uncomfortable similarities between the hapless protagonist and livestock or road kill. The fact that Chris is black also lends the trope an even more sinister historical resonance: slavery, after all, essentially reduced African American captives to the status of human "livestock" who could be tortured, put to work, and "bred" as their owner wished.

Once Rose and Chris arrive at her parents' house, the wider Armitage clan begins to take center stage, and *Get Out*'s pointed inversion of the most significant backwoods horror film trope of all—that of the monstrous "White Trash" family—begins. Within the wider "rural gothic" tradition, narratives often pivot upon ill-fated encounters between degenerate locals tied to one place and naïve middle-class visitors who, like Chris, are "just passing through." As David Bell has noted, alongside the many representations of "idyllic" rural life in British and American popular culture, there runs a parallel tradition of films in which the countryside serves as a "perfect backdrop for terror." These films "have spawned a peculiar species, usually referred to in US horror films as hillbillies, rednecks or mountain men. Trading on assorted cultural myths—of inbreeding, insularity, backwardness, sexual perversion (especially incest and bestiality)—these rural 'white trash' are familiar popular culture icons" that serve as "symptoms of social, cultural and economic processes having profound impact upon rural regions in the USA."[15] In their discussion of the origins of the term "White Trash," Annalee Newitz and Matt Wray trace it back to the early nineteenth century and to a derogatory slur allegedly used by black slaves as a way

15. Bell, "Anti-Idyll," 94, 96–97.

of contemptuously referring to white servants.[16] As Jaqueline Zara Wilson expands, however, "With the abolition of slavery . . . the original White Trash category expanded and diffused to embrace a wide variety of White groups and communities, mostly rural, and became identified chiefly with the 'backwoods' yokels of areas such as the southern Appalachians."[17]

Supposedly "scientific" studies from the late nineteenth and early twentieth centuries gave temporary legitimacy to the prejudices undergirding those designations of "White Trash" that would persist in the traditional backwoods horror movie and are reconfigured in a particularly interesting way in *Get Out*. As Newitz and Wray note, between 1880 and 1920, the Eugenics Records Office produced fifteen "Eugenic Family Studies" that "sought to demonstrate scientifically that large numbers of rural poor whites were 'genetic defectives.'"[18] Their standard methodology was to begin with an individual who was already incarcerated and then trace back their genealogy to a supposedly "defective" source—often a distant or not-so-distant ancestor who was suspected of having "mixed blood."[19] Newitz and Ray further observe, "Many of these accounts became popular with the American public, and family clans like 'The Jukes' and 'The Kallikaks' became widely known, entering the public imagination as poor, dirty, drunken, criminally minded, and sexually perverse people."[20] More recently, Nancy Isenberg cites a widely read 1868 *Putman's Magazine* article that "told the history of a family," tracing "a corrupted genealogical tree back to its roots" as the precursor to a "host of studies" that helped shorten "the line from delinquency to eugenic sterilization in the late-nineteenth and early twentieth-century America."[21]

The offensive stereotypes these supposedly "scientific" studies helped perpetuate left an imprint upon the post-1970 rural horror movie, as evidenced by the unmistakably degenerate backwoods dwellers seen in such films as *Deliverance, The Texas Chain Saw Massacre, The Hills Have Eyes* (1977), *Wrong Turn* (2003), *House of 1000 Corpses* (2003), *Timber Falls* (2007), and

16. Newitz and Wray, Introduction, 2.

17. Wilson, "Invisible Racism," 389.

18. Newitz and Wray, Introduction, 2.

19. Ibid. This kind of discovery was often employed by H. P. Lovecraft. In stories such as "The Shadow Over Innsmouth" (1931) and "The Facts Concerning the Late Arthur Jermyn and His Family" (1920), his characters are horrified to discover that they themselves are related to the monstrous and degenerate beings that they have been investigating. Interestingly, "Armitage" is the name of a character in another tale of rural degeneracy by Lovecraft, "The Dunwich Horror" (1928).

20. Newitz and Wray, Introduction, 2.

21. Isenberg, *White Trash*, 181.

in novels such as *Off Season* by Jack Ketchum (1980), *The Woods are Dark* by Richard Laymon (1981), *The Bighead* by Edward Lee (1997), and more recently, *The River at Night*, by Erica Ferencik (2017). The presence of some degree of physical deformity and/or mental disability amongst the local antagonists is a given in the backwoods horror movie, and it tends to pose a striking contrast with the obvious good health of their conventionally attractive middle-class victims. This physical divide is even more pronounced when the antagonists are part of the same slovenly and possibly inbred clan. If we take two famous examples of "backwoods" families that would come to pop culture prominence in the 1970s—the Waltons (from Earl Hamner Jr.'s 1972–1981 television show) and the deranged, all-male cannibal clan from *The Texas Chain Saw Massacre* (unnamed in the original film, but given the surname "Sawyer" in the 1986 sequel), we see the qualities associated with one are the flipside of those manifested by the other.[22]

The "Good" White Trash Family:

1. Agreeable folks with their own home-spun wisdom
2. Family-oriented
3. Members of a close-knit rural community even beyond the nuclear family
4. Representative of the "Real" America
5. God-fearing and moral
6. Poor, but happy
7. Close to nature
8. Hardy and physically resilient
9. Pragmatic and unashamedly individualistic
10. Proud owners of their own ramshackle but beloved homestead filled with cherished homemade furniture, furnishings, heirlooms, etc.
11. Self-sufficient—rearing their own animals for slaughter, pickling and preserving their own fruits and vegetables

The "Bad" White Trash Family:

1. Racist and ignorant/uneducated
2. Inbred and incestuous
3. Insular and xenophobic
4. Representative of the "Other" America—and not in a good way
5. Fanatical and intolerant
6. Deeply resentful of those who have more economic power

22. This discussion has been adapted from Murphy, *Rural Gothic*, 133–50.

7. Feral, savage, and degenerate
8. Physically and psychologically misshapen
9. Brutal, callous, and psychotically idiosyncratic
10. Deeply attached to a squalid, filthy, nightmarish hovel furnished with Ed Gein–style trophies from previous victims and other signifiers of deviancy (such as the oddly unsettling sight of a chicken in a tiny cage in *The Texas Chain Saw Massacre*)[23]
11. Treat fellow human beings like animals reared for slaughter, and preserve their remains as smoked meats or barbeque—generally not recognizing the line between human beings and other animals

What is fascinating about the way in which Peele represents the Armitage family in *Get Out* is the way in which it both replicates and inverts so many of the characteristics of the "Bad" White Trash clan, although this connection is not immediately apparent. While the Armitages are, it turns out, deeply racist, their racism tends not to be openly expressed for much of the film (except by a drunken Jeremy) and initially takes the form of a condescending fetishizing of racial difference. Like her parents, Rose would no doubt also be highly offended if she were accused of being racist, even though her horrific mistreatment of Chris and her other love interests/victims underlines her refusal to see African Americans as anything other than exploitable objects. Furthermore, far from being uneducated, the Armitage clan is notable for its high educational attainment. Dean is a neurosurgeon (with a handy home operating theater), Missy is a therapist, and Jeremy is a medical student. Whilst Rose's professional status is never identified, she is clearly also affluent and most likely college educated. Dean and Missy use their professional skills to turn the racist dream of a "superior" white mind in control of an "exceptional" black body, which began with Dean's father Roman (defeated in the 1936 US Olympic team trials by Jesse Owens), into a horrific reality.

While the accomplished and well-connected Armitage clan certainly does not represent the eugenicist's worst nightmare in the obvious sense, the aims of the secret society they belong to are grounded in eugenicist principles. As Isenberg notes of this movement during the early twentieth century, "Evolution rested on nature's law, whereas eugenics found nature wanting. Galton's adherents stressed the necessity for human intervention to improve the race through better breeding. . . . Almost as a mantra, eugenicists compared good human stock to thoroughbreds, equating the wellborn with superior

23. Murphy, *Rural Gothic*, 149–50.

ability and inherited fitness."[24] In this instance, rather than embodying insidious myths about the dangers of the degenerate working-class rural family (a trait that makes many backwoods horror films deeply troubling when we stop to consider these narratives usually endorse this perspective—the rural poor really *are* monsters in these films), the rural white Armitages are *themselves* modern day eugenicists whose self-aggrandizing credo emboldens them to engage in the systematic abuse of racial "others" such as Chris.

Although they do not conform to the "inbred and incestuous" descriptor either, it is clear that the Armitages are extremely close, as attested to by the fact that they are happy coconspirators in the same atrocious scheme. Indeed, for much of the film, three generations of the same family inhabit the same home, as is the case in *The Texas Chain Saw Massacre*. Although we don't know it until the end of the film, both "Georgina" and "Walter" are victims of the Coagula procedure who have been "taken over" by Dean's elderly mother and father. Like the horrific, barely alive figure of "Grandpa" (John Dugan) in Hooper's film, Walter and Georgina represent the Armitages' decision to keep their elderly relatives alive at any cost.

It must be admitted, however, that the Armitage family is certainly not poor, and as such, their relationship to Chris inverts another common backwoods horror trope, whereby the obvious economic disadvantage of the locals inflames their desire to persecute well-off outsiders. Here, Chris is at a social, economic, and demographic disadvantage, a fact that is perhaps made most obvious at the garden party during which he is fawned upon by the wealthy white baby-boomers openly sizing up his physical attributes. The wealth and social standing of Rose's family have given them license to carry out acts of extreme criminality almost in plain sight. Yet although they have certainly not been in any way "left behind" by the modern world, like their backwoods predecessors, the Armitages have also clearly marked out their own territory—a space in which anything goes—amidst the solitude of the rural setting. Indeed, Dean even stresses this "total privacy" when he gives Chris a tour of the property, noting that "the nearest house is across the lake."

The style and the contents of the Armitage home also provide evidence of the film's nuanced debt to the backwoods horror tradition. Although it is in upstate New York, the house, which comes complete with sprawling porch, obedient black staff, and Doric columns, obviously evokes a Southern plantation. Peele has stated that he deliberately did not set the film in the South, explaining, "'It was really important for me to not have the villains in

24. Isenberg, *White Trash*, 175.

this film reflect the typical red state type who is usually categorized as being racist. It felt like that was too easy,' he said. 'I wanted this film to explore the false sense of security one can have with the, sort of, New York liberal type.'"[25] Nevertheless, both the plot and the setting obviously evoke the Southern dependence upon slavery. (As Steve Erickson notes in his *Cineaste* review, the movie is "full of antebellum imagery.")[26] The vast majority of American backwoods horror movies are explicitly set in the South, which for many decades has been seen, as Alison Graham puts it, as the "'dark' underbelly of the nation"; as "the reversed image in the mass-media mirror, the South was and is America's repellent yet all too compelling Other."[27] Somewhat akin to the appurtenances of the Ed Gein–style psychotic pack-rats of *The Texas Chain Saw Massacre,* the ornaments and paintings that tastefully adorn the Armitage home not only emphasize the provenance of the family (including, as they do, antique maps, photographs, and portraits of their ancestors) but also provide an important clue as to their inherently acquisitive nature. For instance, upon seeing Chris notice an object "picked up" in Bali, Dean remarks that it is "such a privilege to be able to experience another person's culture." It's an important early indication of the mind-set that leads them to believe that literally hijacking the body of someone from another race is perfectly acceptable.

The final and most significant way in which *Get Out* intersects with the conventional backwoods horror film inheres in the "Bad" White Trash Family's treatment of its hapless victims in a deeply dehumanizing, degrading manner. Time and again, young city dwellers are hunted down like animals and tortured in ways that signal that their abusers see them as livestock. (Think for instance of the first killing in *The Texas Chain Saw Massacre,* carried out as if Leatherface were dispatching a steer in the slaughterhouse.) This relationship is horribly emphasized when the bodies of the victims are subsequently "processed" and their flesh is sold for human consumption. The Armitage clan and their confederates are not cannibals in a *literal* sense of the word, but their business nonetheless revolves around the processing and selling of (black) flesh to greedy white consumers. Like their more economically disadvantaged backwoods brethren then, the family have completely abdicated all moral and humane considerations in favor of their own depraved desires. Here, however, the slaughterhouse has been upgraded to the operating theater.

25. Herbert, "Hit New Movie."

26. Erickson, "Get Out," 52.

27. Graham, "South," 335.

This easy access to high-tech medical equipment and a well-heeled clientele willing to pay top dollar to be "reborn" in command of an unwilling but helpless black body is part of what makes the behavior of the Armitage family even more disturbing than that of their 1970s counterparts. They are clearly the linchpins of a wider group—the Coagula Society—happily reconciled to the concept of reducing African American captives to mindless slaves if it helps expand the lifespan of their own consciousness. Whilst the poverty and marginal social status of the Sawyer clan obviously informs their horrific actions, Leatherface and his family arguably pose much less of a threat to the world at large than the articulate, professional, and well-connected Armitage clan. Rose and the rest of her kin have power, money, and obvious social and educational capital. They can also move from city to suburb to exurb with ease. It's all part of the reason why, although emotionally satisfying, the film's cathartic climax—famously changed from the much bleaker original conclusion—comes as such a thematic surprise.[28]

Nevertheless, although Chris manages to escape, leaving the bodies of the Armitage clan in his wake, he is still returning to a United States that is economically and politically dominated by upper-middle-class white folks with a mobility denied to many of their nonwhite fellow citizens. By way of contrast, in the final moments of *The Texas Chain Saw Massacre,* it is made clear that Leatherface and the rest of his family will remain defined by and contained within the specific cultural and physical geography of their godforsaken place of origin. As a result, we know that once the film's "Final Girl" Sally Hardesty (Marilyn Burns) is driven away by a passing motorist, she is at least physically safe, even if her future mental stability may understandably be in some doubt. Leatherface remains in the middle of the sun-baked Texas highway, mindlessly roving in circles and revving his chainsaw, forever stuck in one place (at least, until the sequel . . .).

There can be no such certainty in *Get Out,* despite the relief we feel when Rod comes to the rescue. Certainly, the Armitage clan has (seemingly) been eliminated, but as the well-attended garden party demonstrates, they have many wealthy associates. They were not isolated, psychotic loners lashing out at naïve outsiders who accidentally stumbled into their territory; they were instead part of a well-organized and well-funded group of individuals who "rationally" justify the horrific mistreatment of their fellow human beings for purely selfish reasons. For that reason, our joy at Chris's survival should be tempered by the awareness that he and Rod are still citizens of a nation in which previously antiquated notions of "white supremacy" now

28. Goldberg, "'Get Out.'"

have more mainstream currency than they have had for generations. Though their actions are hyperbolically extreme, the Coagula Society's worldview is a satiric but incisive distillation of attitudes that have shaped North America since the very beginning of European settlement. Although Chris is finally able to escape the Armitage estate, as the spatial underpinnings of the film have underlined from the very first scene, the dehumanizing racial attitudes that have shaped America for centuries remain embedded in the nation's political, environmental, and psychological landscape.

Bibliography

Aguilar, Louis, and Christine MacDonald. "Detroit's White Population up after Decades of Decline." *Detroit News*, September 17, 2015. https://www.detroitnews.com/story/news/local/detroit-city/2015/09/17/detroit-white-population-rises-census-shows/72371118/.

Bell, David. "Anti-Idyll: Rural Horror." In *Contested Countryside Cultures: Otherness, Marginalisation, and Rurality*, edited by Paul Cloke and Jo Little, 91–103. New York: Routledge, 1997.

Blow, Charles M. "The Curious Case of Trayvon Martin." *New York Times*, March 16, 2012. http://www.nytimes.com/2012/03/17/opinion/blow-the-curious-case-of-trayvon-martin.html.

Clover, Carol J. *Men, Women, and Chain Saws: Gender in the Modern Horror Film*. Princeton, NJ: Princeton University Press, 1992.

Erickson, Steve. "Get Out." *Cineaste* 42, no. 3 (Summer 2017): 51–53.

Get Out. Directed by Jordan Peele. USA: Universal Pictures, 2017. DVD.

Goldberg, Matt. "'Get Out': Darker Alternate Ending Revealed by Jordan Peele." *Collider*, March 3, 2017. http://collider.com/get-out-alternate-ending/#poster.

Graham, Allison. "The South in Popular Culture." In *A Companion to the Literature and Culture of the American South*, edited by Richard Gray and Owen Robinson, 335–52. London: Blackwell, 2004.

Herbert, Geoff. "Hit New Movie 'Get Out' Turns Racial Issues into Horror Story in Upstate NY." *Syracuse.com*, February 28, 2017. https://www.syracuse.com/entertainment/index.ssf/2017/02/get_out_movie_jordan_peele_upstate_ny.html.

Hoberman, J. "A Real American Horror Story." *New York Review of Books*, March 13, 2017. http://www.nybooks.com/daily/2017/03/13/a-real-american-horror-story-get-out/.

Isenberg, Nancy. *White Trash: The 400-Year Untold History of Class in America*. New York: Viking, 2016.

Levin, Ira. *The Stepford Wives*. New York: HarperCollins, 2002. First published 1972.

Means Coleman, Robin R. *Horror Noire: Blacks in American Horror Films from the 1890s to the Present*. New York: Routledge, 2011.

Murphy, Bernice M. *The Rural Gothic in American Popular Culture: Backwoods Horror and Terror in the Wilderness.* Basingstoke, UK: Palgrave Macmillan, 2013.

———. *The Suburban Gothic in American Popular Culture.* Basingstoke, UK: Palgrave Macmillan, 2009.

Newitz, Annalee, and Matt Wray. Introduction. In *White Trash: Race and Class in America,* edited by Newitz and Wray, 1–12. London: Routledge, 1996.

Transportation Safety Administration. "Mission." https://www.tsa.gov/about/tsa-mission.

Wilson, Jacqueline Zara. "Invisible Racism: The Language and Ontology of 'White Trash.'" *Critique of Anthropology* 22, no. 4 (2002): 387–401.

CHAPTER 6

THE BODY HORROR OF WHITE SECOND CHANCES IN JOHN FRANKENHEIMER'S *SECONDS* AND JORDAN PEELE'S *GET OUT*

ROBYN CITIZEN

THE SUCCESS of Jordan Peele's *Get Out* (2017) is credited with sparking conversations about liberal racism and the myth of postracial America through the framework of horror. This chapter situates *Get Out* somewhat differently, within a larger generic history of body-swap films, a subgenre with multiple points of intersection with horror. Typically, body-swap films feature a white male protagonist getting a second chance at life or a privileged view into the lived experience of an ethnoracial or gendered Other. A version of the body-swap film, *Get Out* tracks Chris's discovery that his girlfriend Rose has been luring black men (and at least one black woman) to her family's upstate enclave where their bodies become hosts for brain transplants (consciousness transfers) from rich elderly and/or disabled white people, thus giving elderly and infirm whites a second chance at life in what they perceive to be physically superior black bodies. I argue that while *Get Out* is most clearly a hybrid horror/social problem film, it also makes explicit the ways in which the body-swap subgenre, and what J. P. Telotte observed as the lingering belief in Cartesian dualism at the core of body-swap plots, has *always* been racialized and has often served as a device to examine social problems.[1]

1. Telotte, "Human Artifice," 44–51.

Along these lines, John Frankenheimer's cult science-fiction film *Seconds* (1966), in which a dissatisfied, affluent, middle-aged white man undergoes transformational plastic surgery to give him a young new identity, may be viewed as an unlikely progenitor for *Get Out*'s exploration of the body-swap subgenre's core themes. *Seconds* illustrates how the concept of second chances—with its assumption of *inter*corporeal motility from an unmarked position—is linked to whiteness; this "swap" is temporalized and spatialized, in other words, within the matrix of ethnoracial and socioeconomic identity formations specific to the United States.[2]

Sandra Meiri and Odeya Kohen-Raz provide a helpful taxonomy of what they term "body-character breach films," a taxonomy predicated on the cause and type of body swapping:

1. *Body switch*—"the co-presence of two swapped bodies, each containing two opposite characters (good/evil; young/old; female/male; married/single; active/passive, and so on)";
2. *Reincarnation*—"a deceased body occupies the body of another in the present";
3. *Body transformation*—"one character whose body has been radically transformed, hence played by two different actors. The oppositions (old/young; female/male; refined/common; fat/thin) are manifested, like in the body-switch category, in the perceptual contradiction between body and character";
4. *Multiple-body character*—"the main character is played by one or more actors (one character, multiple bodies). The oppositions are manifested in the difference between the physique and attributes . . . of the actors who play the main character."
5. *Body host*—"epitomized in *Being John Malkovich* (Spike Jonze, 1999), where we have one actor-body (John Malkovich) occupied, alternately, by three different characters."[3]

As Meiri and Kohen-Raz's taxonomy makes clear, "body-character breach film" is more precise than "body swap" for describing this subgenre, since there is not always an exchange of bodies. Meiri and Kohen-Raz argue

2. These themes of race and class within the body-swap (sub)genre appeared in *Angel Heart* (1987) and *The Skeleton Key* (2005) before Peele made them explicit in the narrative of *Get Out*. Looking back still further, however, the filmic "body-swap" genre is a distillation of themes of doubling originating in gothic literature such as Mary Shelley's *Frankenstein* (1818), Edgar Allan Poe's "William Wilson" (1839), and Robert Louis Stevenson's *The Strange Case of Dr. Jekyll and Mr. Hyde* (1886), as well as Sigmund Freud's "The Uncanny" (1919).

3. Meiri and Kohen-Raz, "Mainstream," 204–5.

that the breaches generally have two functions: first, a fantasy fulfillment, in which the "scripted scenarios of the films' plots enable the characters to gain access to the Other's desire";[4] and, second, a function tied to social identity and status: the swappers, "acquire her/his privileges: the young get to be older, black get to be white, female characters get to be male, and vice versa."[5] The authors never provide any instances of blacks getting to be white, however, and there are just as many examples of swaps that result in an ostensible loss of privilege. Because of the importance of psychosexual development and socialization to their Lacanian argument, Meiri and Kohen-Raz focus on gender/sex swaps, to the exclusion of interpreting the effects of racialized identity swaps.

Earlier foundational texts on speculative genre films with body-swap plots, which also fall in the body invasion category, similarly overlooked the role that racial identity played, implicitly or explicitly, in the narrative. In "Human Artifice and the Science Fiction Film," Telotte claims that the common thread in films of the 1970s and early 1980s—among them Philip Kaufman's *Invasion of the Body Snatchers* (1978), John Carpenter's *The Thing* (1982), Bryan Forbes's *The Stepford Wives* (1975), and Ridley Scott's *Blade Runner* (1982)—is the question of what it means to be human. Telotte mentions race in only one sentence, noting the uniqueness of the *The Thing*'s racially differentiated survivors:

> The confrontation with which the film ends, as McReady and a black man, the only other survivor of the group, eye each other suspiciously, each equally sure that the other is only a double fashioned by the alien, metaphorically points up the distrust and fear which already typically mark modern society, and particularly its race relations.[6]

Body invasion films often address the problem of social hierarchies (*The Faculty* [1998]), personal interests (*The Stepford Wives, Body Snatchers*), ethnoracial identities (*The Thing, They Live* [1988], *The Stuff* [1985]), and economic backgrounds (*Alien* [1979] series) by forcing disparate people to work together and fight against a monstrous threat relative to which their human differences pale. Protagonists fight the indignity and violence of corporeal imposition by creatures who claim superiority on the basis of brute force or advanced technology—a scenario that cannot help but evoke the ethos of the colonial project from indigenous genocide to the Middle Passage. Indeed, *Get Out* makes this sociohistorical analogy explicit in its focus on a

4. Ibid., 206.
5. Ibid.
6. Telotte, "Human Artifice," 47.

descendant of slaves, Chris, resisting being sold into body hosting through the racialized Coagula procedure. In the end, then, *The Thing*'s casting suggested what would later become a more explicit congruence between the generic production of the monster's otherness/alienness and the cultural processes of racialization (and gendering), a metaphor that is usually a structuring absence in the horror genre.[7]

An analysis of *Seconds* lays the foundation for understanding how body-character breaches, particularly body switches, body transformations, and body-host types, are racialized in the subgenre: even in the near absence of black bodies, whiteness is associated with mind/subjectivity within the Cartesian split. Since, unlike other possession or magic-related body swaps, *Get Out*'s body-character breach is mainly the result of brain transplant surgery, it is necessary to explain how "mind" and the physical brain have been differentiated historically. The body-switch, reincarnation, and body-host categories of the body-character breach subgenre are grounded in a lingering belief in Cartesian dualism or the "ghost in the machine," which claims that the mind and the body are discrete "substances" in spite of the fact that they are "ordinarily harnessed together."[8] Thus, someone's mind may exist beyond corporeal death and a mind may even exist in another body, commandeering it as a captain does a ship. This dualistic imagining of human existence intersects with discourses that have conflated certain ethnoracial identities with only one part of the body/mind dyad. The implications of *Get Out*'s reveal depend on how this mind/body split is mapped onto other binaries including civilized/uncivilized and mobility (agency)/stasis.

In *Black Skin, White Masks,* Frantz Fanon noted that the results of a word association test given to five hundred white subjects demonstrated how blackness was overdetermined by the physical body: "Almost 60 percent gave us the following answers: Negro = biological, sex, strong, athletic, powerful, boxer, Joe Louis, Jesse Owens, Senegalese infantryman, savage, animal, devil, sin."[9] Five years after Fanon's *Black Skin, White Masks,* Norman Mailer offered a description of and prescription for the growing dissatisfaction with establishment norms of postwar America and the romanticization of social outsiderness in his essay "The White Negro." Sexual excess, personal violence, rebelliousness, and "philosophical psychopathy" are infamously attributed to the titular Negro, who is the primary referent for the

---

7. According to Isabel Pinedo, "If the racial Other is marked as monster in the larger culture, then to do so in the horror film is to tread too closely to prevailing anxieties." See Pinedo, *Recreational Terror,* 112.

8. Ryle, *Concept of Mind,* 11.

9. Fanon, *Black Skin,* 103.

ethos of hipsters/Bohemians.[10] For Mailer, the "Negro's" supposed indulgence of bodily pleasures and "infantile fantasy"[11] is a posture that others should adapt to revolutionize a culture too dependent on conformity and the suppression of individual self-expression. Fanon and Mailer illustrate how racial hierarchies are underpinned by the belief that whiteness is partially defined by a healthy relationship between body and mind, with the former at the service of the latter's higher functions (e.g., intelligence, agency, and discipline), while blacks are merely flesh, reproducing and laboring body-machines—neither subjects nor persons.[12]

Although *Get Out* takes place over sixty years later, it is striking how Fanon's findings and Mailer's supposedly celebratory descriptions of black bodies in American culture find their respective parallels in the microaggressions perpetrated by the upstate locals who frequent the Armitage home and the eugenic arguments about blacks' nature used to justify the body swaps. In a tense dinner scene, Rose's brother Jeremy seems fixated on the possibility of Chris's physical potential—and it is a mere assumption, because he has just met Chris who has been introduced as a professional photographer and has already stated that he's never been particularly into sports. Yet Jeremy speculates at length on how far someone with Chris's "frame and genetic makeup" could "be a beast" in UFC fighting or martial arts if only he trained. Jeremy continues, to everyone's growing discomfort, explicitly to foreground sports, from his own practice of jiu-jitsu, which requires mental strategy "like chess," implying that this is an area that favors *his* "genetic makeup."[13] Later in the film, the family patriarch, Roman, emphasizes this dichotomous black body/white mind in the video explaining the Coagula procedure: "You were chosen because of the physical advantages you've enjoyed your entire life. I'm certain that with your *natural gifts* and *our determination* we'll soon both be a part of something greater."

Therefore *Get Out*'s plot twist, in which (mainly) white consciousnesses vie to commandeer black bodies that are perceived to be physically superior yet mentally deficient, represents Peele's artful synthesis of prior horror

10. Mailer, "White Negro," 280.

11. Ibid., 283.

12. In terms of gender, the female, including the white female, is overdetermined by her body, as she cannot transcend its "limitations," namely the reproductive processes that historically define it. Thus, a film like *The Stepford Wives* plays on this belief in its employment of men longing to separate "extraneous" individual traits and personal agency from the physical functions and social roles historically assigned to women as reproducers, sexual objects, housekeepers, and caretakers in general. Elizabeth Grosz's concept of corporeal feminism discusses this dualism at length and proposes a way to surpass it. See Grosz, *Volatile Bodies*, 19–22.

13. *Get Out*. All further references to the film are to this DVD.

texts, overlaying a thin veneer of the fantastic onto the historical realities of chattel slavery, eugenics programs, and the material and psychosocial effects of institutionalized racism. *Get Out* does offer a more ambiguous view of the Cartesian split than others of the body-swap subgenre, however, precisely because the transference of the new consciousness/mind happens as a result of a brain transplant, suggesting a materialist view of consciousness as located in or arising from the brain. Roman explains that a small part of the host brain, mainly the stem, must remain to connect the new brain to the host body, which supposedly explains the lingering copresence of the black consciousness. And yet, in combination with the aforementioned dialogue, details of the Coagula procedure—including subtle references to the occult (i.e., the candles and other props in the operating room, allusions to the Knights Templar[14]) and the sunken place scenes in which Missy (Rose's psychiatrist mother) hypnotizes Chris to prepare his body for Jim's copresence—demonstrate the film's investment in exploring the effects of discourses that have historically defined blackness as insufficient quality of mind.

The fact that the mind is immaterial and that white as an ethnoracial category has historically been constructed as transcendent—"the subject without properties . . . unmarked, universal, just human . . . pure spirit"—enables the intercorporeal mobility central to many body-character breach films.[15] For instance, in *Get Out* there is no suggestion that the white characters undergo a similar process of hypnosis in order to prepare for the transplant/consciousness transfer. They do not need to be taught how to take physical or cognitive control of a body of color (although one wonders how the Coagula clients respond to being seen in a black body outside of the confines of their own community, where everyone knows who they "really" are). *Seconds* develops this purported "transcendence" of whiteness in its temporalization as future-oriented, by default relegating blackness and certain other nonwhite identities to a state of embodied objectivity and what scholar James Snead called, "metaphysical stasis," adding that "the black—particularly the black woman—is seen as eternal, unchanging, unchangeable."[16] This relentless future-orientation of whiteness is actively rejected by the protagonist in *Seconds,* but at a cost.

Seconds was released in 1966, one year before the "Summer of Love" and the year that youth and bohemian culture exploded into the mainstream. Only two years after the Civil Rights Act, 1966 was marred by multiple race uprisings in various American cities, among them Lansing, Chicago,

14. *Get Out,* "Special Features."

15. Dyer, *White,* 38–39.

16. Snead, *White Screens,* 3.

and Cleveland. In *Seconds,* family man Arthur Hamilton (John Randolph) approaches retirement alongside his aging wife (Frances Reid) in their airless upper-class community. A strange man pushes a note into Hamilton's hand on his daily commute into Manhattan; then he is contacted by an old friend who supposedly died years earlier. The film's depiction of Hamilton's life in the early scenes is one of crushing ennui and alienation. Soon, Hamilton is lured into becoming a client at a company specializing in "second chances."

Seconds's intertexts can be traced to racialized and classed American notions of morality and action, Mailer's prediction of a new youth culture for disaffected whites, and European male crisis films about otherwise privileged men. In their video essay on the film, R. Burton Palmer and Murray Pomerance identify the source of Arthur's malaise—the social problem as it were—as "the American myth, the national belief of the real possibility of second chances and self-remaking. And the American nightmare, the unfulfilling boredom of a life lived according to the rules with its expectation of constant compliance and mitigation of self that *even members of the white Anglo-Saxon Northeastern ruling elite,* the Wall Street masters of the universe, find increasingly impossible to fulfill."[17]

If *Get Out* uses the legacy of black slave labor as a bit of a red herring in the film to conceal the real twist, *Seconds,* in a departure from most body-character breach films, shows how the utopian promise of starting again actually entails a significant amount of both visible and invisible labor. The film attends to the details of how individuals legitimate their identities not only through their appearance but via social, medical, and legal institutions. It begins with faking the client's death and using a cadaver for insurance identification purposes, then radical surgical transformation, and finally producing the personal and legal documents that Hamilton will need to navigate the world. This labor allows Hamilton, now Tony Wilson (Rock Hudson), to start over in his ideal profession of painter. As part of the contract, the company continues to work on his behalf, including hiring a servant to help with his transition. However, this labor is exclusively performed by other whites—either the professionals in the company or the white working-class butchers and dry cleaners who provide cover for the company's location and true purpose. Black male extras in *Seconds* are extras in business suits retrieving briefcases from the baggage claim at Los Angeles Airport. In *Get Out,* on the other hand, the overeager servility of the black help at the Armitage home and those in the larger community has a different narrative function. The black characters appear to have been brain-

17. Palmer and Pomerance, "Special Features"; emphasis added.

washed into subservience by the white privileged class to reinstate blacks as an involuntary servile class for sexual (Logan) and labor purposes (Walter and Georgina). This conceals both the "why?" and the true extent of the Armitages' exploitation—thus, the body-host category only becomes salient at the end of the film before the attempted transference of Jim's consciousness into Chris's body.

In *Seconds,* on a plane to his new home, Wilson contemplates the guidance advisor's parting words, that the company is giving him what "every middle-aged man in America wants: freedom, real freedom." But, if men like Hamilton—whose identities were privileged within the ethnoracial, regional, class, gender, and sexuality configurations of 1966 American institutions—were not free, then *what kind* of freedom, *whose* freedom is the point of reference here? Precisely because characters like Arthur Hamilton occupy so much space in the *Bildungsroman* literary and filmic canons of the West—although we meet him at the endpoint of that typical character arc—the viewer is primed to fill in the sociocultural obstacles that discouraged his pursuit of artistic occupation. An attractive neighbor, Nora (Salome Jens), brings him to a Bacchanalian party, but the youthful wildness of the festivities initially disturbs Wilson. A subsequent party, which reveals that Nora and Wilson's neighbors are also "seconds," sent to help him integrate, highlights the superficiality of the second chances offered by the company and the limits to the self-remaking fantasy offered by the body-character breach film in general. Wilson's transition is arranged to give him the pleasures of "second chances" without the concomitant struggles; he starts over with a ready-made reputation and backlog of artistic work, he is financially set, and, most ironically, he lands in a community of all-white, primarily male, upper-class others nearly indistinguishable from those in his previous life.

Seconds challenges the assumption that well-bred white men can adapt every perspective to their supposedly unmarked identity position, as if changing one's identity and radical bodily transformation were merely extreme iterations of practicing empathy, cultural appropriation, or cosmopolitanism.[18] This depiction of how the perspectival differences imprinted by the social and cultural processes of racialization are also not so easily overcome is echoed in *Get Out.* In nonspeculative genre body-swap films, the violation of social norms, bodily comportment, and disruptions in personality continuity that occur after the swap due to differences between the characters' ages, values, and/or gender are either mitigated as the narrative progresses or accepted by those around them as a beneficial transition. However, Wilson's mind cannot transcend the relatively modest

18. Thanks to Leigh Goldstein for this analogy.

disjuncture between his transformed body—more conventionally attractive and endowed with youthful bohemian credibility but still presenting as white, male, affluent, and educated—and the cumulative effect of choices and experiences from his previous life. In this sense, it is possible to read *Seconds* as placing more limitations on white heteropatriarchal males than other body-swap films, even *Get Out*, as Wilson finds himself in a roomful of failed "seconds" of his own demographic. Hamilton and others like him may be "trapped by the geography of their own choices," but for a while they benefitted from those choices that perpetuated institutions which have always been someone *else's* "American nightmare" of systemic "mitigation of self."[19] By comparison, the Coagula participants in *Get Out* have much more to acclimate to, transitioning from a socioculturally unmarked body to one with visible difference.

Just as *Get Out* complicates the mind/body split at the heart of many body-character breach films, it also briefly introduces a character who seemingly transgresses the black/white binary of American racial ideology. The only non-body-host person of color at the auction, the Japanese/Japanese American character, Hiroki Tanaka, foreshadows the contradictory eugenics-based and "colorblind" rationalizations of the Coagula process.[20] The geopolitical history between Japan and the US, as well as model minority discourse, is relevant to the body-swap subgenre—and specifically to *Get Out*'s reveal. Among nations with majority nonwhite populations, Japan was an exception, begrudgingly "admitted . . . to the circle of 'civilized nations'" by Roosevelt after defeating Russia in the Russo-Japanese War.[21] Both "Japaneseness" and model minority attributes in general align with characteristics that supposedly distinguish whites from racial others, namely, work ethic, intelligence, and ambition. The film explicitly references eugenics and other cultural ideologies that naturalized white supremacy, not least though exposition about the Coagula procedure originating after

19. Palmer and Pomerance, "Special Features."

20. In the screenplay, Tanaka's first line is in Japanese and Dean answers him back in Japanese, which suggests that the old alliances of WWII's ethnoracial nationalism have been maintained through secret societies. See Peele, "*Get Out.*" Furthermore, the suburban parts of the film are set in fictional Lake Pontaco, which likely references Lake Pocantico in Westchester County. Westchester County has a majority white demographic, but the next most populous group is Asian and particularly a small Japanese diaspora. Japanese began migrating to Westchester County in the 1980s. As businessmen settled with their families in the suburbs, there were alarmist articles in the early 1990s about the "Japanning" of Scarsdale. See Handelman, "Japanning," and Berger, "Our Towns." Therefore, Peele rewards viewers with insider knowledge about local demographics, offers another layer of verisimilitude, and likely pokes fun at the conspiracy-filled Japan Panic of his youth.

21. Kowner, "Becoming," 36.

Rose's grandfather, Roman, lost to Jesse Owens in the qualifying rounds of the Olympics. Owens's victory was an iconic setback for claims to Aryan physiological superiority during the rise of Axis powers, of which Japan represented the only Axis power of color. The appearance of an Asian character, outed as specifically Japanese through the mention of his name, is a subtle reminder of the grandfather's World War II story introduced earlier in the film. Tanaka's presence also speaks to the tension between Asians as the model minority group and other people of color, particularly blacks. Richard Dyer explains that whiteness can include other groups, who are sometimes "assimilated into the category of whiteness" and sometimes "treated as a 'buffer' between the white and the black or indigenous."[22]

Thus, in terms of how the mind/body dyad has been historically racialized, Tanaka and the Japanese, unlike the cognitively infantile, laboring body-machines of blacks, have been positioned as having the inherent qualities to be collaborators in the Coagula group as well as tokens whose racial "buffer" status diverts from the white supremacist beliefs and racial revenge at the root of the procedure. Perhaps it is this racially and nationally liminal status that emboldens Tanaka to ask Chris a direct question about race—"Do you find that being African American has more advantages or disadvantages in the modern world?"—whereas the white characters mask racial microaggressions with compliments about black physicality.[23] For clients like Jim, who thinks of himself as colorblind, the Coagula process is not about antiblackness but the belief that "they," who just *happen* to be white, are uniquely equipped to tap into the unrealized potential contained in black bodies. When Chris asks why the victims of the Coagula process have to be black, Jim demurs, "I could give two shits about race. I don't care if you're black, brown, green, purple . . . whatever." He suggests that people just want "a change," but the changes Jim mentions are specifically linked to stereotypes about black physicality, "stronger, faster, cooler." And even what he covets, Chris's "eye," as in his artistic vision, seems linked to his idea of an authenticity steeped in black bodily suffering—Chris's work is "brutal" and "melancholic." When he states that he and Chris are in a category of "real people" that the Armitages "don't understand," Jim is assuming that his

22. Dyer, *White,* 19. Although Dyer does not mention Asians specifically, others have extrapolated on this "buffer" group idea: activist Scot Nakagawa observes that within the system of white supremacy "Asians are the wedge."

23. I include national identity here because Tanaka has an accent suggesting he is a first-generation immigrant rather than a later-generation Asian American. And, as I mentioned above, in the screenplay he first speaks in Japanese.

acquired disability, which he characterizes as "unfair," is analogous to that of being born black in a racist society.

Peele draws on Nazism and other historical discourses of race, as well as the current, contradictory cultural phenomena of colorblind denial amidst the groundswell of resistance against, not least, racialized policing, in order to innovate the genre's typical narrative and stylistic methods of building suspense. Because current discussions of racism and the generic drift of the horror film focus on working-class and/or individual whites with explicitly malicious intent, for many viewers the suburban Armitages do not initially fit the typical perpetrators of racial exploitation. However, the Armitages are not really progressive; their performance of liberal allyship exists only at the level of textual address to show a target demographic the moral deferrals underlying the mainstream racial discourse in which they participate. This performance simultaneously fulfills the generic imperative of delaying the plot twist, which is essentially that we have been watching the aftereffects of a body-swap conspiracy (the odd behavior of those already hosting) and the preparations to make Chris another victim. The Armitages' explanation for having exclusively black help seems problematic but benign enough, as is the racial awkwardness of their friends and neighbors. However, it is easy to forget that much of the awkwardness seems to be performed *for Chris's sake* in the film. When Missy and Rose cringe at the father's use of antiquated African American slang, and Rose eye-rolls the various comments at the auction party, the awkwardness and the faux-horrified reactions have happened in some variation before. When Jeremy plays a ukulele on their suburban porch in a surprising homage to the dueling banjo scene in John Boorman's *Deliverance* (1972), the film subverts the depiction of the family's genteel visage both on the level of the text and metatextually. They might be part of the act every single time, but why? Wouldn't it be easier for the Armitages to subdue a subject who has not been repeatedly put on edge by days of microaggressions and attempts at psychoanalysis by the family matriarch?

These encounters, I argue, are necessary because they force Chris to see himself through another's eyes over and over again in a process that mirrors Fanon's description of blackness as beginning with interpellation (i.e., "Look a Negro!"). More importantly, due to Chris's position as protagonist, the ideal white liberal spectator constructed by the textual address must experience this process through his point of view. Musser eloquently paraphrases this hailing process:

> [It] disrupts the narrator's sense of himself as a sovereign subject, a subject who could possess mastery over the world. Instead, he discovers that he is

> an object, which is to say that he has no agency and is controlled by other people's images of him. This moment of objectification catches the narrator by surprise and undoes his sense of self. Fanon describes the loss of agency and subjective coherence in physical terms: "I burst apart."[24]

Chris is arguably first objectified during the interrogation by the police officer, then through the aforementioned racial gaffes, which "burst apart" his mind/subjectivity from his body just enough for Missy to implant the hypnotic suggestions that lay the groundwork for his "sunken place." That blacks must be always aware of "other people's images of [them]"[25] is made clear in the opening scene when we meet Andre—later Logan after his operation—who is lost in a predominately white suburb and on the phone: "I'm out here like a sore thumb and shit." Indeed, the blatant aggressiveness of Jeremy's character (who was also the one to abduct Andre) is an intentional part of this objectification process, as well as a bit of misdirection drawing Chris's attention away from the larger conspiracy, similar to racial discourses that overemphasize the threat of racist individuals in order to avoid addressing systemic and institutional racism. This concept of black identity being shaped by others' stories and preconceptions evokes the struggles around black representation and racialized tropes in American media, which is perhaps why screens and flash photography recur in the film. In his sunken place, Chris is shown looking back at Missy through a space that resembles a screen, and which thus functions as a spatial representation of how he felt when his mother disappeared while he watched TV, too paralyzed to alert anyone to her absence. This play of racialized histories, semantics, and discourses dovetails with the generic trope of flash photography, as having magical soul-capturing qualities. And, of course, the "soul" invokes the contradictory articulations of soul as an aspect of the immaterial mind and spirit or soul-as-the-bodily-emoting associated with blacks.

Indeed, creating a hybrid medical-occult method for commandeering black bodies seems superfluous after the past three hundred years of colonization: slavery, *de jure* and *de facto* discrimination had already accomplished the physical ownership of black bodies, degradation of black culture, and the aforementioned colonization of black psyches in the form of interpellation, internalized racism, and Du Boisian doubleness. While *Get Out* integrates the psychosocial processes of racial interpellation with the narrative conventions of horror in a way that is more explicit than typical American

---

24. Musser, *Sensational Flesh*, 89–90.
25. Ibid., 90.

horror, which tends to displace racialization onto monstrousness, as in *King Kong* (1933) and *Bride of Frankenstein* (1935), there is precedent in other, less well-received, modern body-swap horror films such as *Angel Heart* (1987), *The Skeleton Key* (2005), and *Jessbelle* (2014) that peripherally engage the nation's legacy of racial terror.[26]

Ultimately, through its generic hybridity of black comedy, horror, and the social problem film, *Get Out* is able to comment on the limitations of its predecessors in the larger body-swap genre. If comedy and drama body-swap films tend to rely on "fish out of water" scenarios in order to create humor and pathos from the way "walking a mile in another's shoes" generates empathy that leads to personal growth, then *Get Out*'s depiction of white characters whose values are utterly unchanged despite their newfound black embodiment and having access to its original consciousness with its reservoir of memories, traumas, and racial socialization is revealing. In the speculative genres—fantasy, sci-fi, horror—body-character breach films such as *The Thing* and *Invasion of the Body Snatchers* typically emphasize the horrific vulnerability of the human body and mind, displacing monstrousness onto racial and gendered others or confining race to a structural absence. However, *Get Out*'s plot not only incorporates concrete references to how America's systematic psychic, physical, and epistemic violence toward African Americans has already cleaved the black mind from its body but also imprints the monstrosity and "stranger within" paranoia endemic to the genre onto aberrant whites and whiteness in general. For example, Chris is alerted that something is amiss when talking to Walter, Georgina, and Logan in private. When confronted with modern African American Vernacular English (AAVE) colloquialisms, they pause and then translate the terms into mainstream English, such as when Georgina substitutes "tattle" for Chris's "snitch." This is not only a racial disjuncture but a generational one. In other instances, Chris's attempts to commiserate with these characters about experiences of racism are indiscreetly dismissed. Chris comments to his friend Rod that the blacks in this neighborhood "missed the [civil rights] movement," because they exhibit such a profound lack of racial socialization and consciousness. Indeed, *Get Out* and the texts here that are among its predecessors—including *Seconds*, "The White Negro," *Angel Heart*, and others—show how white second chances, and even maintenance of the

26. See Young, "Here Comes the Bride," 403–37. It should be noted that *The Skeleton Key* reverses the typical racialized associations of body-swap films in that, through hoodoo, the black conjurers achieve the corporeal motility usually reserved for white protagonists.

privileged status quo, have always depended on the desire for the racial other and their physical and/or cultural labor and sacrifices.

Bibliography

Berger, Joseph. "Our Towns; Scarsdale Woman Helps Ease the Strain When Cultures Clash." *New York Times,* February 9, 1993. https://www.nytimes.com/1993/02/09/nyregion/our-towns-scarsdale-woman-helps-ease-the-strain-when-cultures-clash.html.

Dyer, Richard. *White.* London: Routledge, 1997.

Fanon, Frantz. *Black Skin, White Masks.* New York: Grove Press, 1952.

Get Out. Directed by Jordan Peele. USA: Universal Pictures, 2017. DVD.

Grosz, Elizabeth A. *Volatile Bodies: Toward a Corporeal Feminism.* Bloomington: Indiana University Press, 1994.

Handelman, David. "The Japanning of Scarsdale." *New York Magazine,* April 29, 1991. https://books.google.ca/books?id=BOkCAAAAMBAJ&pg=PA3&dq=the+japanning+of+scarsdale+NY+magazine+april+1991&hl=en&sa=X&ved=0ahUKEwjouLqco8HeAhUCrlkKHcZyDuEQ6AEILjAB.

Kowner, Rotem. "Becoming an Honorary Civilized Nation: Remaking Japan's Military Image during the Russo-Japanese War, 1904–1905." *Historian* 64, no. 1 (2001): 19–38.

Mailer, Norman. "The White Negro." *Dissent Magazine* 4 (Spring 1957): 276–93.

Meiri, Sandra, and Odeya Kohen-Raz. "Mainstream Body-Character Breach Films and Subjectivization." *International Journal of Psychoanalysis* 98, no. 1 (2017): 201–17.

Musser, Amber Jamilla. *Sensational Flesh: Race, Power, and Masochism.* New York: New York University Press, 2014.

Nakagawa, Scot. "Asians Are the Wedge." *Race Files,* May 29, 2012. https://www.racefiles.com/2012/05/29/asians-are-the-wedge/.

Palmer, R. Burton, and Murray Pomerance. "Special Features: Visual Essay" *Seconds.* Directed by John Frankenheimer. USA: Paramount Pictures, 1966. DVD.

Peele, Jordan. "*Get Out.*" Unpublished screenplay.

Pinedo, Isabel Christina. *Recreational Terror: Women and the Pleasures of Horror.* Albany: State University of New York Press, 1997.

Ryle, Gilbert. *The Concept of Mind.* Chicago: University of Chicago Press, 2002.

Seconds. Directed by John Frankenheimer. USA: Paramount Pictures, 1966. DVD.

Snead, James A. *White Screens/Black Images: Hollywood from the Dark Side 1953–1989.* New York: Routledge, 1994.

Telotte, J. P. "Human Artifice and the Science Fiction Film." *Film Quarterly* 36, no. 3 (1983): 44–51.

Young, Elizabeth. "Here Comes the Bride: Wedding, Gender, and Race in *Bride of Frankenstein.*" *Feminist Studies* 17, no. 3 (1991): 403–37.

CHAPTER 7

JORDAN PEELE AND IRA LEVIN GO TO THE MOVIES

The Black/Jewish Genealogy of Modern Horror's Minority Vocabulary

ADAM LOWENSTEIN

WRITER/DIRECTOR JORDAN PEELE geared up for the premiere of *Get Out* (2017) by programming a slate of films that influenced him at New York's Brooklyn Academy of Music under the series title "The Art of the Social Thriller." The films Peele selected were *Night of the Living Dead* (1968), *Rosemary's Baby* (1968), *The Shining* (1980), *Candyman* (1992), *The 'Burbs* (1989), *Scream* (1996), *Rear Window* (1954), *Funny Games* (1997), *The Silence of the Lambs* (1991), *The People Under the Stairs* (1991), and *Guess Who's Coming to Dinner* (1967). It's a striking and telling array of influences, but only one of the two films that hang most heavily over *Get Out* is included: *Rosemary's Baby*. The other, as this chapter will illustrate, is *The Stepford Wives* (1975). These are both famous modern horror films, but they began as bestselling novels (published in 1967 and 1972, respectively) by the Jewish American author Ira Levin.[1]

The fact that *Get Out* would find so much inspiration in a Jewish author's work is fascinating in its own right and suggests that the horror genre may

1. For Jordan Peele's own thoughts on his debts to *The Stepford Wives*, *Rosemary's Baby*, and what he calls "the Ira Levin school of writing," see Peele, "*Get Out*." Ira Levin, who was born in 1929 and died in 2007, was a master of suspenseful, paranoia-inducing horror. During his remarkable and underappreciated career, he also wrote the novels *The Boys from Brazil* (1976) and *Sliver* (1991), as well as the Broadway smash *Deathtrap* (1978), among others.

have some important things to teach us about how social minority positions have more in common than we might imagine—that those who lack social power and suffer from majority prejudice can find common ground in horror. This extends not just to Jews and blacks, but also to women, since *Rosemary's Baby* reads like a Jewish nightmare of religious oppression in the same way that *The Stepford Wives* reads like a feminist nightmare of gender oppression.[2]

What Peele gets from Levin is that paranoia, when you are a social minority, can be real, lived horror even if it can only be treated as absurd fantasy by the social majority. As Rosemary Woodhouse says in *Rosemary's Baby* when she tries to convince others who refuse to believe that she has become the victim of an elderly band of Satanists, "Now and then there *are* plots against people, aren't there?"[3] What Rosemary voices here is the horror of minority experience within a majority society that marginalizes the legitimacy of that horror, that dismisses real pain as imagined paranoia. In Levin's fiction and in *Get Out*, being paranoid is not a delusional state, but an anguished way of waking up to the way things actually are.

This chapter explores the affinities between *Get Out* and Levin's work in order to theorize what I will call modern horror's minority vocabulary: the genre's ability to articulate the experience of social minorities as real pain rather than paranoid fantasy. The horror film has often been regarded as thriving negatively on "otherness," usually by aligning its monstrous threats with social others. For example, Robin Wood's landmark argument that the structure of horror films can be boiled down to the formula "normality is threatened by the Monster" assumes that the monster resembles the minority others that majority society fears—those deemed different in terms of race, class, gender, sexuality, nationality, ethnicity, or political beliefs.[4] What Wood and those in his wake have been less willing to argue is that horror's relation to social otherness may be closer to acknowledging actual minority experience rather than converting it into fantastic monstrosity. Yet this is precisely what a closer look at the relationship between Peele and Levin reveals—the power of horror as a vocabulary for the illumination, not the demonization, of the pain endured by social minorities.[5]

---

2. One might add that *Deathtrap* could be read as a queer nightmare of sexual oppression, but space does not permit more thorough investigation of this argument.

3. Levin, *Rosemary's Baby*, 206.

4. Wood, "Introduction," 117; 111–15.

5. Of course, this claim condenses a number of issues that would need more thorough elaboration in a longer version of this chapter. For the history of relations between blacks and Jews in America, see Sundquist, *Strangers;* for the history of relations between

Get Out is at least as much a product of 1968 as it is of 2017. Peele's use of horror as a minority vocabulary stems directly from two watershed modern horror films released in 1968: *Rosemary's Baby* and *Night of the Living Dead*. Although both of these films have long been considered central to shaping modern horror cinema, they have most often been perceived as inhabiting opposite ends of the horror spectrum. *Rosemary's Baby* is the glossy, big-budget, star-studded, Hollywood-produced, auteur-driven horror film that paved the way for *The Exorcist* (1973), *The Omen* (1976), *The Silence of the Lambs, The Sixth Sense* (1999), *Zodiac* (2007), and *The Shape of Water* (2017). *Night of the Living Dead* is the gritty, low-budget, starless, independently produced, unknown-directed horror film that opened the doors for *The Last House on the Left* (1972), *The Texas Chain Saw Massacre* (1974), *Shivers* (1975), *Halloween* (1978), *The Blair Witch Project* (1999), *Paranormal Activity* (2007), and *Get Out*. What is lost when focusing on these differences, however, is how much the two films share in terms of their investments in social otherness.[6] *Night of the Living Dead* features an African American protagonist, Ben (Duane Jones), who survives the zombie onslaught only to be murdered by the all-white militia that has supposedly come to his rescue. *Rosemary's Baby* is less straightforward in its presentation of social otherness, but pairing Roman Polanski's film with Levin's source novel uncovers just how much *Rosemary's Baby* is rooted in the dynamics of a Jewish nightmare.

In Levin's novel, one of Rosemary's friends reacts to her emaciated appearance during her pregnancy with a telling line: "You look like Miss Concentration Camp of 1966."[7] A hint, among others, that Rosemary's struggle is not limited to being sold out by her husband to a coven of Satanists and impregnated with the Antichrist. Her struggle also transforms her from a literal Catholic into a figurative Jew. Already a fish out of water in 1960s New York due to her Midwestern background and residual attachment to her Catholic faith, Rosemary becomes truly other as she draws closer to the Jewish elements in her life. First, her ostensibly Protestant husband Guy Woodhouse is already tainted in the eyes of her Midwestern Catholic family for having divorced parents and a mother who remarried a Jew. It's even possible that Guy changed his name from Sherman Peden for reasons not solely to do with his acting profession. After all, he criticizes his fellow

blacks and Jews in Hollywood cinema, see Rogin, *Blackface;* and for the history of black representation in the American horror film, see Means Coleman, *Horror Noire.*

6. It is also worth noting how the presence of William Castle as the producer of *Rosemary's Baby* for Paramount suggests an intersection between "high" and "low" horror traditions.

7. Levin, *Rosemary's Baby,* 154.

actor Donald Baumgart for holding on to his Jewish-sounding name, a name Guy makes a point to ridicule; it is Baumgart, moreover, whom Guy blinds with the help of the coven in order to secure his own break in the acting business. Like the Jewish Bobbie Markowe in Levin's *The Stepford Wives,* who changes her surname from Markowitz to Markowe in order to conceal her Jewishness, it's possible that Guy's background is not Protestant at all. Although Levin does not make this suggestion explicit, he does make it clear that one of Guy's partners in the coven, Abe Sapirstein, is a Jew. Sapirstein, the famous obstetrician who becomes Rosemary's doctor at the behest of the coven, is praised by the coven's leader, Roman Castevet, as "brilliant, with all the sensitivity of his much-tormented race."[8] The Jews as a "much-tormented race" who might have something to gain from Roman's promises that Satan "shall redeem the despised and wreak vengeance in the name of the burned and the tortured!" is underlined by having Roman hide behind his own false name (Roman Castevet is, as Rosemary discovers, an anagram for his true name Steven Marcato, son of the infamous Satanist Adrian Marcato).[9] Rosemary, who is as uncertain about her own name (she veers between her married name and her maiden name, Reilly) as she is about the name of her unborn child, at one point tells Sapirstein that she wants to name her baby after him. Sapirstein's response: "God forbid."[10]

Sapirstein's reply is emblematic of Levin's humorously ironic but cutting juxtaposition of the fantastic and the realistic in his work. On the one hand, Sapirstein as Satanist is suggesting to Rosemary, "If only you knew how little agency you will have in the identity of your baby and how little God will have to do with it." On the other hand, Sapirstein as Jew is also saying, "Why would you saddle your child with such a Jewish-sounding name when it will undoubtedly result in social suffering?" The fact that Adrian, Andrew, and Abe all begin with the same letter and compete as possible names for Rosemary's baby points toward a certain interchangeability between the positions of Satanist and Christian (Adrian dies in a stable, Christ is born in a manger) as well as Satanist and Jew (Sapirstein, named after the father of the Jewish people, delivers babies for others while his namesake was willing to kill his own miraculously born child to prove his faith in God). It's as if Levin, with his nearly obsessive exchanging of "true" and "false" names (even Rosemary's trustworthy friend Hutch writes adventure stories for boys under three different pseudonyms), is arguing that everyone is in danger of becoming an other—Christ is only so far

8. Ibid., 110.
9. Ibid., 236.
10. Ibid., 184.

from the Antichrist, the Christian only so far from the Jew, the God-fearing believer only so far from the Satanist. Simply scratch the name and a different identity appears. In this logic of precarious naming, Rosemary as figurative Jew makes alarming sense—there *is* a plot against her, she *could* suffer the fate of those condemned to the concentration camps. She is not a Jew, but she has come to occupy the social position of Jew as persecuted other.

It may seem surprising at first that writer/director Polanski, as both a Polish Jew and a Holocaust survivor, drains much of Levin's explicitly Jewish content from his adaptation of *Rosemary's Baby.* Gone is the "Miss Concentration Camp" line, along with Guy's Jewish-tainted family history and the explicit identification of Sapirstein as a Jew. But since Polanski's own survival as a child depended in part on concealing his Jewishness, it makes sense that it is not really until *The Pianist* (2002) that he grapples with Jewishness in any overt, straightforward way.[11] But nearly all of his films draw much of their power from channeling precisely the sort of paranoia that anchors Levin's Jewish-inflected vision. In fact, Levin has called Polanski's *Rosemary's Baby* "possibly the most faithful film adaptation ever made."[12] Levin may foreground Jewishness in a way that Polanski does not, but both men convey the pain of paranoia's reality for the social other. In short, there is a shared feeling for Jewishness as a persecuted minority position in both Levin and Polanski, even if one expresses it explicitly and the other implicitly. For example, it is noteworthy that Polanski replaces Levin's description of Minnie Castevet's "hoarse midwestern bray" with Ruth Gordon's nasal, stereotypically New York-Jewish cadences.[13]

Get Out nods to *Rosemary's Baby* in a number of ways, including naming the patriarch of the white Armitage clan "Roman," but perhaps the most powerful connection between the two texts (and here I am combining Levin's novel and Polanksi's film as a collective reference point) are the affinities between Chris and Rosemary (Mia Farrow). Both of these protagonists veer between knowing and not knowing what is happening to them, between trust and distrust of their own gut feelings, between wishful desires about those who surround them to steely recognition of the dangers they pose. In short, they both oscillate between denying their observations, feelings, and experiences as paranoid to embracing them as truth.

Of course, there are dissonances between Chris and Rosemary as well. Chris fights and even kills some of his enemies (although he relents from strangling his betraying girlfriend Rose to death), while Rosemary's knife-

11. For context on Polanski's Jewishness, see Sandford, *Polanski.*

12. Levin, "'Stuck with Satan,'" 17.

13. Ibid., 24.

wielding revenge on her tormentors is cut short by her maternal instincts toward her baby. Rosemary loses her only real ally in the conspiracy against her when her perceptive friend Edward "Hutch" Hutchins (Maurice Evans) is placed in a coma by the coven, resulting in his eventual death. Chris's Hutch, his TSA officer friend Rod, not only uncovers the conspiracy against Chris but also saves him from it when he arrives to rescue him at the film's conclusion.[14]

In fact, the biggest difference between Chris and Rosemary emerges when Chris, accompanied by Rod, is able to leave the nightmare of the country behind and return to a community in the city. Where *Rosemary's Baby* concentrates its horror in the seemingly civilized urban setting of a stately Manhattan apartment building, *Get Out* discloses the exurban space of the country—with its isolation, wealth, emptiness, and whiteness—to be much more frightening than the city. In fact, Chris's foundational trauma, the loss of his mother in a hit-and-run accident when he was a child, is about this divide: in the racially diverse city, you are connected to other people and *should* call for help (which Chris, as a child, was too frightened to do); in the racially homogenous country, you (especially when you're nonwhite) are alone and no one will help. When Rod saves Chris, the city comes to the country, where the sense of a black community finally gets established, against all odds, in a place that is entirely inhospitable to it.

The dissonances between Chris and Rosemary diminish when Chris is placed alongside Joanna Eberhart, the heroine of Levin's *The Stepford Wives.* Joanna is a stronger, more self-aware version of Rosemary. She is an accomplished professional woman, successful homemaker, and awakened feminist who moves with her husband and two children from New York City to the suburb of Stepford, Connecticut. The conspiracy against Joanna and the other women of Stepford is a plot hatched by the men of the town to replace their wives with animatronic robots that desire only to indulge the decidedly prefeminist whims of their husbands. Joanna, like Chris, is a photographer, and the two even share some of the same photographic subject matter. Chris's intimate portraits of urban African American life are anticipated by one of Joanna's most prized photographs: a well-dressed young black man attempting to hail a ride, ignored by an empty taxicab that passes him by. Joanna not only captures the scene, but also the expression of the black man "glaring venomously" as the cab drives away.[15]

Joanna's photograph, which she later titles "Off Duty," paired with her deep friendship with the Jewish Bobbie Markowe and her budding friend-

14. *Get Out.* All further references to the film are to this DVD.

15. Levin, *Stepford Wives*, 13.

ship with Stepford's first black resident, Ruthanne Hendry, posits her, like Rosemary, as a figurative racial minority. Joanna's figurative role is compounded not only by her literal status as a gendered minority (she is a feminist woman in an environment where women are subordinate to men and feminism is treated like an infection) but also by the symbolic transference of her anticonspiratorial mission to Ruthanne in the novel's final act. Ruthanne, who already shares with Joanna an artist's sense of observation concerning her surrounding social reality (she is an author and illustrator of children's books), becomes the last chance for Joanna's discoveries about the true Stepford to come to light. One of Joanna's last thoughts before she succumbs to robotic replacement is that she must warn Ruthanne, and it is through the eyes of Ruthanne that we see the transformed Joanna at the end of the novel. If Joanna's soul lives on, then it is through the black body of Ruthanne.

Chris must be understood, in the final analysis, as a composite of Joanna and Rosemary. Through his connections to them, he inherits horror's vocabulary of social otherness as a fabric interwoven across black, Jewish, and female strands. By extension, Peele's *Get Out* must be understood as building on Levin's earlier creations through an expanded articulation of minority paranoia as lived pain in the horror vernacular. What Peele achieves in *Get Out* by making blackness the explicit subject rather than the implicit subtext of minority otherness is comparable to the move Levin himself makes in his novel *The Boys from Brazil* (1976), where Jewishness moves from the background to the foreground.[16] *The Boys from Brazil,* like *Rosemary's Baby,* includes a conspiracy against the innocent: this time the conspirators are Nazis who survived World War II. And like *The Stepford Wives, The Boys from Brazil* includes a technological plan to put minorities back in their place: now it is genetic engineering masterminded by Josef Mengele that produces newly born clones of Adolf Hitler.

In both *The Boys from Brazil* and *Get Out,* a past that is not even past returns to haunt and humiliate the minority protagonists. Jews who survived the Holocaust must face the prospect of reliving it through a new genetically engineered Hitler; Chris as a modern black man is sold to the highest bidder in a slave auction and must resort to cotton picking (plugging his ears with it to ward off hypnosis) in order to escape. These ghostly revivals of the traumatic past underline how much minority "paranoia" in the present is not a matter of hysteria but a reckoning with how the unresolved past shapes today's world. Levin and Peele speak the language of horror precisely because they want to convey how minority paranoia is not para-

16. It is also worth mentioning that Jewishness is similarly foregrounded in Levin's play *Cantorial* (1988), a dramatic-comedic variation on the famous dybbuk story of supernatural possession descended from Jewish folklore.

noia at all. The true monster for Levin is not a genetically engineered Hitler clone but the world's inability to comprehend how anti-Semitism did not die in Hitler's bunker. The true monster for Peele is not a white neurosurgeon who resuscitates slavery, but today's racism that still objectifies blacks as if they were less than fully human.

Turning to the African American novelist and critic Ralph Ellison clarifies how Levin and Peele merge historical and fantastic horror. When Ellison meditated in 1949 on the state of black representation in American films of the 1940s, he turned to the distinction between "the shadow" and "the act." Film is the shadow, the realm of the image, and the act is history, the realm of action. For Ellison, the act precedes the shadow and cuts a sharp divide between the two; to treat the shadow as if it were the act would be "to confuse portrayal with action, image with reality."[17] Distinguishing shadow from act allows Ellison to find symptomatic value and emotional power in social problem films that address race, such as *Home of the Brave* (1949) and *Pinky* (1949), no matter how blinkered or even absurd they might be in their imagining of actual black experience and subjectivity. The fact that these films are focusing on race at all strikes Ellison as worth noting, despite their many limitations. Their value stems from the opportunity they provide, especially for white viewers, to connect to "the deep centers of American emotion" touched by the films. As Ellison observes, "One of the most interesting experiences connected with viewing [these films] in predominantly white audiences is the profuse flow of tears and the sighs of profound emotional catharsis heard on all sides. It is as though there were some deep relief to be gained merely from seeing these subjects projected upon the screen."[18]

What happens when we move from social problem films like *Home of the Brave* and *Pinky* to a horror film like *Get Out*? When tears, sighs, and relief become screams, gasps, and discomfort? Do the shadow and the act remain as neatly distinct as Ellison suggests? Or does the shadow, accruing the full power of its darkest connotations, which horror understands as a matter of course, transform our very relation to the act rather than separating itself from it? Perhaps we feel the act through the shadow in a way that horror makes visceral, through fear and unease, in a territory of the imagination where social problem films do not dare to tread. By availing themselves of the particular resources of horror, of minority paranoia made experientially real, Levin and Peele bring the shadow and the act into an affective proximity that Ellison cannot yet detect in the films he studies.

17. Ellison, "Shadow," 276.

18. Ibid., 280.

What we can see in Levin and Peele together as they reconfigure the boundary between Ellison's shadow and act is a definition of minority experience as not only human but *shared*; something carried collectively (even if unequally) by blacks, Jews, and women. One way that Levin and Peele accomplish this feat is by modulating the dynamics of voice and silence so that minority positions become figurative instead of solely literal. We have already seen how Rosemary and Joanna become figurative Jews in Levin, how the plots against them attempt to relegate their own voices and their own pain to silence. Some of *Get Out*'s most powerful scenes generate a similar effect by operating deftly between silence and voice. When Chris's body is put up for auction as a vessel for the surgical transplant of an aging white brain, it is quite literally a silent auction. Rose's father, the auctioneer, does not speak; the participants indicate their bids by raising their bingo cards wordlessly; and Chris himself is silent, as he is represented by a large framed photographic portrait that stands in for his physical presence (see figure 4). The silence lends a genteel air to the proceedings, almost as if the horror of a slave auction could somehow be ameliorated by simply not speaking its racism—reducing the act of the auction to a silent shadow. But Peele, utilizing the logic of what I have called horror's "allegorical moment," makes the silence curdle, turning its gentility into uncanniness as viewers face the silence as an historical act of racism's horror, not just its fantastic shadow.[19] Chris as a silent, disembodied photograph accurately conveys the attitude of the white bidders toward him: he is not human at all, only property to be purchased or traded, much like the exchangeable bodies of Rosemary (impregnated against her will) and Joanna (replaced with a robot). And the silence of the bidders in turn relieves them of the distasteful task of speaking—admitting—their racism.

But since Peele intercuts the auction with shots of Chris speaking with Rose about his suspicions concerning the true nature of her family and friends, we are reminded of the voice under the silence. We think again of Chris's earlier exposure to "the sunken place," a mental pit of quicksand where Rose's mother is able to send Chris by hypnotizing him and where Chris's consciousness would reside forever if the surgical replacement of his brain with the brain of an old white man were performed successfully. In the sunken place, you are aware but powerless; you become a spectator of your own body, your own life, your own words and actions now beyond your

19. Lowenstein, *Shocking*, 1–16. My concept of the "allegorical moment" relates cinematic horror to the horrors of history, where "a shocking collision of film, spectator, and history" allows "registers of bodily space and historical time" to become "disrupted, confronted, and intertwined" (2).

FIGURE 4. The silent auction. *Get Out* (Jordan Peele, 2017).

control. This is the essence of horror's minority vocabulary as developed by Levin and Peele, for what could be scarier than knowing what's happening to you without the ability to convince others that it is happening to you? To try to speak, but for your listeners to hear only silence rather than a black, Jewish, or female voice?

This is what Chris experiences not only in the supernatural sunken place, but at all of those times when he wearily, resignedly faces the familiar, everyday social humiliations that surprise only others, not himself: the racist cop who demands his identification even when it's his white girlfriend who is driving the car; his polite acceptance of Rose's parents' liberal but still racist "open-mindedness" about his blackness; and finally the sinking feeling we share with him near the end of the film when a police car pulls up to him amidst the carnage of the dead and dying bodies of those who have been trying to kill him. The sinking feeling, which transports *us* to the sunken place vicariously, comes because Chris, like us, does not yet know that Rod is inside the police car. What Chris knows as well as we do is that the chances of a black man explaining the corpses that surround him as a sign of his innocence rather than his guilt are just about nil when faced by the white law and the white majority privilege of "rational" explanation versus minority "paranoia." When Rod reveals himself, we are as exhilarated as Chris is dumbfounded. "How did you find me?" he asks Rod incredulously.

In that moment, we understand Chris's question as a variation on Rosemary's question about the existence of plots against people, a question tinged with the desperation of minority experience where pain gets dismissed as paranoia. For those who feel invisible or unacknowledged, who live in a world that they are told does not truly belong to them or in a body that they are told is not valued as fully human, the possibility of being seen and even saved is all too often beyond imagining. But we need to imagine it. And what Levin and Peele show us is that one of the places we can go to imagine it is a place that may at first seem very unlikely indeed: the horror genre.

What Levin and Peele accomplish in terms of horror's minority vocabulary is as critically sophisticated as it is affectively powerful and forces us to question the conventional wisdom surrounding horror's relation to social otherness. But the accomplishments do not come without a certain price. Peele's decision to abandon the original ending of *Get Out*, where Chris ends up in prison rather than making a getaway with Rod, indicates one kind of price: the need for an audience escape hatch, for shadow and act to diverge rather than converge. But the price I want to conclude by considering is something we might call the mathematics of difference, where forging affinities between blacks, Jews, and women, as we see across the work of Levin and Peele, comes with a need for another other: the Asian.

Among the white bidders at the auction in *Get Out* is a lone Asian man named Hiroki Tanaka. Hiroki does not win the auction, but he gets a brief moment in the spotlight earlier that same day when he asks Chris, in Japanese-accented English, "Do you find that being African American has more advantage or disadvantage in the modern world?" Chris does not answer the question, but Hiroki's presence is striking in that he provides a rare moment within the film where the "modern world" is not divided into exclusively black and white (a Latino police officer, Detective Garcia, also appears briefly at one point).[20] Is this Peele's gesture toward acknowledging racial difference as something more than a black and white issue? If so, then why does Hiroki occupy such a fleeting, tokenistic, perhaps even borderline cartoonish role (the stereotypical Asian accent)? At least one Asian American critic has accused Peele of disappointing insensitivity in his portrayal of Hiroki, but another way of analyzing Hiroki's presence in *Get Out* is as yet one more echo of *Rosemary's Baby*.[21]

Like Hiroki among the bidders in *Get Out*, Levin also includes a Japanese man, named Hayato, among the Satanists who celebrate the birth of the Antichrist at the end of *Rosemary's Baby*. Hayato's presence seems slightly more motivated than Hiroki's in that Levin wants to convey the worldwide reach of the Satanists, but his portrayal comes off as similarly cartoonish. Hayato speaks in the same heavily accented English as Hiroki and reproduces another common Asian stereotype: a touristic obsession with taking photographs. In fact, Hayato's photos of Rosemary and her child are the note on which Levin ends his novel. Why?

---

20. Zadie Smith's thoughtful review of *Get Out* argues that the film stumbles when it resorts to a black vs. white, us vs. them logic. See Smith, "Getting In."

21. Lee, "*Get Out*."

Perhaps the need for another other at the conclusion of *Rosemary's Baby* is necessitated by the disappearance of Rosemary herself. She has struggled mightily throughout the novel as the minority protagonist, the exploited woman and figurative Jew, but her acceptance of her maternal role finally aligns her with the very Satanists who have oppressed her. In transferring the point of view from Rosemary to Hayato, Levin preserves a minority perspective even as his minority protagonist is absorbed into the majority. A similar move occurs at the end of *The Stepford Wives,* as we see the robotic Joanna through the eyes of her black friend Ruthanne Hendry. The move is stronger and more meaningful in *The Stepford Wives* because Ruthanne is someone we know; Hayato barely registers as a person in *Rosemary's Baby,* as he is sometimes referred to simply as "the Japanese."[22]

But here is where looking at Levin and Peele as *conjoined,* in the manner this chapter has argued throughout, reveals something potentially deeper than the tokenistic impressions of Asians in their work. Hiroki lacks the camera of Hayato, but Hayato's function as a photographer is taken on by Chris. Indeed, shortly after Chris's brief exchange with Hiroki, he photographs the one other black man (Logan) attending the party and inadvertently frees his surgically imprisoned subjectivity from the sunken place through the flash of his camera-phone. For a brief moment, Logan's consciousness returns to inhabit his own body and warns Chris to "get out," to avoid the same fate. In a complicated series of exchanges performed in the poetics of horror's minority vocabulary, Chris's photographic gesture as an amalgam of Rosemary and Joanna animates Hayato as Hayato animates Hiroki. The liberating vision of the camera, its ability to unmask minority paranoia as pain, is enacted by Chris but prefigured by Joanna and suggests how Hayato's photographic vision of Rosemary may have points of contact with Chris. Hiroki's presence, then, initially so jarring, becomes not just an intertextual cue between *Get Out* and *Rosemary's Baby,* but an invitation to connect the dots between Chris, Rosemary, Joanna, Ruthanne, Hayato, and Hiroki as those who see the horror of minority experience for what it is. None of them can see the big picture alone; they need each other's visions, just as we need theirs. Just as Peele needs Levin, and vice versa.

Analyzing Peele and Levin together shows us how and why horror matters for experiences of social difference. Horror can awaken us to fearful experiences that are our own but that we may not have the courage to face, or fearful experiences that are not our own that we don't have the courage to acknowledge. In Peele as in (and through) Levin, we can see the strug-

22. Levin, *Rosemary's Baby,* 245.

gle and the opportunity to imagine the pain of minority experience in an American society where social justice for all is still a dream awaiting fulfillment. This is a dream that matters, and horror is a genre that matters to that dream.

Bibliography

Ellison, Ralph. "The Shadow and the Act." In *Shadow and Act*. New York: Quality Paperback Book Club, 1994. First published 1949.

Get Out. Directed by Jordan Peele. USA: Universal Pictures, 2017. DVD.

Lee, Marie Myung-Ok. "*Get Out* Shows That Even the Most Intelligent Films Can Fall Prey to Asian-American Stereotypes." *Quartz*, March 31, 2017. https://qz.com/945493/get-out-shows-that-even-the-most-intelligent-films-can-fall-prey-to-asian-american-stereotypes/.

Levin, Ira. *Rosemary's Baby*. New York: Random House, 1967.

———. *The Stepford Wives*. New York: William Morrow, 2002. First published 1972.

———. "'Stuck with Satan': Ira Levin on the Origins of *Rosemary's Baby*." *Rosemary's Baby* DVD Booklet. Criterion Collection, 2012. First published 2003.

Lowenstein, Adam. *Shocking Representation: Historical Trauma, National Cinema, and the Modern Horror Film*. New York: Columbia University Press, 2005.

Means Coleman, Robin R. *Horror Noire: Blacks in American Horror Films from the 1890s to Present*. New York: Routledge, 2011.

Peele, Jordan. "*Get Out* Sprang from an Effort to Master Fear, Says Director Jordan Peele." Interview by Terry Gross. *Fresh Air*. National Public Radio, March 15, 2017. https://www.npr.org/sections/codeswitch/2017/03/15/520130162/get-out-sprung-from-an-effort-to-master-fear-says-director-jordan-peele.

Rogin, Michael. *Blackface, White Noise: Jewish Immigrants in the Hollywood Melting Pot*. Berkeley: University of California Press, 1996.

Sandford, Christopher. *Polanski: A Biography*. New York: Palgrave Macmillan, 2008.

Smith, Zadie. "Getting In and Out: Who Owns Black Pain?" *Harper's Magazine*, July 2017. https://harpers.org/archive/2017/07/getting-in-and-out/.

Sundquist, Eric J. *Strangers in the Land: Blacks, Jews, Post-Holocaust America*. Cambridge, MA: Harvard University Press, 2005.

Wood, Robin. "An Introduction to the American Horror Film." In *Planks of Reason: Essays on the Horror Film*, revised ed., edited by Barry Keith Grant and Christopher Sharrett, 107–41. Lanham, MD: Scarecrow Press, 2004. First published 1979.

CHAPTER 8

RACISM THAT GRINS

African American Gothic Realism and Systemic Critique

SARAH ILOTT

FOR AIMÉ CÉSAIRE, colonialism is vampiric, a gothic invasion. Karl Marx draws on the specter, the vampire, and the werewolf as shorthand for describing the mechanisms of capitalism.[1] The zombie has been employed by authors, directors, and economists alike as a parodic critique of neoliberal economics and consumer culture.[2] Beyond providing useful metaphors, we might think of the use of these gothic tropes as signifying the failure of realist modes of representation to capture the horror, violence, or absurdity of the structures under critique. Despite this, the gothic is still regularly dismissed as frothy, fantastic, and therefore ill-suited to comment on serious social ills. What this chapter argues, through analysis of Jordan Peele's 2017 film *Get Out*, is that gothic is in fact *ideally* suited to structural and systemic critique, its forms and tropes defamiliarizing the economic structures that underpin systemic racism. This is not to suggest that the gothic has not frequently been employed as a vehicle for challenging racism in African American literature and film. Rather, I suggest that the nature of this critique has shifted from a focus on historical violence, albeit with psychological and epistemic legacies in the present day, to that systemic and material violence that proceeds unabated into the contemporary moment. This

1. See Césaire, *Discourse;* Marx, *Capital.*
2. See Aldana Reyes, "Contemporary Zombies."

critique is enacted through what I term a "gothic realism" that provides a discourse and aesthetic suited to uncovering hidden mechanisms of violence and oppression. In so doing, the gothic also registers the failure of realist frameworks of representation to recognize and critique the systems that perpetuate racial violence in the present day.

The failure to recognize and address the continuation of racial violence in the US is due in large part to what sociologists Alana Lentin and Gavan Titley have described as "racial neoliberalism," in which the problem of racism is understood through the framework of neoliberalism's individualizing logic. Lentin and Titley trace the historical success of neoliberal approaches to race back to the confusion created by a "conflict between a lived reality of multiculturalism, coupled with the real gains of the civil rights movement [. . .] and what is essentially the rejection of these facts by a new right that fears the loss of white privilege," all of which leads to "confusion over how to define racism today." Furthermore, a concomitant investment in the notion of postracialism, which has won considerable traction since the election of Barack Obama in 2008, is expressed as "an already achieved reality, because capitalism, it is held, gains no advantages in reproducing racisms."[3]

The foundations of Western capitalism in the exploitation of enslaved Africans and indentured laborers drawn from the colonies, coupled with the racial logic that justified European colonization and the looting of material wealth from nations across the world, is effectively whitewashed from history. What is worse, the imagined decoupling of racial discrimination and capitalism denies the necessity of systemic critique in the present, and individuals are therefore held solely responsible for their own disadvantage and/or their own racism: "The focus on capital as a social corrector, rather than as a participant in the perpetuation of discrimination, inequality and poverty, is based on a denial of the reciprocal relationship between state and neoliberal capital."[4] As such, everyday challenges to racism tend to function on the level of the individual: Donald Trump is racist, Roseanne Barr is racist, those people in the South are racist, and so on. Or, by offering a multicultural résumé—"I voted for Obama," or "some of my best friends are black"—white people attempt individually to excuse themselves from the functioning of a racist society. Such microinvalidations allow white liberals to feel comparatively superior and, crucially, to do nothing, as they are not figured as part of the problem. This means that a more insidious systemic racism is allowed to proceed unchecked.

---

3. Lentin and Titley, *Crises*, 168.

4. Ibid.

In terms of literary critiques of racism, postcolonial and African American gothic has frequently focused on questions of psychology and epistemology. The legacy of crucial anticolonial thinkers and activists such as Frantz Fanon, Aimé Césaire, and Ngũgĩ wa Thiong'o has been to think of race primarily in psychological terms as the colonization of the mind, a psychic battle between self and Other that contemporary gothic literature frequently functions to foreground and deconstruct.[5] Meanwhile, epistemological questions—how to speak the unspeakable, how to uncover repressed histories, how to challenge structures of knowledge that fix black peoples as monstrous in their otherness—are answered through gothic tropes of haunting and monstrosity. Building on the work of gothic literary critics including Allan Lloyd Smith, Teresa Goddu, and Maisha Wester, who have pointed to the sympathies between the gothic and African American histories and subjectivities, I aim to extend the frames of reference from the predominantly psychological and epistemological to the economic and structural in order to analyze material systems that function to create hierarchy, division, and inequality.[6] By locating a reading of Peele's film in the Marxist world-literary approach of the Warwick Research Collective (detailed below), I demonstrate what the gothic can do to reveal and challenge systemic racism, a racism that grins, and in which we are all implicated if we fail to listen, recognize, and act.

In order to rethink the nature of racism today, both in terms of unthinking the individualizing logic of racial neoliberalism and in terms of restating its centrality to contemporary modes of disenfranchisement, it is necessary to draw on critical models that recenter systemic critique. For critics such as Neil Lazarus, postcolonial studies have become increasingly ill-suited to such a task due to theorists' habitual tendency to describe imperialism as "a process of cultural and epistemological subjugation, whose material preconditions have been referred to only glancingly, if at all."[7] Lazarus has subsequently joined the Warwick Research Collective, which has been influential in reviving the category of world literature as "*the literature of the modern capitalist world-system.*"[8] In revitalizing this demoded critical category, they argue that we should conceive of world literature "as neither a canon of masterworks nor a mode of reading, but as a *system*," a system

5. See, for example, Fanon, *Black Skin;* Césaire, *Discourse;* Ngũgĩ, *Decolonising the Mind.*

6. See Lloyd-Smith, *American Gothic;* Goddu, *Gothic America;* Wester, *African American Gothic.*

7. Lazarus, *Postcolonial Unconscious,* 17.

8. WReC, *Combined,* 15.

that is "structured not on *difference* but on *inequality*."[9] This materialist turn has been significant for postcolonial scholars as a means of recentering the capitalist roots of colonialism and challenging the slide in the canon of postcolonial literature and theory into the "pomo-postcolonialist" cultural tendency exemplified by the likes of Salman Rushdie and Homi Bhabha.[10] It gets to the heart of an imperialist politics driven by capitalist accumulation while also providing a rationale for the dominance of certain literary forms at particular moments. As they state: "We prefer to speak then not of literary forms spreading or unfolding across empty time . . . but of forms that are brought into being . . . through the long waves of the capitalisation of the world—not of *modernism* (or even *modernisms*) but of the *dialectics of core and periphery* that underpin all cultural production in the modern era."[11] What is particularly notable in their discussion of world literature is that the styles and tropes that they identify as exemplifying moments of systemic crisis are frequently those common to fantastic genres such as sci-fi, magic realism, and the gothic. Pertinent in particular to the gothic is their identification of the unusual, the alienating, and the surreal, as well as the use of "spatio-temporal compression" that collapses past and present, here and there, registering ways in which "invisible forces act[] from a distance on the local and the familiar."[12] As such, their identification of the common means by which modernity's combined and uneven development are registered find a natural home in the gothic.

The texts that the Warwick Research Collective examine as examples of such world literature share a range of formal features that they designate "irrealist," drawing on the terminology of the Marxist sociologist and philosopher Michael Löwy. Challenging the Lukácsian notion that only realist artwork can function to critique contemporary society, Löwy argues that irrealist (fantasy, gothic, surreal) works can "help us understand and transform reality."[13] Building on this, the Warwick Research Collective suggests that irrealist writing is a pervasive feature of world literature produced at moments of systemic crisis, which they suggest is due to its "in-mixing of the imaginary and the factual," which is "more sensitive" to registering "specific circumstances of combined and uneven development."[14] Understood as such, the gothic is not a means of escape but a means of reengage-

9. Ibid., 7.
10. Lazarus, *Postcolonial Unconscious*, 34.
11. WReC, *Combined*, 50–51; emphasis in original.
12. Ibid., 17.
13. Löwy, "Current," 206.
14. WReC, *Combined*, 70.

ment with the lived realities of twenty-first-century societies in the face of systemic violence and the structural exclusion of minority voices. The collective crucially notes, "Irrealist aesthetics might then be presented as corresponding not to any depreciation of realism, but to a refinement of it."[15] Defined as such, irrealist literature rightly becomes an extension of realism in its function as social critique, and one that is ideally suited to the representation of those marginalized within and because of capitalist systems. Though the Warwick Research Collective's publication is strategically limited to literature, it is nevertheless applicable to a range of cultural forms that register the systemic crises of modernity, such as the gothic film considered in this collection. In so doing, I suggest that the gothic provides an ideal language and framework for reengaging with the political realities of the present, speaking truths that are structurally repressed elsewhere in a challenge to the individualization of racism central to neoliberalism and recentering the material, economic basis of contemporary racisms in the US.

Peele's film functions as a gothic satire on contemporary race relations in America that calls to mind the history of the slave trade alongside the contemporary systems that continue to disenfranchise African Americans in the present. Its gothic mode tallies precisely with Chris Baldick's recipe for the gothic tale, that it "should combine a fearful sense of inheritance in time with a claustrophobic sense of enclosure in space, these two dimensions reinforcing one another to produce an impression of sickening descent into disintegration."[16] This effect is achieved through the layered presence of historical and contemporary modes of racial violence in the domestic space of the Armitage family residence, which provides the setting for the majority of the film, and in the polysemic significations of the central character's name. Chris's surname (Washington) calls to mind the first US president, who used and sanctioned slavery to preserve his wealth and supported policies to protect the financial interests of slave owners, Booker T. Washington, a controversial African American activist whose accommodationist social policies pursued economic self-determination as the key to social equality over and above political and civil rights, and the ingrained racism at the center of American political institutions today.

The film's gothic mode might be read as a riposte to the individualizing logic of the romcom, in which, as I have argued elsewhere, the romantic couple are made to "bear the burden for problems of social division."[17] In this case, the happy relationship between Chris and Rose might be interpreted

15. Ibid.

16. Baldick, Introduction, xix.

17. Ilott, "British Multiculturalism," 62.

as signifying a promise of racial harmony in the future. There are early nods to the romcom in the film's opening scenes, in which Rose comically knocks on Chris's door with her forehead, her hands overladen with bags and coffee. The final opening titles play over a medium shot of the couple, locked in a kiss at the threshold of Chris's apartment. True to romcom convention, the ensuing discussion highlights the problem that the romantic couple must surmount in order to emerge united: Chris asks Rose whether her parents know he is black, setting up their potential racism as obstacle. The discussion is sealed with another kiss, in a moment that is recalled as the couple debrief at the end of the first day at Rose's family home, during which it has become apparent that her family are indeed racist in the assumptions that they make about Chris. Rose—attired in her lover's shirt and brushing her teeth between angry outbursts in a manner that both domesticates her and signals her intimacy with Chris—laments her family's actions, drawing the couple closer together in unity against the archaic values represented by her parents and offering hope for a different future. So far, so romcom. Yet Peele's film takes a darker turn at this juncture, demonstrating that there is a great deal that (the individualizing logic of) romantic love cannot conquer in contemporary America. It becomes increasingly apparent from here that, far from offering Chris a way out of the racism represented by her family, Rose is colluding with them in a plan to torture and enslave him.

Early encounters with the Armitage family's black servants, Georgina and Walter, demonstrate the film's engagement with the racism of the past. Their dated diction, anachronistic apparel, and passive subservience to their white masters portray them as visitors from a pre–civil-rights era America. Jump cuts and screeching sound effects to mark their sudden appearance draw on genre conventions to implicate them as the source of horror—and in a sense they are, insomuch as they represent a period of American history that rudely intrudes upon the present moment. Yet it is revealed that the film's spectral black servants, initially figured as haunting, are in fact themselves haunted by versions of African American identity the nostalgic white folk project onto them: through lobotomy, black characters are recreated in the image of a historical period in which their agency was more recognizably curtailed through the institutions of slavery and Jim Crow segregation. Moments of anachronism that crop up repeatedly in the film suggest the power of nostalgia to return people to a glorified image of the past. The opening sequence, for example, records the stalking and kidnapping of a black man named Andre Hayworth in the modern suburbs of an unnamed upstate New York town to the haunting and darkly comic accompaniment of "Run Rabbit Run." This is a song that was popularized during World

War II and often used to poke fun at the German Luftwaffe, and here it plays through the car stereo of the kidnapper, Jeremy Armitage. The music functions to imply that Jeremy's actions belong to another time. Georgina's failure to understand Chris's use of the word "snitch," to which she offers the alternative "tattletale," proves equally anachronistic.

The Warwick Research Collective provides an alternative means of reading these moments of anachronism, not as a haunting but as a revelation of the conditions of the present. "Tradition," they argue, "comes into existence not as the lingering forms of the past but as the coeval other of 'modernity.'"[18] Peele's film works on this principle, revealing the repressed horrors of the present—the dependence of the American economy on the historical and continuing disenfranchisement of African Americans—and refusing to locate the horrors of racial hatred in other times or other places. This is reminiscent of what Sheri-Marie Harrison terms the "new black gothic" with reference to Peele's film, Jesmyn Ward's 2017 novel *Sing, Unburied, Sing,* and Childish Gambino's "This is America." Identifying a renewed trend for "the spectral reappearance of America's violent history in recent fiction," Harrison suggests that it "is neither about recovery nor representation," unlike canonical African American gothic texts such as Tony Morrison's *Beloved* (1987). Like Ward's ghosts, who "speak to an ever-present and visible lineage of violence that accumulates rather than dissipates with the passage of time," Georgina and Walter's spectral presence registers what Harrison suggests is a defining feature of "new black gothic"—that "gothic violence remains a part of everyday black life."[19]

Set in upstate New York rather than in the Southern states, the film critiques racism derived from liberal ignorance, a racism that grins, in which Rose's incongruous, near-permanent smile is one of the film's most chilling tropes. The smile is rendered sinister as it functions to mask a character's true feelings: Chris is instructed to smile as he is paraded around the Armitages' party and quizzed by the various guests in increasingly intrusive and bigoted ways, while Georgina continues to smile as tears run down her face when she is forced to apologize to Chris for disconnecting his phone charger. The smile as mask interacts with gothic's ongoing concern with the interplay of depth and surface.[20] *Get Out* follows in this gothic tradition in its preoccupation with screens, not just as a call to recognize concealed depths but to recognize the power of the surface. To screen means both to display for an audience and to conceal or hide, and Peele's film is alert to these contradic-

18. WReC, *Combined*, 76.
19. Harrison, "New Black Gothic."
20. See Sedgwick, *Coherence.*

tory meanings, foregrounding screens as a means of rendering visible the mechanisms of liberal racism. This is a film *about* screens, from the smiles, costumes, bodies, and masks that people wear, to the television screen that functions to engender passivity. Chris's moment of childhood trauma is that, transfixed by his TV, he failed to alert the emergency services that his mother had not returned home, meaning that she was found on the side of the road following a hit-and-run, too late to save her. This instance of inactivity—the failure to look beyond the screen—is turned into punishment for Chris, as Rose's mother returns him to this moment during hypnosis before attempting to reduce him to the role of "audience" in his own life by lobotomizing him and sending him to the "sunken place." The film is a prompt to look beyond surface niceties to recognize the veiled malice of the series of assumptions the family makes: that Chris will be a strong athlete; that he must be patronized with a change in language—apparent in the father's incongruous repetition of "my man"; that he will want to talk endlessly about Obama. Yet it is also a call to recognize the screens—of wealth, position, geography, social standing, and neoliberal ideology—that allow racism to be considered a problem of another time, another place.

Screens are central to the film's engagement with the hidden mechanisms of racial violence, as the setup of Chris's invitation to Rose's home to coincide with a family party functions as a screen for his auction to the highest bidder. Parallels with historical slave auctions are writ large, yet the auction is conducted silently: Dean Armitage indicates a price through hand gestures and party guests hold up bingo cards to signify their interest. The unnatural diegetic silence of the scene serves to indicate the repression of the mechanisms of economic enslavement and racial violence rather than their demise. Teresa Goddu has articulated the tensions in rendering gothic the subject of slavery, as it can equate the witnessing of slavery with the firsthand experience of the slave's horror, just as the act of giving testimony translates the experience of horror from object to observer of violence. She cites white abolitionist Sarah Grimké's account of the South in gothic terms as "abstracting and co-opting the slave's horror" and departicularizing the horror of the South to encompass the slave and slaveholder for the titillation of a white audience as a means of establishing her own authority.[21] Peele's film works in quite a different way: audiences are made to witness systemic violence without the bloody spectacle of visceral horror. Comparable to the postmodern horror of *The Cabin in the Woods* (Drew Goddard, 2012) in which the Ancient Ones who dictate the nature of the horror are metonyms for the unquench-

21. Goddu, *Gothic America*, 135.

able thirst for new spectacles of horror expressed by the cinema audience, Peele's audience are implicated in the quotidian racism of the film: the experience of watching a film such as *Get Out* is not to be equated with an antiracist outlook, let alone activism. Instead, inactivity is associated with complicity, and unlike Chris—glued to his chair through hypnosis—the audience is free to move, to react, to respond. Gothic is not employed here to subsume realities by drawing upon brutal histories for artistic inspiration, as Goddu has rightly argued was the case in Harriet Beecher Stowe's fictionalization of slavery.[22] Instead, the gothic mode articulates and renders visible political realities through a process of fantastical defamiliarization. What a reading of this film rejuvenated with a more materialist approach to African American gothic reveals is the collusion of capitalism and structures of inequality with the imperialist mindset that values the labor provided by black bodies while disregarding their humanity. It reveals the engine of capital behind oppositions all-too-readily constructed as cultural in order to foreground inequality, rather than difference, as the crucial inheritance of African Americans.

The irrealist aesthetic of the gothic combines with taboo comedy in Peele's film, as a means of expressing truths not recognized or articulated elsewhere. The film's classification as comedy has courted controversy since it was included in the "Best Musical or Comedy" category at the Golden Globes. Though renowned for his comedy work as part of the comedy duo Key and Peele, the director has challenged the film's award classification, describing it as "documentary" and questioning what there is to laugh at.[23] This in part points to a failure to consider the comic a serious mode, but it also registers that received knowledge about dark comedy does not apply to this film. Peele's variety of gothic humor differs considerably from the celebratory lightness of tone that Catherine Spooner identifies in a particular strain of postmillennial "happy gothic," and it exists at the margins of the comic turn in the gothic explored by Avril Horner and Sue Zlosnik, which encompasses a spectrum ranging from "horror-writing containing moments of comic hysteria or relief" to "works in which there are clear signals that nothing is to be taken seriously."[24] For Horner and Zlosnik, the function of humor in the comic gothic texts that they explore is to "help to make the modern condition livable," to "celebrate the possibilities" offered by an otherwise horrifying "shifting and unstable world" and to hold horror "in abeyance."[25]

---

22. Ibid., 136.
23. Peele cited in Kohn, "Jordan Peele."
24. See Spooner, *Post-Millennial;* Horner and Zlosnik, *Gothic,* 4.
25. Horner and Zlosnik, *Gothic,* 18, 9, 3.

By contrast, I would argue that humorous moments in *Get Out* are deployed as a means of reengaging with (rather than escaping or finding relief from) a terrifying world. The techniques of humor, like the tropes of gothic, offer a new framework for interpreting social realities—a realism for when mainstream discourse fails to capture the horrors of lived realities. Following Elliott Oring, who recognizes the function of dark humor to conjoin "an unspeakable, and hence incongruous, universe of discourse, to a speakable one," I suggest that comedy and the gothic combine in new ways in this film to register what popular discourse seeks to repress and, crucially, to make visible the mechanisms of repression.[26] It represents what Harrison has described as "the laughter of the new black gothic," which is "always proximate to the ways in which daily black life can suddenly descend into horror. This shit is not supposed to be funny, but we laugh uncomfortably anyway."[27] What is represented as absurdity—this comic gothic film suggests—could all too easily become horrific reality.

The film's key comic signifier is the casting of standup comedian Milton "Lil Rel" Howery as Chris's friend, Rod. The casting and dialogue combine to depict Rod as the film's comic relief, as he is the mouthpiece for a series of seemingly outrageous suspicions regarding the dangers represented to Chris by the Armitage family. Audiences are condoned in their laughter at Rod's allegations about the Armitages—"I believe they've been abducting black people, brainwashing them, and making them work as sex slaves and shit"—when the police officer tasked with taking the report seeks out her colleagues so they can hear his statement before they all collapse in laughter. The dramatic irony, of which the viewing audience is aware, is not only that the institution of slavery has a clear historical precursor, but that Rod is the only character who has been reading the situation accurately from the outset; it is Chris's unwillingness to distrust his girlfriend that almost seals his fate as lobotomy victim.

The film's comic gothic mode does not offer cathartic release from the horrors of reality. This is particularly evident in the final scenes, in which Chris finds himself unexpectedly rescued by Rod, who arrives in a police car. A close-up of the car door opening indicates that it is a moment of tension, and that the ending will be decided by the person who steps out. The relief in Chris's face allows the tension to dissipate momentarily. Once Chris is seated in the car, Rod continues to lighten the mood, joking, "I mean, I told you not to go in that house" and "I'm T. S. motherfucking A. We handle

26. Oring, *Jokes*, 35.

27. Harrison, "New Black Gothic."

shit. Consider this situation . . . handled." However, Chris's face remains haunted, and his failure to collude with the sentiment of Rod's comments by acknowledging them as jokes and laughing along means that the relief the audience may otherwise have been afforded at this point is denied. Instead, a parting shot of Rose's still-living face does not rule out her being found by a police officer more likely predisposed to believe her version of events. As such, the combined comic and gothic modes provide a framework for expressing what Peele in interviews describes as "an expression of my truth, my experience, the experiences of a lot of black people and minorities."[28] It is, in effect, a form of realism in which the gothic horror of possession renders visible the mechanisms by which the systemic racism of the present day preserves the legacy of slavery, and in which expressions of the absurd are the only accurate descriptions of reality.

The systemic nature of the racism experienced is most clearly registered in the film's iconic "sunken place" as an effective and metaphorical prison. Following a slow-motion fall to an ominous soundtrack, the music cuts and the camera zooms in to capture Chris's screaming face, rendered uncanny through the white noise that accompanies the image. This functions as metaphor for the literal and systemic silencing of minorities fighting to make their oppression heard. As Peele tweeted, the sunken place highlights processes of marginalization, saying, "No matter how hard we scream, the system silences us."[29] It is the prison cell that African Americans are incarcerated in at five times the rate of their white counterparts, six times the rate for a drug charge.[30] Furthering their discussion of racial neoliberalism, Lentin and Titley indicate the centrality of literal and metaphorical prisons to lock up or lock out "undesirables" (people of color and migrants, respectively) when the neoliberal state is charged with ensuring its citizens' security, rather than their welfare (in accordance with free market logistics).[31] The collusion of the American judiciary system in the perpetuation of the racial hierarchies and economic disparities of the slave trade is evident through the system by which falsely imprisoned African Americans, unable to pay the fines for their own living expenses while in custody, were trapped in the judiciary system and leased to entrepreneurs, farms, and corporations, and thereby kept in involuntary servitude;[32] it is evident in the Executive Order required

28. Peele cited in Kohn, "Jordan Peele."

29. Jordan Peele, @Jordan Peele, Twitter, March 17, 2017, https://twitter.com/jordanpeele/status/842589407521595393?lang=en.

30. "Criminal Justice Fact Sheet," National Association for the Advancement of Colored People, https://www.naacp.org/criminal-justice-fact-sheet/.

31. Lentin and Titley, *Crises*, 172–73.

32. See Blackmon, *Slavery by Another Name.*

to enforce desegregation in the place of legislation or judicial review;[33] and it is evident in the "new Jim Crow," which sees racial control enacted through the mass incarceration of African Americans in the purportedly "colorblind" era following Barack Obama's election in 2008.[34] It is the specter of prison that haunts the film, its title even referencing the slang for prison release. The specter of prison as shorthand for systemic violence is referenced through Chris's early brush with the police in which he is treated with suspicion even as a passenger in the car involved in a collision with a deer; through Rod's reference to the Jeffrey Dahmer case in which the serial killer's disproportionate targeting of African Americans pointed both to Dahmer's racism in seeing black men as disposable and to the police's racism for failing to pursue their disappearances; and in the film's alternative endings, both those included on the DVD extras and those implied through the final frames. The irrealist gothic aesthetic of the film makes visible (and audible) the lived realities of African Americans: the paradox of living in a purportedly postracial society in the context of the enduring necessity of the Black Lives Matter movement and the renewed nationalism and xenophobia in the era leading up to the election of Donald Trump.

In a post-truth society, in which black Americans are so frequently misrepresented or systemically silenced, a genre that questions the nature and representation of reality becomes necessary. This is a realism for when "ideal type" realism fails: a gothic realism. Framing the gothic as a genre ideally suited to registering systemic critique and the failure of realist representation also shifts the function of criticism. To follow the work of the Warwick Research Collective, what we should then be reading for is "the self-conscious transformation by authors of [textual] fissures into sources of innovation which transform the genre of realism," rather than for a text's political unconscious.[35] This allows for a renewed understanding of the gothic, which also follows Goddu's advice that "instead of accepting traditional readings of the gothic as unrealistic and frivolous, thereby excluding African-American narratives from the genre, we should use the African-American gothic to revise our understanding of the gothic as a historical mode."[36] Through an examination of Peele's film, I have demonstrated that the gothic is ideally suited not only to register the haunting violence of the past, but the systemic violence of the current moment.

33. Kymlicka, *Multicultural Odysseys*, 117.
34. See Alexander, *New Jim Crow.*
35. WReC, *Combined*, 97.
36. Goddu, *Gothic America*, 140.

Bibliography

Aldana Reyes, Xavier. "Contemporary Zombies." In *21st-Century Gothic*, edited by Xavier Aldana Reyes and Maisha Wester, 89–101. Edinburgh: Edinburgh University Press, 2019.

Alexander, Michelle. *The New Jim Crow: Mass Incarceration in the Age of Colorblindness.* New York: New Press, 2012.

Baldick, Chris. Introduction. In *The Oxford Book of Gothic Tales*, edited by Chris Baldick, xi–xxiii. Oxford: Oxford University Press, 2009.

Blackmon, Douglas. *Slavery by Another Name: The Re-enslavement of Black Americans from the Civil War to World War II.* New York: Anchor Books, 2009.

Césaire, Aimé. *Discourse on Colonialism.* Translated by Joan Pinkham. New York: Monthly Review Press, 1972.

Fanon, Frantz. *Black Skin, White Masks.* Translated by Charles Lam Markmann. London: Paladin, 1972.

Goddu, Teresa A. *Gothic America: Narrative, History, and Nation.* New York: Columbia University Press, 1997.

Harrison, Sheri-Marie. "New Black Gothic." *LA Review of Books*, June 23, 2018. https://lareviewofbooks.org/article/new-black-gothic/#!

Horner, Avril, and Sue Zlosnik. *Gothic and the Comic Turn.* Basingstoke, UK: Palgrave Macmillan, 2004.

Ilott, Sarah. "British Multiculturalism, Romantic Comedy, and the Lie of Social Unification." In *Comedy and the Politics of Representation: Mocking the Weak*, edited by Helen Davies and Sarah Ilott, 61–77. Basingstoke, UK: Palgrave Macmillan, 2018.

Kohn, Eric. "Jordan Peele Challenges Golden Globes Classifying 'Get Out' as a Comedy: 'What Are You Laughing At?'" *Indie Wire*, November 15, 2017. https://www.indiewire.com/2017/11/jordan-peele-response-get-out-golden-globes-comedy-1201897841/.

Kymlicka, Will. *Multicultural Odysseys: Navigating the New International Politics of Diversity.* Oxford: Oxford University Press, 2009.

Lazarus, Neil. *The Postcolonial Unconscious.* Cambridge: Cambridge University Press, 2011.

Lentin, Alana, and Gavan Titley. *The Crises of Multiculturalism: Racism in a Neoliberal Age.* London: Zed Books, 2011.

Lloyd-Smith, Allan. *American Gothic Fiction: An Introduction.* New York: Continuum, 2004.

Löwy, Michael. "The Current of Critical Irrealism: 'A moonlit enchanted night.'" In *Adventures in Realism*, edited by Matthew Beaumont, 193–206. Oxford: Blackwell, 2007.

Marx, Karl. *Capital: A Critique of Political Economy*, volume 1. Translated by Ben Fowkes. Harmondsworth: Penguin, 1976. First published 1867.

Ngũgĩ wa Thiong'o. *Decolonising the Mind: The Politics of Language in African Literature.* Martlesham, UK: James Currey, 2011.

Oring, Elliott. *Jokes and Their Relations.* Lexington: University of Kentucky Press, 1992.

Sedgwick, Eve Kosofsky. *The Coherence of Gothic Conventions.* New York: Methuen, 1986.

Spooner, Catherine. *Post-Millennial Gothic: Comedy, Romance and the Rise of Happy Gothic.* London: Bloomsbury, 2017.

Wester, Maisha. *African American Gothic: Screams from Shadowed Places.* New York: Palgrave, 2012.

WReC (Warwick Research Collective). *Combined and Uneven Development: Towards a New Theory of World-Literature.* Liverpool: Liverpool University Press, 2015.

PART 2

The Horror of Politics

CHAPTER 9

REVIEWING *GET OUT*'S REVIEWS

What Critics Said and How Their Race Mattered

TODD K. PLATTS AND DAVID L. BRUNSMA

FILM REVIEWERS and critics play vital roles in the promotion and consumption of individual films. Among these roles, production companies regularly use positive reviews to promote films;[1] they have the potential to influence a film's box office returns;[2] they play a factor in how long a film is exhibited;[3] and they can help audiences understand the meanings of a particular film.[4] While this list is far from comprehensive, and scholarly research devoted to each role is far from settled, it is the last one that concerns this chapter. Here, film reviewers and critics serve as publicly visible and often authoritative interpreters of cinematic texts for the mass of potential viewers. They constitute cinematic tour guides, a role that is magnified when dealing with complex and difficult film texts. The study of film reviews can thus allow us to observe how the interpretive and rhetorical practices of reviewers construct the meaning of films for lay audiences.

1. Baumann, *Hollywood Highbrow,* 137–48; Debenedetti, "Role of Media Critics" 37.

2. Basuroy, Chatterjee, and Ravid, "How Critical," 103–17; Duan, Gu, and Whinston, "Do Online Reviews," 1007–16. For a critique see, Berg and Raddick, "First You Get,"101–29.

3. Legoux, Larocque, Laporte, Belmati, and Boquet, "Effect of Critical Reviews," 357–74.

4. Austin, "Critics' and Consumers' Evaluations," 156–67; Cameron, "On the Role," 323–24.

Previous studies have found that the production and consumption of film reviews is structured by class, gender, sexuality, and race. A series of works by Matthew Hughey and colleagues, for instance, argues that film critics interpret film texts from a white normative perspective that uncritically accepts dominant racial frames and/or fails to critique them.[5] Alecia Anderson and Scott Grether discovered that white and nonwhite reviewers interpret the racial content of films differently. They argue that white reviewers speak of race in more vague terms and rarely provide readers with historical or contemporary commentary regarding race relations or racial domination—even when the films are clearly about race. By contrast, nonwhite reviewers included more nuanced and vivid discussions, often supplying readers with richer social, cultural, political, and experiential context for understanding race and, therefore, the film in question.[6]

Jordan Peele's *Get Out* (2017) provides an illuminating case study here. Virtually everyone understands that the film offers a less-than-subtle skewering of contemporary racism. Despite tackling such a touchy subject in a genre (horror) that rarely garners critical acclaim,[7] *Get Out* has received near unanimous high praise from film critics,[8] including some 142 nominations for some of the most coveted industry and critical awards both nationally and internationally (e.g., Golden Globes' Best Motion Picture, The Black Reel Awards' Outstanding Motion Picture). Indeed, it won almost 60% of these nominations (e.g., AFI Awards' Movie of the Year, African-American Film Critics Association's Best Picture). Pushing beyond this acclaim, however, one must ask just what reviewers are noticing in a horror film that so overtly addresses race? What lenses are they using to guide viewers through the complex realities and ideological quagmires of race in the United States? And, more particularly, do white and nonwhite reviewers highlight different aspects of the film for readers to consider?

Data and Methods

To answer the above questions, we conducted a qualitative content analysis of twenty-six reviews of *Get Out*: thirteen reviews from white review-

5. Hughey, "White Savior Film," 475–96; Hughey, *White Savior Film*, 72–124; Gonzalez-Sobrino, Goss, and Hughey, "Rise of the Racial Reviewer," 165–81; Hughey and Gardner, "Film Reviewers."

6. Anderson and Grether, "Reviewing the Reviewers," 188–204.

7. Grierson, "From *Psycho*."

8. Ruimy, "AD Critics Poll."

ers and thirteen reviews from nonwhite reviewers, pulled from a selective nonrandom sample. Because mainstream media outlets netted few reviews from nonwhite critics, we located additional reviews from nonwhite critics by canvassing publication outlets catering to African American audiences (e.g., *Vibe, Ebony, Jet, Washington Informer,* and *New Orleans Tribune*). The reviews informing our analysis are displayed in Appendix 1 at the end of this chapter.

When analyzing the reviews, we utilized an inductive qualitative content analysis insofar as we allowed analytic categories to surface from the data rather than approaching it with preconceived categories.[9] Formal coding of reviews underwent several stages. To start, each author carefully read each review, taking notes on patterns and themes emerging from the data. Through this process we identified the three levels at which reviewers focused their reviews—the textual level, the meaning level, and the commentary level. As we developed our analysis, we identified sublevels within each level. These were fleshed out with further readings of each review, which, in turn, informed our coding scheme. Appendix 2 shows the breakdown of each level as well as the sublevels in each.

Reviewing *Get Out*'s Reviews

Before getting to the specifics of how white and nonwhite reviewers differed across the three levels of analysis, it is worth providing more detail about each level. The *textual level* assessed how reviewers handled the narrative, plot, and individual scenes of the film. This consisted of how they related key events of the film such as the interactions between Chris and the Armitages, the awkwardness of the Armitages' annual get-together, the actions of Georgina and Walter, etc. General discussions of the film's tone were also considered in this level, as when reviewers mentioned the creepiness or genuine scariness of *Get Out*. The *meaning level* gauged how reviewers related the broader themes of the film to readers. It also included how critics discussed Peele's intent, whether through interviews with the director or actors, stories around *Get Out*'s production history, and/or drawing parallels between the story of the film and contemporary realities of race. Mentions of the film's self-conscious bending of conventions or stereotypes such as the abduction of Andre Hayworth by an unknown white assailant (which

9. Hsieh and Shannon, "Three Approaches," 1277–88; Neuendorf, *Content Analysis Guidebook,* 11–13.

challenges the stereotype of black dangerousness) at the film's beginning were also coded within this level. Finally, the *commentary level* documented how reviewers diverged from the script of a standard film review in order to offer readers personal anecdote or testimony (e.g., relating their own first-hand experiences with racism), to discuss race or racism (e.g., discussing high-profile black victims), or to highlight problems revealed by the success of *Get Out* (e.g., the lack of opportunities for black directors in Hollywood).

Get Out's Narrative—The Textual Level

The storyline of *Get Out* was relayed differently by white and nonwhite film critics. Both groups of reviewers colloquially understood liberal racism as the awkward and unintentionally insulting attempts by whites to relate to minorities, and both groups spent a comparable amount of space detailing Peele's satirizing of it. Despite these similarities, the comments from white critics tended to spotlight how liberal racism was a byproduct of "well-intentioned" white people, while nonwhite critics expressed their frustration with the persistence of the practice. Consider John DeFore's review for the *Hollywood Reporter,* "All [white people at the Armitages' get-together] are overfriendly to Rose's new boyfriend, and the faux pas they make with him are like a condensation of all the awkward things uttered by white people who don't encounter many people of color in their social lives."[10] Likewise with Peter Travers's *Rolling Stone* review:

> Dean, a self-congratulating liberal ("I would have voted for Obama for a third term"), winks when he asks how long their "thang" has been going on. He also pointedly shows off a photo of his own father running alongside black gold-medalist Jesse Owens in the 1936 Olympics. He's got well-meaning liberal bona fides, in other words.[11]

In each case, the reviewers elide the deeper psychosocial impact of liberal racism, treating it, instead, as just an awkward attempt to be friendly. By contrast, nonwhite critics were more pointedly critical of the interpersonal impact of liberal racism. Danielle Young of *The Root* succinctly summarized this facet of the film: "Peele reveals the routine racism that many of us have to push to the back of our minds every day."[12] Aisha Harris of *Slate* points to

10. DeFore, "'Get Out.'"
11. Travers, "'Get Out.'"
12. Young, "Get Out."

how *Get Out* reveals that "even surface-level 'admiration' for black culture on the part of white people can give way to insidious interactions that are, at best, a persistent annoyance black people must learn to laugh off, and, at worst, the kind of fetishizing that only conceals deadlier preconceptions."[13] From here, the job of informing would-be audiences about *Get Out* diverged even more along racial lines.

Any review of a horror movie would be remiss if readers were not informed of how the film achieved the genre's central function: "to scare and/or disturb its audience."[14] White reviewers described the effect of *Get Out*'s masterfully crafted atmosphere. Nonwhite critics, however, pinpointed how the horror of the film arises from telling the story from the perspective of a black man. The film's tension, *USA Today*'s Brian Truitt suggested, was something that cut across racial lines: "No matter your race, creed or color, you're bound to feel in your bones the extreme discomfort of *Get Out*'s African-American protagonist walking into a garden party of freaky old white folks smiling weirdly at him."[15] Writing for *The Atlantic*, David Sims told how *Get Out* builds tension through the use of familiar horror tropes, "The opening scene of *Get Out* is a familiar horror-movie image—a stranger walking an unfamiliar street, in the dead of night, nervously looking over their shoulder at every rustle of sound."[16] Sims later acknowledged that Peele "is clearly playing on the discomfort a young African American man might have in visiting a largely white community," but he fails to explore further the reason for this discomfort.

Nonwhite reviewers saw *Get Out*'s scares as emanating specifically from its dramatization of the experience of black men in contemporary America. Kyra Kyles of *Ebony* quoted lead-actor Daniel Kaluuya, "It captures the fear you feel being a Black man in America. It's this paranoia, and [you] wonder what people are saying and feeling about you."[17] *Slate*'s Aisha Harris pushed the analogy of lived black apprehension further: "This is the essence of *Get Out*, which only grows more darkly relevant as the main story gets going, masterfully unfurling all of the real-life anxieties of Existing While Black while simultaneously mining that situation for all its twisted absurdity."[18] Perhaps because nonwhite reviewers delved deeper into the racial dynamics of *Get Out*, they alone acknowledged the presence of microaggressions

13. Harris, "*Get Out*."
14. Clasen, *Why Horror*, 3.
15. Truitt, "Review."
16. Sims, "*Get Out*."
17. Kyles, "Bigotry Is the Monster," 21.
18. Harris, "*Get Out*."

in the film. To cite one example, Justin Chang's *Los Angeles Times* review lauded Jordan Peele for "a deadpan compendium of racial microaggressions . . . forced references to Tiger Woods and fondl[ing] Chris' muscles with the sort of relish that brings Southern slave traders to mind."[19] In short, there was a subtle, but significant difference occurring across the reviews. White reviewers related how *Get Out* used racial tension to create fear; nonwhite reviewers envisioned *Get Out* as giving voice to the fear and anxiety created by racial tension. This, in turn, created differences in how both sets of critics related the message of the film to readers.

Get Out's Message—The Meaning Level

When relaying the message of *Get Out,* white reviewers favored vague references to race and racism, while nonwhite reviewers afforded much richer critiques. Exemplifying white reviewers' vagueness, Brian Truitt wrote in *USA Today,* "Peele imparts a great deal about his thoughts on race, culture and humanity in the face of doom, and makes a successful play for being horror's essential new voice."[20] Relatedly, Peter Debruge's review for *Variety* noted, "Comedian Jordan Peele's race-based horror movie combines genuine thrills with a no-holds-barred critique of black-white relations."[21] While these reviewers are correctly identifying the film's central subtext, they fail to comment further on "Peele's thoughts on race" or exactly how *Get Out* is a "no-holds-barred critique of black-white relations."

To be sure, several white reviewers did delve into deeper discussions of race. Richard Brody noted in the *New Yorker,* for example, how Peele expertly made "commonplace, banal experiences burst forth like new to convey philosophically rich and politically potent ideas about the state of race relations in America."[22] In contrast to other white reviewers, Brody did not stop there; he pinpointed how specific scenes in the movie dovetailed with ongoing racial issues:

> The sight of a police officer and his request for I. D., the very notion of genetic qualities, and, for that matter, the very concept of seeing and being

---

19. Chang, "Jordan Peele's Clever."
20. Truitt, "Review."
21. Debruge, "Film Review."
22. Brody, "'Get Out.'"

> seen—or of not being seen—emerge in *Get Out* as essentially racialized experiences, fundamentally different from a white and a black perspective.[23]

Brody was joined by Alan Scherstuhl (*Village Voice*)[24] and Manohla Dargis (*New York Times*)[25] as the only white reviewers to venture beyond superficial discussions of race. Much like *Wall Street Journal* critic Joe Morgenstern commented of the film itself—"No preachments are preached, no parables are dwelled on"[26]—the vast majority of white reviewers did not dwell on any of the film's overt and covert messages. This lack of elaboration on the part of white reviewers is revealed more starkly when compared to those of nonwhites.

Over half of nonwhite reviewers engaged in a deeper dialogue about race and racism. Kristian Lin of *Fort Worth Weekly* instructed readers how *Get Out* conveys black fears to nonblack audiences, offering a commentary that has largely been absent from the horror genre:

> Peele's flair for the genre helps bring home the fears that come with being African-American in a racist society to a non-black audience, as in the opening scene with Stanfield when the clean, leafy suburb he's walking through reveals its menace ("You know how they like to do motherfuckers out here," he mumbles to himself), or a late one when Chris looks to be the latest unarmed black man to be shot by an overzealous white cop.[27]

Similarly, writing for *The Root,* Danielle Young pointed to white privilege as an animating force behind the film's message: "Black people will never be able to relate to white privilege, and it's obscenely displayed with violence and complete entitlement in *Get Out* in a way that's sure to make folks uncomfortable, but isn't that a testament to true artistry?"[28] After noting how *Get Out* "does a magnificent job of presenting the current flawed race relations that darken America,"[29] *Vibe*'s Richy Rosario focused on the scene in which a police officer asks to see Chris's identification: "It gets one thinking, would this have been the same outcome if Rose was a black woman

23. Ibid.
24. Scherstuhl, "You Won't Believe Hollywood."
25. Dargis, "Review."
26. Morgenstern, "'Get Out.'"
27. Lin, "*Get Out.*"
28. Young, "*Get Out.*"
29. Rosario, "Review."

instead?"[30] In these examples, the reviewers provide readers with explicit examples of how the film taps into race. Much like Clay Cane of *BET* notes how "*Get Out* manages to simultaneously educate and disturb you,"[31] nonwhite reviewers educate audiences on how the film disturbs.

Digging into the deeper significance of *Get Out*'s narrative allowed some nonwhite reviewers the opportunity to highlight how Jordan Peele played with various genre and cultural tropes, including white saviorism and the criminal blackman. Focusing on the opening scene, Aisha Harris's *Slate* review quipped, "You need no more than a passing awareness of the past five years' news cycle—or what it's like to inhabit a black body in America—to immediately recognize the way in which Peele cleverly repurposes those tropes."[32] This insight was echoed by Justin Chang of the *Los Angeles Times*—"The [opening] scene is a jolting piece of suspense craftsmanship and a clever dismantling of several decades' worth of racist stereotypes"—before he explicitly laid the nature of the inversion out to readers: "The black guy walking alone on a dark street, so routinely depicted as a figure of fear, menace and criminality, is here recast as a frightened, vulnerable innocent."[33] Writing for the *New Orleans Tribune* and summarizing *Get Out*'s overall message, Morgan Lawrence informed readers, "Ultimately, Jordan Peele successfully illuminated the perception of Black men as dangerous when in fact, they are the ones in danger."[34] This level of analysis was not matched by white reviewers.

The nebulous discussions of race relations by white reviewers, in contrast to the way nonwhite reviewers drew concrete parallels to current racial issues, was a consistent feature in our data. While this finding corroborates Anderson and Grether's study that found nonwhite reviewers willing to paint lines between filmic text and social context and an unwillingness of white reviewers to follow suit, we can add an important qualification. Anderson and Grether suggest two reasons for nonwhite reviewers' willingness to press discussions of racism onto readers—more experience with racism, and, therefore, greater comfort writing about it and the fact that nonwhite film reviewers often wrote for nonmainstream media outlets where the pressure to eschew mention of a film's racial implications would be minimized.[35] However, in our dataset, the nonwhite reviewers writing for

30. Ibid.
31. Cane, "'Get Out.'"
32. Harris, "*Get Out*."
33. Chang, "Jordan Peele's Clever."
34. Lawrence, "*Get Out*."
35. Anderson and Grether, "Reviewing the Reviewers," 194.

predominantly white publication outlets were no less pointed than reviewers writing for traditionally black media outlets. As we show next, not only were nonwhite reviewers more willing to broach the subject of race, they were also more willing to voice a distinctly personal commentary.

Speaking Past *Get Out*—The Commentary Level

Film critics can use their status as cultural authorities to invite readers to consider their views on contemporary social issues. Indeed, in 2007, *Forbes* named the late Roger Ebert "the most powerful pundit in America" because he was "viewed by the public as intelligent, experienced and articulate."[36] In a climate of high-profile racial incidents and the resurgence of white nationalism, a rich text like *Get Out* could have provided an ideal platform for critics, in the role of pundits, to offer informed political commentary. Despite this, only a minority of white reviewers pushed past the textual level to tackle issues of broader importance. By contrast, only one nonwhite reviewer failed to do so. In particular, nonwhite reviewers chose to give voice to black victims of extralegal shootings like Trayvon Martin, to critique current race relations, and to protest the lack of opportunity afforded to black creative personnel in Hollywood.

The focus on black victimization by nonwhite reviewers was triggered by two scenes: the opening sequence in which Andre Hayworth is abducted from a wealthy suburb and the scene in which a white police officer harasses Chris after Rose hits a deer with her car. In the former scenario, *The Root*'s Danielle Young noted how she was reminded of the circumstances behind Trayvon Martin's death: "Stanfield is first seen at the beginning of the movie, nervously stranded in a suburban utopia. My mind wandered to Trayvon Martin and how his killer passed judgment on him that he didn't belong there."[37] In the latter instance, *Vibe*'s Richy Rosario asked readers to ponder a different scenario, "After, the police, of course, leave. It gets one thinking, would this have been the same outcome if Rose was a black woman instead? Personally, Sandra Bland instantly came to mind."[38] These sorts of observations did not slip the minds of all white critics. In her *New York Times* review, Manohla Dargis also drew parallels to Trayvon Martin, "except that when this man anxiously looks for a way out, the scene grows discordantly

36. Van Riper, "Top Pundits."
37. Young, "Get Out."
38. Rosario, "Review."

disturbing because you may, as I did, flash on Trayvon Martin."[39] This was reverberated by Peter Debruge of *Variety,* who noted that "the opening scene (in which an uneasy black man walking alone in a predominately white suburb) recalls the fate of Trayvon Martin."[40] However, such observations were disproportionately in the purview of nonwhite film critics.

With *Get Out* openly satirizing modern race relations, numerous nonwhite reviewers pushed their readers to reflect more deeply on these relations. Merecedes Howze of the *Pittsburgh Courier,* for instance, posited, "The movie's ideas and topics are racially-motivating and thought provoking" and then told readers, "While many current films are now playing it safe when [it] comes to discussing race relations, 'Get Out' pushes the envelope and forces the audience to evaluate the role of White people in the modern-day oppression of Black people."[41] Danielle Young from *The Root* chose to critique Donald Trump's comments to reporter April Ryan, which took place less than a week before *Get Out* premiered: "It's the same type of racism that has President Donald Trump believing that if you're black, you know and can set up meetings with the Congressional Black Caucus because we're all friends, right? Wrong. That's the real horror we're living in."[42] *Ebony*'s Kyra Kyles asked readers to consider Black Lives Matter because, "Interwoven within these scares is a social message not unlike the eerily Black Lives Matteresque conclusion of the original *Night of the Living Dead* (1968)."[43] *Slate*'s Aisha Harris also evoked Black Lives Matter in her review, "But, not unlike the black teen whose name became a rallying cry for the Black Lives Matter movement, [Stanfield's character] can't avoid trouble."[44] Though some white reviewers did mention the current racial climate, they failed to pinpoint specific events like their nonwhite counterparts. John DeFore's *Hollywood Reporter* review only cryptically referenced rising racial animus: "[*Get Out*'s] timing couldn't be better, as it exploits racial fears that have become substantially more potent (not to mention more comprehensible for many white Americans)" since Donald Trump won the 2016 presidential election.[45]

While a few white critics joined nonwhite reviewers in isolating black victimization as an important issue to address, and even spoke to current racial hostility, only nonwhite reviewers drew attention to another vexing issue: the lack of diversity behind the camera. After noting *Get Out*'s box

39. Dargis, "Review."
40. Debruge, "Film Review."
41. Howze, "'Get Out.'"
42. Young, "Get Out."
43. Kyles, "Bigotry Is the Monster," 21.
44. Harris, "*Get Out.*"
45. DeFore, "'Get Out.'"

office success, D. Kevin McNeir from the *Washington Informer* asked, "Who says Black directors can't make it in Hollywood?"[46] *BET*'s Clay Cane made the point more forcefully: "I am certain some Hollywood exec thought a movie like this would 'never' sell. Not only will it sell, but I predict Peele's movie will blow up the box office this weekend."[47] Though film reviews are not necessarily meant to be vehicles for the personal observations of critics, it is surprising to document such a disparity between white and nonwhite reviewers at this level of analysis, especially for a film that so "meaningfully reflect[ed] a culture's latent fears and anxieties."[48] Here, nonwhite reviewers are pushing readers beyond the safety of escapist entertainment and challenging them to see the correspondence between movie and real-life events.

Discussion/Conclusion

While film reviewing is often seen as an individual act of evaluating the cultural merit and entertainment value of a film, our chapter echoes prior scholarship by documenting differences in assessment across racial lines. In sum, our analysis of *Get Out*'s reviews shows that white reviewers opted to focus on the film's construction of atmosphere when relating its major plot events. By contrast, nonwhite reviewers zeroed in on the subjective position of the film's black protagonist, Chris. Both sets of reviewers picked up on the racial messaging of *Get Out*, but nonwhite reviewers were more likely to elaborate on that messaging. Finally, where only a few white reviewers provided readers with commentary external to the film, a majority of nonwhite reviewers chose to do so. Taken together, these results suggest that white reviewers collectively mute in-depth discussions of race, preferring, instead, a superficial handling of the subject—even with a film that lends itself to deeper analysis. Nonwhite film reviewers, regardless of publication outlet, were more willing to tackle *Get Out*'s racially weighted text. The particular approach of white reviewers, Anderson and Grether argue, "reinforces the idea that race is simply a describing mechanism and not one that affects life experiences and outcomes."[49] Providing more opportunities to nonwhite reviewers may not overturn entrenched and institutionalized racism, but, by offering critically informed interpretations of the (often lived) racial aspects of films, minority critics can help push those conversations that so many are unwilling to have.

46. McNeir. "Editor's Column."
47. Cane, "'Get Out.'"
48. Chang, "Jordan Peele's Clever."
49. Anderson and Grether, "Reviewing the Reviewers," 199.

Bibliography

Anderson, Alecia, and Scott Grether. "Reviewing the Reviewers: Discussions of Race by Film Reviewers." *Sociological Spectrum* 37, no. 3 (2017): 188–204.

Austin, Bruce. "Critics' and Consumers' Evaluations of Motion Pictures: A Longitudinal Test of the Taste Culture and Elite Hypotheses." *Journal of Popular Film and Television* 10, no. 4 (1983): 156–67.

Bauman, Shyon. *Hollywood Highbrow: From Entertainment to Art.* Princeton, NJ: Princeton University Press, 2007.

Basuroy, Suman, Subimal Chatterjee, and S. Abraham Ravid. "How Critical Are Critical Reviews? The Box Office Effects of Film Critics, Star Power, and Budgets." *Journal of Marketing* 67, no. 4 (October 2003): 103–17.

Berg, Jeremy, and M. Jordan Raddick. "First You Get the Money, Then You Get the Reviews, Then You Get the Internet Comments: A Quantitative Examination of the Relationship Between Critics, Viewers, and Box Office Success." *Quarterly Review of Film and Video* 34, no. 2 (2017): 101–29.

Brody, Richard. "'Get Out': Jordan Peele's Radical Cinematic Vision of the World through a Black Man's Eyes." *New Yorker,* March 2, 2017. http://www.newyorker.com/culture/richard-brody/get-out-jordan-peeles-radical-cinematic-vision-of-the-world-through-black-eyes.

Cameron, S. "On the Role of Critics in the Culture Industry." *Journal of Cultural Economics* 19, no. 4 (1995): 321–31.

Cane, Clay. "'Get Out' Movie Review: 'The First Must-See Film of the Year.'" *BET,* February 23, 2017. https://www.bet.com/celebrities/news/movie-reviews/2017/02/get-out-movie-review.html.

Chang, Justin. "Jordan Peele's Clever Horror-satire 'Get Out' is an Overdue Hollywood Response to Our Racial Anxiety." *Los Angeles Times,* February 23, 2017. http://www.latimes.com/entertainment/movies/la-et-mn-get-out-review-20170223-story.html.

Clasen, Mathias. *Why Horror Seduces.* New York: Oxford University Press, 2017.

Dargis, Manohla. "Review: In 'Get Out,' Guess Who's Coming to Dinner? (Bad Idea!)." *New York Times,* February 23, 2017. https://www.nytimes.com/2017/02/23/movies/get-out-review-jordan-peele.html?_r=0.

Debenedetti, Stéphane. "The Role of Media Critics in the Cultural Industries." *International Journal of Arts Management* 8, no. 3 (Spring 2006): 30–42.

Debruge, Peter. "Film Review: 'Get Out.'" *Variety,* January 24, 2017. http://variety.com/2017/film/reviews/get-out-review-jordan-peele-1201968635/.

DeFore, John. "'Get Out': Film Review." *Hollywood Reporter,* January 24, 2017. http://www.hollywoodreporter.com/review/get-review-967922.

Duan, Wenjing, Bin Gu, and Andrew B. Whinston. "Do Online Reviews Matter?—An Empirical Investigation of Panel Data." *Decision Support Systems* 45, no. 4 (November 2008): 1007–16.

Gonzalez-Sobrino, Bianca, Devon R. Goss, and Matthew W. Hughey. "The Rise of the Racial Reviewer, 1990–2004." In *Race and Contention in Twenty-First Century U. S. Media,* edited by Jason A. Smith and Bhoomi K. Thakore, 165–81. New York: Routledge, 2016.

Grierson, Tim. "From *Psycho* to *Get Out*: A History of Horror at the Oscars." *Rolling Stone*, January 30, 2018. https://www.rollingstone.com/movies/news/from-psycho-to-get-out-a-history-of-horror-at-the-oscars-w516044.

Harris, Aisha. "*Get Out.*" *Slate*, February 23, 2017. http://www.slate.com/articles/arts/movies/2017/02/get_out_jordan_peele_s_horror_movie_reviewed.html.

Howze, Merecedes J. "'Get Out' Depicts White Privilege and Black Depreciation." *Pittsburgh Courier*, February 27, 2017. https://newpittsburghcourieronline.com/2017/02/27/get-out-depicts-white-privilege-and-black-depreciation/.

Hsieh, Hsiu-Fang, and Sarah E. Shannon. "Three Approaches to Qualitative Content Analysis." *Qualitative Health Research* 15, no. 9 (November 2005): 1277–88.

Hughey, Matthew W. "The White Savior Film and Reviewers' Reception." *Symbolic Interaction* 33, no. 3 (Fall 2010): 475–96.

———. *The White Savior Film: Content, Critics, and Consumption.* Philadelphia: Temple University Press, 2014.

Hughey, Matthew W., and Sheena Gardner. "Film Reviewers and Framing Race: Recuperating a Post-Racial Whiteness." *Dark Matter* 9, no. 2 (November 2012). http://www.darkmatter101.org/site/2012/11/29/film-reviewers-and-framing-race-recuperating-a-post-racial-whiteness/.

Kyles, Kyra. "Bigotry Is the Monster in Jordan Peele's New Film." *Ebony* (March 2017): 20–21.

Lawrence, Morgan. "*Get Out*: The Escape from Black Misconceptions." *New Orleans Tribune*, March 22, 2017. http://www.theneworleanstribune.com/main/film-review/get-out-the-escape-from-blackmisconceptions/.

Legoux, Renaud, Denis Larocque, Sandra Laporte, Soraya Belmati, and Thomas Boquet. "The Effect of Critical Reviews on Exhibitors' Decisions: Do Reviews Affect the Survival of a Movie on Screen?" *International Journal of Research in Marketing* 33, no. 2 (June 2016): 357–74.

Lin, Kristian. "*Get Out*: I Am Not Your Negro." *Fort Worth Weekly*, February 28, 2017. https://www.fwweekly.com/2017/02/28/get-out-i-am-not-your-negro/.

McNeir, Kevin D. "Editor's Column: Peele's Film on Race, 'Get Out,' Shows How Far We Haven't Come." *Washington Informer*, April 12, 2017. http://washingtoninformer.com/editors-column-peeles-film-on-race-get-out-shows-how-far-we-havent-come/.

Morgenstern, Joe. "'Get Out' Review: Black, White and Terrific All Over." *Wall Street Journal*, February 23, 2017. https://www.wsj.com/articles/get-out-review-black-white-and-terrific-all-over-1487874658.

Neuendorf, Kimberly A. *The Content Analysis Guidebook.* Thousand Oaks, CA: Sage, 2002.

Rosario, Richy. "Review: Jordan Peele's 'Get Out' Examines the Plight of Black Men in a Horrifying Way." *Vibe*, February 22, 2017. http://www.vibe.com/2017/02/review-jordan-peele-get-out/.

Ruimy, Jordan. "AD Critics Poll: 'Get Out' Tops the Chart of 2017 Favorites, So Far." *Awards Daily*, July 12, 2017. http://www.awardsdaily.com/2017/07/12/ad-critics-poll-get-best-movie-2017-far/.

Scherstuhl, Alan. "You Won't Believe Hollywood Let Jordan Peele Get Away with 'Get Out.'" *Village Voice*, February 21, 2017. https://www.villagevoice.com/2017/02/21/you-wont-believe-hollywood-let-jordan-peele-get-away-with-get-out/.

Sims, David. "*Get Out* Is a Funny and Brilliantly Subversive Horror Film." *The Atlantic*, February 23, 2017. https://www.theatlantic.com/entertainment/archive/2017/02/get-out-jordan-peele-review/517524/.

Travers, Peter. "'Get Out' Review: Scares Meet Racially Charged Satire in Instant Horror Classic." *Rolling Stone*, February 22, 2017. http://www.rollingstone.com/movies/reviews/peter-travers-get-out-movie-review-w468003.

Truitt, Brian. "Review: Give in to the Fear Factor of Jordan Peele's Satirical 'Get Out.'" *USA Today*, February 23, 2017. https://www.usatoday.com/story/life/movies/2017/02/23/review-jordan-peele-get-out-movie/98249818/.

Van Riper, Tom. "The Top Pundits in America." *Forbes*, September 24, 2007. https://www.forbes.com/2007/09/21/pundit-americas-top-oped-cx_tvr_0924pundits.html#7d79a0bb54c4.

Young, Danielle. "Get Out Is a Refreshing, Creepy, Stress-Filled Thriller Unafraid to Comment on Race." *Root*, February 24, 2017. http://www.theroot.com/get-out-is-a-refreshing-creepy-stress-filled-thriller-1792645766.

Appendix 1
Reviews Analyzed

NONWHITE REVIEWS		
Reviewer	*Publication*	*Date*
Cane, Clay	*BET*	2/23/2017
Chang, Justin	*Los Angeles Times*	2/23/2017
Cruz, Lenika	*Atlantic*	3/3/2017
Harris, Aisha	*Slate*	2/23/2017
Howze, Merecedes	*Pittsburgh Courier*	2/27/2017
Johnson, Todd	*Grio*	2/23/2017
Kyles, Kyra	*Ebony*	3/2017
Lawrence, Morgan	*New Orleans Tribune*	3/22/2017
Lin, Kristian	*Fort Worth Weekly*	2/28/2017
McNeir, Kevin	*Washington Informer*	4/12/2017
Rosario, Richie	*Vibe*	2/22/2017
Shahid, Shah	*Blank Page Beatdown*	5/27/2017
Young, Danielle	*Root*	2/24/2017

WHITE REVIEWS		
Reviewer	*Publication*	*Date*
Brody, Richard	*New Yorker*	3/2/2017
Coyle, Jake	*Associated Press*	2/22/2017
Dargis, Manohla	*New York Times*	2/23/2017
Deburge, Peter	*Variety*	2/24/2017
DeFore, John	*Hollywood Reporter*	1/24/2017
Phillips, Michael	*Chicago Tribune*	2/22/2017
Morgenstern, Joe	*Wall Street Journal*	2/23/2017
Scherstuhl, Alan	*Village Voice*	2/21/2017
Sims, David	*Atlantic*	2/23/2017
Smith, Kyle	*New York Post*	2/22/2017
Travers, Peter	*Rolling Stone*	2/22/2017
Truitt, Brian	*USA Today*	2/23/2017
Zacharek, Stephanie	*Time*	2/23/2017

Appendix 2
Levels and Sublevels of Commentary within Reviews

	NONWHITE REVIEWS	WHITE REVIEWS
I. Textual Level		
Black POV	10	8
Colorblind	0	1
Foreboding	3	11
Liberal Racism	11	13
Microaggressions	4	0
Symbolism	0	1
Use of Prior Films	7	6
White Privilege	1	1
Whitewashing	1	2
II. Meaning Level		
Commentary on Racism	11	13
Inversion of Tropes	5	2
III. Commentary Level		
Black-White Divide	1	1
Black Victims	8	2
Blacks and Horror	1	2
Critiques of the Film	3	0
Lack of Creative Opportunities	4	0
Political Climate	11	3

CHAPTER 10

SPECTERS OF SLAVE REVOLT

SARAH JULIET LAURO

RECENTLY, I was surprised by a protest sign. It read: "Not Today—Nat Turner." I was struck by this invocation of Nat Turner in the context of political resistance because of how rarely we in the United States talk about violent slave uprisings in public discourse as compared to other former slaveholding societies—like Cuba, Guadeloupe, and Haiti—where rebel slaves are overtly celebrated as freedom fighters.[1] Nat Turner was an enslaved person who, in 1831, led an uprising in Southampton, Virginia, that would swell to (by some accounts) over eighty rebels, attacking various plantations across the region and resulting in the assassination of fifty-one white slaveholders and their family members. This description of the man, from History.com, which is one of the first options presented by a simple Google search, reveals many of the problems with the way we talk about Nat Turner:

> Nathanial "Nat" Turner (1800–1831) was a black American slave who led the only effective, sustained slave rebellion (August 1831) in US history.

1. In Cuba, there is a monument to rebel slaves commemorating an insurrection on a sugar plantation in Matanzas; in Guadeloupe, a statue celebrates a maroon who mobilized forces against the French in 1802; in Haiti, such monuments are prevalent across the country. One of these is a mural that stands at Bois Caïman, where slaves took an oath to carry out rebellions on their neighboring plantations.

> Spreading terror throughout the white South, his action set off a new wave of oppressive legislation prohibiting the education, movement, and assembly of slaves and stiffened proslavery, antiabolitionist convictions that persisted in that region until the American Civil War (1861–1865).[2]

To call Turner's revolt the "*only* effective, sustained slave rebellion" is immediately problematic, for inherent in it is a value judgment about what constitutes efficacy. Perhaps the metric by which these authors measured success is body count, but such a statement elides other major slave rebellion events, like the Stono Rebellion (1739) and the German Coast Uprising (1811).[3] It diminishes some 250 slave revolts that the same website (albeit, on another page) estimates occurred prior to the Civil War, implicitly deeming them *ineffective*.[4] The use of the word "only" erases a rich history of slave revolt even as it paints Turner as a man who failed if the goal was to improve his people's treatment.

This website echoes two of the main points we often hear repeated about Turner, that he was a terrorist (but, somehow, also a coward), and that his revolt, despite high casualties, was actually a dismal failure, for it resulted in the execution and expulsion from the state of many persons, both involved and uninvolved, and otherwise brought about a crackdown that was antithetical to all of his goals for the uplift of the enslaved. "His action set off a new wave of oppressive legislation," History.com tells us, effectively shifting the blame for slave-owners' cruelty to Turner himself.[5]

Simply put, we don't seem to know how to talk about Nat Turner, a man who was responsible for the deaths not only of slave-holding men but of their wives and children, too. This may be due to the fact that our society is comprised of the ancestors of both the oppressed and the oppressor, of the rebel slave and the slain master, or merely a sign that we inhabit a culture that *still* has not accepted what John Brown knew in 1859, that slavery was war.[6] However, by drawing on a longstanding practice in the Afrodia-

---

2. "Nat Turner."

3. The Stono Rebellion, also called Cato's rebellion, occurred in South Carolina and was one of the largest slave revolts in the mainland at the time, with twenty-five white persons killed. The German Coast uprising of 1811 was carried out in Louisiana; although only two white persons were killed, it is sometimes called the largest revolt because of the territory covered and the number of enslaved persons involved, which some accounts number in the hundreds.

4. Fick, *Making*, 71.

5. "Nat Turner."

6. For a sample of views of Turner, including testimonials from people claiming to be related both to the man himself and his victims, see the "Talkback" on "Nat Turner: A

sporic black radical tradition—that is, recourse to the marvelous, the fantastic, or the surreal—Jordan Peele found with *Get Out* a way to talk about slave revolt without talking about slave revolt. One might say that Peele's latest film, *Us* (2019), continues this theme by depicting the uprising of the "tethered." But in *Get Out,* Peele links his narrative specifically to the history of slavery.

Migration

Get Out calls attention to police discrimination, to the exploitation of black domestics in white suburbia, and to the devaluation of black lives in US society, generally, but it also highlights the pervasive racism of our society *as* the legacy of slavery. Peele accomplishes this by means of an allegorical structure that links a tale of capture, occupation, and revolt with its historical parallel in the transatlantic migration of the enslaved, their oppression, and their diverse acts of resistance.

More than just a revision of the horror tropes of films like *The Stepford Wives* (1975), or *Invasion of the Body Snatchers* (1956), to which the film admits comparison, the body-snatching theme is used in *Get Out* to recall that "peculiar institution" in which white people historically commandeered black lives. On the surface, the film's narrative concerns Chris's navigation of various tensions as he meets his white girlfriend's family for the first time; from the start, it is clearly about race relations in the US, well before Chris discovers that Rose's family has a nefarious agenda. What Chris uncovers in the film is a gruesome family business: the Armitages perform body snatching of African Americans through a kind of hypnotic zombification and brain transplantation, in order to give control of young black bodies over to aging white people who pay handsomely for this privilege. As the narrative begins to take a twist, the significance of the plot likewise corkscrews, revealing a layer beneath, one that tacitly communicates that black lives *don't* matter to the powers that be—as seen in the poisoned drinking water of Flint, Michigan, and the exoneration of George Zimmerman for the murder of Trayvon Martin—and connects this devaluation to the plantation's complete mastery of the enslaved person's life. It is necessary to understand this allegory, in which the original inhabitant of the body remains trapped within, but powerless, in the lineage of similar "death-in-life" figures metaphorizing slavery.

Troublesome Property," PBS, Independent Lens, including an anonymous comment on February 25, 2009, that he was an "antebellum Charles Manson." https://www.pbs.org/independentlens/natturner/talkback.html.

From the soul capture mythologies of Western Africa to the Caribbean Vaudou zombie, such incarnations dramatize the incomprehensible sorcery that gave over control of one person's life to another.[7] At the same time, the metaphor recalls theoretical work on the "social death" of the enslaved, which we must remember to trouble by paying attention also to the enslaved's persistence and acts of resistance within a disempowered state.[8]

Peele's film begins with a scene of capture. An African American man is wandering at night on a darkened street in "the suburbs." A white car begins to follow the young man, eerily blasting the 1939 song "Run, Rabbit, Run" from its speakers, and the audience watches as the victim is placed in a chokehold and forced into the trunk of the car by a figure wearing a strange mask. The song only incidentally resembles the nineteenth-century folksong "Run, Nigger, Run," but its parallelism signals nonetheless that this is a scene of slave capture. The viewer will rediscover this captured character later in the film, when our protagonist meets him at a garden party, but the man appears altered, vacant-eyed, formal, and nearly unrecognizable in this depersonalized state. After the scene of this abduction at the beginning of the film, haunting music plays with lyrics in Swahili that translate to "listen to your ancestors / something bad is coming, run!" (a song that recurs at the film's climax), and the credit sequence rolls over a swift tracking shot of passing woods, as if from the perspective of a moving car.[9] What this opening suggests, I would argue, is the original seizure of the slave in Africa and his forced migration across the Atlantic. Peele is careful at every turn to thread the needle, connecting our past and our present: the abductor's method of subduing his captive, by choking him unconscious, may also recall Eric Garner, the victim of police brutality whose last words—"I can't breathe"—have become a rallying cry for the Black Lives Matter movement.[10] This moment in the film is an example of the kind of "temporal accumulation" that Ian Baucom describes in *Specters of the Atlantic*: it can be read as striated through with both the past and the present.[11]

Directly after this opening scene, the viewer is introduced to our protagonist in his studio apartment in New York, as he prepares for a weekend

---

7. While not a zombie movie *per se, Get Out* does similar work as the original Caribbean zombie myth in that it allegorizes both slavery and slave revolt, what I have elsewhere called the zombie's dialectic. See Lauro, *Transatlantic Zombie.*

8. On slavery as social death, see Patterson, *Slavery,* and Mbembe, "Necropolitics."

9. Peele himself noted the significance of the song's lyrics in an interview. See Weaver, "Jordan Peele." For a full translation of the lyrics, see Gayo, "Sikiliza."

10. This insight was suggested to me by one of my students. "I can't breathe" has since become a slogan printed on T-shirts and protest signs.

11. Baucom, *Specters.*

trip outside the city to meet his white girlfriend's parents for the first time, continuing the theme of migration. He appears nervous and timidly asks Rose: "Do they know? Do they know that I'm black?"[12] Rose reassures him that her parents aren't racists, but the next scene opens with a shot of Chris in the passenger seat of a moving car, and, importantly, the same woods as were previously seen under the film's credits are reflected across his face on the window's surface, as he gazes out. This shot telegraphs subtly to the viewer that Chris is unwittingly making what we will come to find out later is the same journey as the kidnapping victim. In making a journey to which he consents, but without the knowledge of where he is truly being taken, Chris's migration may evoke that of Solomon Northrup, a free man who was lured south, abducted, and sold into slavery, as is chronicled in the memoir *Twelve Years A Slave* (1853) and Steve McQueen's 2013 film *12 Years a Slave.*

Rose is plainly in control at this point in the film, and her charm obscures the danger she represents. Besides the fact that she is driving, she takes Chris's cigarette away from him and tosses it out the window; she also commandeers a phone call with his friend. The motion of the plot is plainly driven by Rose. When Rose hits a deer, Chris looks into the eyes of the wounded creature, which appears alive but is unable to move. It is a state in which he will soon find himself, but also a reminder of the trauma of his mother's death; she too was struck by a car and left for dead when he was a child, a memory that Rose's mother exploits to paralyze Chris when she hypnotizes him, ostensibly to help him quit smoking. The film's structure thus begins with movement but then stalls in a state of paralysis (foreshadowed in the struck deer), when the couple reaches the Armitage house and as the houseguest becomes an imprisoned man.

Plantation

The Armitage homestead evokes "the big house" of the plantation economy not only visually but also because of the centrality of its role in the ensuing drama. The viewer's first sight of the lavish family home, with its Doric columns and rocking chairs, is framed as the car pulls into the driveway of the remote country setting. The camera is situated as if from the perspective of a person sitting with the characters in the backseat of the car. But the camera stays back in the posture of an establishing shot, keeping the full house in the frame. It's a long shot that seems disturbingly removed for an

12. *Get Out.* All further references to the film are to this streaming video.

important plot point wherein the viewer is first introduced to Rose's parents as they greet Chris on the front porch. The viewer is denied, from this distant perspective, an ability to gauge Missy and Dean's reaction to Chris and is forcibly held in place as the characters move in the distance, establishing at first glance the sense of paralysis that we will come to associate with the house. This long shot of the Armitage household (see figure 5), which draws outward to include Walter, the black groundskeeper, in the right of the frame, visually parallels a later shot, when Chris is held captive and forced to watch an informational video about the process he will undergo to give control of his body over to its new owner. Here, too, the house is a focal point. This shot also visually rhymes with the repeated, far away perspective of the "sunken place," when Chris is hypnotized by Rose's mother—placing him completely in her control—and we see through his eyes as he experiences the world at a remove. This spectatorial distance from the diegetic world of the film established in the first shot of the house is akin to the victim's future within his own body, if the Armitages' conquest is successful; the body becomes the prison-house, a concept that itself may resonate with racial slavery. When we return to shots of the home's exterior at several points in the film, especially as it burns in the scene of Chris's revolt against his captors, it recalls the plantation set aflame by rebel slaves.[13]

The house becomes the space that Chris must escape—heeding Andre's warning at the party to "Get Out!"—and, by means of its prominence in the informational video, like the plantation's big house, it serves to represent an oppressive organization. There are only two "servants," Walter the groundskeeper and Georgina the maid, both of whom behave strangely. The fact that Walter is only ever seen outside, and Georgina never strays further than the veranda in her duties, clearly marks them as surrogates for the house and field slaves. The Armitage homestead—note that, related etymologically to "hermitage," the family's last name even means "house"—may most obviously stand in for contemporary America, with its dark past and hidden secret of a pervasive and rankling racism, but for me the attention that Peele devotes to the house signifies on diverse levels.

The space is used to create suspense, foreshadow, and provide important backstory. The layout of the house is mapped out for the viewer via an initial "tour" conducted by Dean, which may cause the viewer to wonder in what context this space will be revisited. During his tour of the house and the grounds, Dean's asides about his travels and collection of souvenirs from foreign cultures become suspect. Foreboding the kind of racial tourism

13. For a discussion of the role of arson in slave resistance, see Genovese, *Roll*, 613.

FIGURE 5. Long shot of the Armitage house as Chris arrives, with Walter in the foreground. *Get Out* (Jordan Peele, 2017).

in which he traffics, he says of his love of traveling, "It's such a privilege to be able to experience another person's culture." It's on this tour that we are given a sense not only of the Armitages' privilege but also of the space that Chris will have to traverse. The rigid control of space, dictating who belongs and does not belong in various rooms—Grandmother's kitchen, Missy's study, Dean's den—tacitly suggests the peculiar use of space on the slave plantation as part home, part factory, and part jail.

A more overt connection to historical slavery is drawn during the auction scene at the gazebo. Rose's parents host a party that we are told is an annual event and a tradition previously held dear by her grandfather, Roman. However, we quickly learn that it is little more than a ruse for potential clientele to examine Chris as a viable commodity—one woman even feels his biceps as she looks him up and down, an echo of the African's examination upon the auction block. As Chris and Rose take a walk in the woods, the rest of the partygoers gather at the gazebo to bid for Chris's body and his life. A low-angled, slow dolly shot tracks back from Dean, who stands beside a large portrait of Chris and makes hand gestures to signify the amount of the bid. Silently raising bingo cards to signal their interest, the crowd of white faces is mostly expressionless, offering tepid and hushed applause to congratulate the winning bidder. Just as the film updates the traditional scene of the slave at auction to this science-fictional premise of a cabalistic organization selling the healthy bodies of black men and women to aged and infirm whites, the plot as a whole alludes to the body snatching of Atlantic slavery, the soul stealing of the plantation, and the perceived living-death of the slave.

But there is one final space that needs to be described in this charting of the Armitage house as plantation: the nonspace of the sunken place. Chris's removal from power over his own body when he is entranced by Missy's spell is represented by shots of him floating helplessly in a black void. Visual space signifies the usurpation of Chris's body: under hypnosis, his perspective is rendered as a distant point-of-view shot framed in darkness, as if he found himself at the bottom of a deep well, or, dare I say, open grave. Although I don't have time to address it here, there is likely also a commentary on colonialism embedded in the allegory: the use of space in the film—including the space of the body and the nonspace of the sunken place to which the victim is banished—calls to mind the occupation of land as well as the conquest of black lives. The victims' bodies, invaded by the consciousness of another, may represent geographic spaces that are physically occupied, just as the nonspace of the sunken place may represent the exiled space of the refugee, the migrant forced from his homeland.

In a similar manner to the way that landforms illustrate geologic time, then, *Get Out* uses space to illustrate that the past is, quite literally, materially visible in the present. Time *and* space are brought together. By resembling the plantation, the house represents America's history, yet it simultaneously makes the case that the devaluation of black lives in the film (but also, plainly, in the United States today) is built upon a bedrock of dehumanizing, commoditizing, and othering the African that goes back centuries. When Chris's very presence in the kitchen, at the end of the film, is seen as an affront—causing Georgina to gasp and run for help—the parallel to the plantation house under attack is clear. Stumbling bloodied through the house as it burns, Chris reminds us of another, too rarely celebrated aspect of our history: that of the rebel slave.

Rebellion

There are not one but four scenes of revolt in *Get Out* that we can read as commenting on diverse strategies of historical slave resistance.[14] In brief, Georgina's internal battle to overpower her occupier, the Armitages' late

14. Elsewhere, I have argued that we can read these various scenes in a manner similar to Paul Gilroy's discussion (in *The Black Atlantic*) of the ways in which Frederick Douglass's battle with the overseer Covey revises the Hegelian Master-Slave dialectic. See Lauro, "*Get Out*."

matriarch, is visible in a scene in which she hysterically cries and smiles at the same time, and this can be interpreted as a struggle against internalized ideology. Georgina's quiet acts of resistance against her body's invader may also be seen elsewhere in the film: the door to a small cubby in Rose's room, for example, is repeatedly left open and eventually offers Chris evidence of the family's sinister intent. Andre, the abducted man of the film's first scene, gains momentary freedom from his condition during the Armitages' party, warning Chris that he must "Get out. Get out. Get out of here! Get the fuck out of here!" This is important for its highlighting of solidarity and protection of one's fellows as a resistive strategy; he might have taken the opportunity to run, but instead, he chooses to warn Chris. In the climax of the film, Walter's quick thinking to cover up the fact that he had been released from his bondage by means of Chris's camera flash, and his acting as he does (shooting Rose and then himself), refers both to the subterfuge of "playing" the master—posing as the loyal slave in order to take advantage of a situation—and, more darkly, to the historical strategy of suicide, which provided a release from enslavement for many.[15] In these examples, we see just some of the enslaved persons' acts of resistance—which could involve: conspiracy, subterfuge, and sabotage; self-defense and self-preservation; solidarity and self-sacrifice; as well as overt rebellion, violence, destruction, infanticide, suicide, and murder.[16] Most strikingly, though, Chris's escape is obviously coded as a scene of slave rebellion as he stalks through the house as it burns, splattered with the blood of his captors, and startling its inhabitants as he comes upon them.

Chris is able to escape because he discovers a way to make himself immune to Missy's hypnotic trance. Stuffing cotton from the armchair to which he is bound into his ears (an obvious reference to the most profitable slave crop in the US), he becomes immune to the sound that subdues her victims. Feigning unconsciousness, Chris gets the drop on Rose's brother Jeremy, who evokes the stock character of the white overseer genuinely enjoying the violence of his work. Jeremy is in the process of transporting Chris to the operating theater for the final stage of his transformation when the latter brains him with a bocce ball, as the African rhythms of the song from the title sequence begin to pound. Part of the way in which the scene maintains its resonance with slave revolt is that Chris is forced to kill the Armitages with his own "brute" force and with the objects he finds immedi-

15. Brown, *Reaper's*, 132–35.
16. See Fick, *Making*, and Genovese, *Roll*.

ately at hand (a bocce ball, a letter opener, the antlers of a taxidermied buck), just as rebel slaves did when they carried out their campaigns.[17]

Standing over Jeremy's bleeding body, Chris removes the cotton from his ears, and at that precise moment, the whispered lyrics of the Swahili song from the opening credit sequence strike up; as if he is hearing his ancestors in this moment, his gaze falls upon the deer's head on the wall. Chris then pierces Dean with the antlers, and, as the patriarch collapses, he accidentally sets fire to the house by knocking over one of the candles in his operating room. That the doctor should have kept lit candles in an operating room is perhaps proof of the director's intent to charge the scene with imagery from slave revolts, as plantation homes and fields were routinely burned; the rebel slaves of Saint Domingue, for instance, followed Jean-Jacques Dessalines's injunction to "coup tet, brule kay," cut off heads and burn down houses.[18]

Chris's revolt weaves together various strategies employed in historical slave resistance, from stopping his ears against the ideology keeping him paralyzed, to the intelligence, resourcefulness, and physical strength he draws from in his escape. Further, collaboration with others is evoked as a resistive strategy in his encounter with Walter, and in the song's appeal to the ancestors. One mechanism that is perhaps missing from this list is *code talking*: enslaved people's skill in speaking to each other about revolt without being understood by those who would oppose their agenda. Code talking was seen in the lyrics of field slaves' songs and in quilt patterns hung on a line, which might convey directions to a safe house on the freedom trail northward, for instance. But of course, we might say that the film itself acts *as* this cipher: like a pattern that will be legible only to some, the film's fantastical scenario, with its resonances both with slavery and revolt, offers us a way to subversively commemorate those who fought valiantly, even violently, against their own enslavement.

It's in this lineage that I read the film's appeal to the marvelous as code talk, a tradition that dates back to the soul-capture myths of Africa but also includes traditions like Magical Realism and even surrealism.[19] Robin Kelley explains that Caribbean artists like Aimé Césaire and Wilfredo Lam

17. See on this point sources on the Haitian Revolution such as Dubois, *Avengers*, and Ott, *Haitian*.

18. For a discussion of Dessalines's importance to Haitian culture, see especially Dayan, *Haiti*.

19. I am interested in a conceptualizing of *Get Out*'s distorted, dystopic fun house mirror of the US as a project in line with many others in the black radical tradition such as Kelley's discussion of surrealism in *Freedom Dreams*. Baucom's discussion of the aesthetic modes of allegory (as a reflection of the commodity) and the speculative (as a reflection of finance capital) in *Specters of the Atlantic* might also be germane here, since

were attracted to European surrealism for its confirmation of what they already knew about the senselessness of the world: "Black people did not have to go out and find surrealism, for their lives were already surreal."[20] It's in this vein, perhaps, that Jordan Peele quipped on Twitter: "*Get Out* is a documentary."[21] This tale of body snatching is both fantastical and real, allegorical and realist, and surreal and historical. It allows us to process the senselessness of slavery, but also gives us the freedom to talk about an aspect of history difficult to discuss in contemporary culture: violent slave rebellion.

Storytelling

My students, and perhaps, *especially* my white students, love to talk about how they cheered as Chris killed each member of the Armitage family, but I'm interested in the way that this film allows us to root for slave revolt in a society that finds fault with rebel slaves like Nat Turner. One way it does this, arguably, is by tempering the violence against women with a depiction of the protagonist's obvious struggle with conscience. There's a strange tenderness to the scene in which Chris kills Missy, with their foreheads resting against each other at one point in the struggle, and his inability to abandon Georgina nearly costs him his life; that the film ends with Chris refusing to kill Rose, instead leaving her to die from Walter's gunshot wound, might seem to some to undercut the film's radicalism. The gendered nature of his revolt is perhaps something that deserves to be taken up in more detail elsewhere, for this is a dense and thorny thicket, one that would have to address the discomfort surrounding violence against women in slave revolt narratives more broadly, but here I just want to make clear my feelings about the limitations that *Get Out* puts on the violence it depicts.

The story we tell ourselves, as a society, about why Nat Turner should not be commemorated while Harriet Tubman can (in statuary and currency) is that Nat Turner and his men "killed women and children," as one woman, who purports to be the descendent of victim Catherine Whitehead, writes on a public forum.[22] It's true that our protagonist in *Get Out* is more gentle with

Get Out lies between allegory and speculative fiction, a sci-fi metaphor that reflects back on the past reduction of humans to commodities.

20. Kelley, *Freedom*, 183.

21. Jordan Peele (@Jordan Peele), Twitter, November 15, 2017, https://twitter.com/jordanpeele/status/930796561302540288?lang=en.

22. See comment by Kelly S., May 13, 2010, in "Talkback" on "Nat Turner: A Troublesome Property," PBS, Independent Lens. https://www.pbs.org/independentlens/natturner/talkback.html.

the women than the men; nonetheless, while Peele may soften the blow, they all end up dead. Even the murder of children is obliquely referenced: when we see Rose and Jeremy as children in the informational video; in Jeremy's chanting of the children's rhyme, "One Mississippi, Two Mississippi," as he battles Chris; and again when Rose is shown eating Fruit Loops and drinking milk right before she is killed. In these moments, the film reminds us of what Turner's men surely knew: children can grow into monsters.

The discomfort around Nat Turner, his willingness to slaughter "innocents"—defenseless women, children, and men asleep in their beds—is a central point of debate surrounding the man, and it is taken up in other renderings of slave revolt in popular culture.[23] For example, in Quentin Tarantino's *Django Unchained* (2012), the titular character (literally) blows away the slave holder's innocuous sister with a blast from a gun, after flatly instructing her slaves to "Tell Ms. Laura 'goodbye.'" By taking pains to show Chris's disgust and discomfort with the violent role into which he has been thrust, Peele offers us something that is missing from the one-sided perspective we get from reading historical accounts of Nat Turner, or Tarantino's stylized orgy. When Chris visibly struggles with the violence he must commit to save himself, *Get Out* offers a more nuanced portrait of the rebel slave. Rather than diminishing the radicalism of the message by portraying the rebel's ethical dilemma, depicting his hesitation, moral conundrum, and *choice* actually enriches the portrait of enslaved peoples as humans who suffered and sacrificed; part of that suffering and sacrifice may have included the sometimes difficult choice to perpetrate violence against others.

Employing diverse strategies of storytelling, the film creates a depiction of the mortal theft of slavery that stands in a long lineage of allegorical representations of the subject, from Angolan soul-capture myths to the Caribbean zombie. It also conjures a portrait of the necessary labor of violent insurrection. The narrative is striated through with the kind of temporal accumulation we associate with the specters of the Atlantic, and it may point equally to our past, present, and future. Operating in the subversive register of allegory to represent a historical subject that remains taboo, the risks of offending the movie-goer are reduced. If the audience mistakes a raised fist for a handshake, well, they weren't meant to be in on the plot.

---

23. Turner's remorselessness is a cornerstone of Thomas R. Gray's 1831 *Confessions;* see Aptheker, *Nat Turner's.* However, an oral history taken as part of the Works Progress Administration suggests that Nat Turner and his men struggled with the decision to murder children; see Allen Crawford's testimony in *Nat Turner* and also "Interview."

Bibliography

Aptheker, Herbert, ed. *Nat Turner's Slave Rebellion, Including the 1831 "Confessions."* Mineola, NY: Dover, 1966.

Baucom, Ian. *Specters of the Atlantic: Finance Capital, Slavery, and the Philosophy of History.* Durham, NC: Duke University Press, 2005.

Brown, Vincent. *The Reaper's Garden: Death and Power in the World of Atlantic Slavery.* Cambridge, MA: Harvard University Press, 2008.

Dayan, Joan. *Haiti, History, and the Gods.* Berkeley: University of California Press, 1998.

Dubois, Laurent. *The Avengers of the New World: The Story of the Haitian Revolution.* Cambridge, MA: Harvard University Press, 2005.

Fick, Carolyn. *The Making of Haiti: The Saint Domingue Revolution from Below.* Knoxville: University of Tennessee Press, 1990.

Gayo, Loyce. "Sikiliza—There is More to the Swahili Song in 'Get Out.'" *Medium,* March 16, 2017. https://medium.com/@loycegayo/sikiliza-there-is-more-to-the-swahili-song-in-get-out-79ebb1456116.

Genovese, Eugene. *Roll, Jordan, Roll: The World the Slaves Made.* New York: Vintage Books, 1976.

Get Out. Directed by Jordan Peele. USA: Universal Pictures, 2017. Streaming video.

Gilroy, Paul. *The Black Atlantic and Double-Consciousness.* Cambridge, MA: Harvard University Press, 1993.

"Interview with Former Slave Allen Crawford, 1937." The Nat Turner Project. Interview conducted June 25, 1937. http://www.natturnerproject.org/allen-crawford-testimony.

Kelley, Robin D. G. *Freedom Dreams: The Black Radical Imagination.* Boston: Beacon Press, 2002.

Lauro, Sarah Juliet. "*Get Out*: From Atlantic Slavery to Black Lives Matter." In *The Aesthetics of Necropolitics,* edited by Natasha Lushetich, 37–54. Lanham, MD: Rowman and Littlefield, 2018.

———. *The Transatlantic Zombie: Slavery, Rebellion, and Living Death.* New Brunswick, NJ: Rutgers University Press, 2015.

Mbembe, Achille. "Necropolitics." *Public Culture* 15, no. 1 (2003): 11–40.

"Nat Turner." *History.com,* December 13, 2018. https://www.history.com/topics/black-history/nat-turner.

Nat Turner: A Troublesome Property. Directed by Charles Burnett. San Francisco, CA: California Newsreel, 2003. Vimeo streaming.

Ott, Thomas. *The Haitian Revolution, 1789–1904.* Knoxville: University of Tennessee Press, 1973.

Patterson, Orlando. *Slavery and Social Death: A Comparative Study.* Cambridge, MA: Harvard University Press, 1982.

Weaver, Caity. "Jordan Peele on a Real Horror Story: Being Black in America." *GQ,* February 3, 2017. https://www.gq.com/story/jordan-peele-get-out-interview.

CHAPTER 11

STAYING WOKE IN SUNKEN PLACES, OR THE WAGES OF DOUBLE CONSCIOUSNESS

MIKAL J. GAINES

THE UNPRECEDENTED commercial and critical success of Jordan Peele's *Get Out* is difficult to overstate, and, for longtime black fans of the horror genre, it is a phenomenon that feels simultaneously well overdue and right on time. Several scholars and critics have chronicled the circumscribed nature of black representation in horror as well as how black audiences have continued to engage with the genre despite (or perhaps because of) its fraught legacy of racial signification.[1] But if part of the horror film's function historically has been to capture the anxieties of the sociocultural moment, then it should come as little surprise that a movie focusing on the monstrosity of racism would resonate with audiences black and otherwise in the era of President Donald Trump. Yet even with these considerations in mind, it seems vital to resist discussing *Get Out*'s thematic concerns as wholly new or as outside of the larger tradition of black thought. In fact, the film's greatest theoretical contribution may very well be how it further elaborates upon older conceptions of black ontology, epistemology, and survival. More specifically, *Get Out*'s urgent preoccupation with upholding a sense of responsive awareness in the face of white supremacy, that is, with the call to "stay woke," bears an ideological affinity to W. E. B. Du Bois's foundational the-

1. See, for instance, Brooks, *Searching;* Means Coleman, *Horror Noire;* Gaines, "Black Gothic" and "Strange Enjoyments"; and Alston, "First to Die."

ory of "double consciousness" in his *The Souls of Black Folk* (1903). Du Bois sought to articulate how being black in America brings about an internal cracking open of the self, a split that ironically renders it impossible to separate questions of subjectivity (one's internal sense of being in relation to the rest the of world) from those of identity (externally imposed and systematically enforced categories of difference). Whether intentional or not, Peele's film about a young black man who goes on a weekend trip with his white girlfriend to meet her family owes as much of a debt to the wellspring of Du Bois's imagination as to the "social thrillers" such as *Rosemary's Baby* (1968) or *The Stepford Wives* (1975) that Peele has name-checked as central influences on his work.[2]

The visualization of "the sunken place" in particular shares an intellectual and conceptual kinship with Du Bois's hypothesis. Having said that, black expressive culture's capacity to adapt established forms for current purposes demands that Peele's construct also complicate and expand upon those ideas. So whereas Du Bois conceives double consciousness primarily as a byproduct of inhabiting a black (male) body with conflicting aspirations, the sunken place signifies more precisely: it literalizes the paralysis that accompanies being forced to occupy a splintered sense of self as a principle condition of life. For Chris, the sunken place also serves as the manifestation of his personal trauma and the guilt he harbors about remaining passive when confronting his mother's death. This internal discord is what makes him susceptible to hypnosis in the first place and what later compels him to *sink*. Still, the paralysis acts as more than an end unto itself, prefiguring the even more horrific "Coagula" brain transplantation procedure that threatens to completely subsume Chris and make him a permanent captive within a body he no longer controls.

Get Out therefore repositions double consciousness as more than just another burden of lived blackness and interprets it as a tool of white supremacy through which white desire for black flesh can be enacted. In the discussion that follows, I examine *Get Out* with Du Bois in mind and consider how his theory can be utilized as part of what Thomas C. Holt describes as Du Bois's "legacy of intellectual tools, a language with which [Americans] might analyze their present and imagine a future."[3] Ultimately, the film draws on Du Bois by positing that the systematic rupture of black consciousness is combined with strategic acts of blinding in order to hold the souls of black folks in captivity.

2. "Jordan Peele."

3. Holt, "Du Bois."

Despite the familiarity of Du Bois's formulation of double consciousness, the eloquence and precision of his language make it challenging to discuss without quoting him at some length:

> The Negro is a sort of seventh son, born with a veil, and gifted with second-sight in this American world,—a world which yields him no true self-consciousness, but only lets him see himself through the revelation of the other world. It is a peculiar sensation, this double-consciousness, this sense of always looking at one's self through the eyes of others, of measuring one's soul by the tape of a world that looks on in amused contempt and pity. One ever feels his twoness,—an American, a Negro; two souls, two thoughts, two unreconciled strivings; two warring ideals in one dark body, whose dogged strength alone keeps it from being torn asunder.[4]

Du Bois's insight into the fabric and constitution of black subjectivity has rightly garnered extensive analysis, but what seems most striking about it in connection to *Get Out* is his emphasis on the unique gift of visual perception or "second sight."[5] We might even go as far as to suggest that the very notion of double consciousness itself rests upon the visual metaphor that Du Bois employs. He imagines the act of looking (and of being seen by others) as inextricably tied to this intensified, friction-filled mode of hyper self-awareness. Putting aside what might prove to be valuable questions about whether Du Bois conceptualizes cognition in ableist terms, the importance he lends to optics seems especially applicable to *Get Out* as a visual text and also because Chris's character is a practicing photographer. As we later learn, his special visual sensibility, even more than his dark-skinned body, marks him as a desirable candidate for the Coagula procedure. The blind art dealer, Jim Hudson, even confesses that what he wants most from Chris is his "eye . . . those things [he] sees through." Hidden then within the almost surreal science fiction premise about brain transplantation lies a more evocative statement about how it is possible to dehumanize black folks while still yearning, deeply, for the perceived extraordinary, even *magical* qualities associated with black corporeality.

---

4. Du Bois, "Our Spiritual Strivings."

5. Elaborations on Du Bois's double consciousness are too numerous to recount here, but some include: Allen, "Ever Feeling"; Dickson, "W. E. B. Du Bois"; Gilroy, *Black Atlantic;* Holt, "Political Uses"; Itzigsohn and Brown, "Sociology"; Lyubansky and Eidelson, "Revisiting Du Bois"; Martinez, "Double Consciousness"; Moore, "Fanonian Perspective"; and Ross, "Race."

Central to *Get Out*'s revision of Du Bois is the way it complicates the psychic architecture of double consciousness. The whites who manipulate Chris look at him and the other black captives not merely with "contempt and pity" but also with a perverse sense of want and admiration. Zadie Smith calls this phenomenon the "obscene love" of oppression in which disgust and passion become intertwined.[6] In Peele's paradigm, then, double consciousness becomes the product of conflicted aspirations on behalf of both the black person experiencing it and the ambivalent white gaze that incites it. Delineating how both of these polarities inform white fantasies about black embodiment grants us a more nuanced understanding of why and how it is that the problem of the twenty-first century continues to be "the problem of the color line."[7] The psychological dynamic that the film highlights, in short, indicates that the demonization of blackness alone cannot explain how many of the same forms of oppression that Du Bois recognized so long ago persist. We must also account for how the projection of hatred toward blackness has always been comingled with lust, fascination, envy, and other unstable patterns of desire.

Get Out's investment in questions about sight, desire, and consciousness evidences itself from the opening scene in which Andre mentions feeling "like a sore thumb" as the camera tracks him through the labyrinthine suburb. Peele utilizes multiple violations of the 180-degree rule in order to emphasize the heightened sense of specularity to which Andre feels subjected. Notably, when Andre nods his head to Jeremy, who remains visually obscured in his white Porsche, Jeremy withholds any form of acknowledgement. By veiling himself in this way, Jeremy ironically unsettles the anticipated visual transaction that double consciousness presupposes. Andre is left without a meaningful gauge by which to determine how he is being viewed "through the eyes of others" and, consequently, which self he is being called upon to perform. Thus, Andre attempts to flee, yes from the mysterious yet obvious danger of the car, but potentially from a more existential dread triggered by Jeremy's unspecified yet overdetermined gaze. Disoriented by Jeremy's play with double consciousness and its dependence on the exchange of visible signs, Andre fails to maintain a line of sight with the threat, resulting in his capture. Peele's opening sequence provides a harrowing occurrence of how it feels to inhabit double consciousness but, at the same time, shows that the distorted expectations it fosters can be further (mis)directed to serve a desiring whiteness.

6. Smith, "Getting In."

7. Du Bois, "Our Spiritual Strivings."

Du Bois's notion of always measuring oneself through others' eyes permeates the other two introductory scenes as well. Peele's visual and sonic iconography implies that Chris is subject to the ambivalent white gaze *and* to the judgment of his ancestors. First, the credit sequence situates the viewer looking out of the window of an unseen moving vehicle as it travels through a heavily wooded area. This symbolic journey into the wilderness functions as a reverse Great Migration back to the kinds of rural Southern enclaves that millions of black folks abandoned in order to escape white terrorism and potentially secure greater access to opportunity in the urban North.[8] A quick cut follows, cueing a montage of Chris's black and white photographs along with the Childish Gambino song "Redbone." The pictures adorn the walls of Chris's apartment establishing his visual acumen while the song lyrics underscore the need to maintain heightened vigilance:

> But stay woke
> niggas creeepin'
> they gon' find you
> gon' catch you sleepin'
> Now stay woke
> niggas creepin'
> Now don't you close your eyes.[9]

While the song seems to focus on safeguarding a romantic relationship from infidelity, its emphasis on consciousness harkens right back to Du Bois. Coupled with the Swahili chant that plays during the credits, "Sikiliza Kwa Wahenga" (roughly translated as "listen to your ancestors"),[10] these auditory messages serve as a kind of psychic warning to Chris, connecting him to the lineage of black diasporic movement and reminding him that he remains under the watchful eye of black folks who came before.

Our visual introduction to Chris conjures up more Du Boisian ideas about the kind of dual surveillance—both internal and external—that so often polices the black body. We meet Chris for the first time as he stands

---

8. As Carol J. Clover and more recently Bernice Murphy have observed, the movement from city to country in horror narratives routinely does the work of making legible latent class, gender, and racial conflicts. See Clover, *Men, Women*, 114–65, and Murphy, *Rural Gothic*. One could argue that this reliance on the city vs. country axis somewhat undermines the film's critique of liberal white racism by still allowing viewers to see the Armitages as "country." See Murphy's chapter in this collection on *Get Out* and rural gothic.

9. Childish Gambino, "Redbone."

10. Moore, "Hidden Swahili Message."

in front of a mirror preparing to shave. What better way to look at oneself through the eyes of others than through a reflection? Introducing Chris in this way immediately distinguishes him as a character for whom questions of subjectivity and identity are instrumental. As Chris proceeds to apply white shaving cream that sits in stark contrast to his dark skin, it is hard not to draw parallels to the blackface minstrel mask. Here, however, the sanitizing, artificial whiteness of the shaving cream replaces the mocking, grotesque blackness of burnt cork. Chris seems less interested in performing stereotypes of blackness than in creating an image of nonthreatening respectability for Rose's family. But this visual substitution nevertheless begs the question of just how much these masquerades truly differ from one another and to what extent the desire for white acceptance dictates black masculine grooming and other practices of self-presentation more generally.

Chris's concern about his self-presentation becomes even more loaded given that we also see Rose for the first time during this opening sequence; she gleefully inspects the merchandise inside a bakery case in much the same way that the potential buyers at the Armitages' garden party-cum-slave auction will later inspect Chris. Crosscutting between Chris's introspective look and Rose's more sinister, investigatory gaze evidences that he is unwittingly preening himself to become a prize buck. That he cuts himself just as the song's chorus crescendos feels like a heavy-handed but appropriate foreshadowing of the hazards awaiting him should he lose himself, as Du Bois might say, "behind the veil." Just as importantly, the sequence ends with Chris looking at pictures on his camera, which reinforces his idiosyncratic ocular gifts—gifts he will need if he is to survive the tests that lie ahead of him later in the film. Chris can *see* in ways that others cannot, and yet clarity of vision alone is not the only challenge standing between him and what Du Bois calls "self-conscious manhood."[11] He must also overcome a deeper psychospiritual paralysis that stems from personal trauma, and, to do that, he must first go to the sunken place.

In addition to his theory of double consciousness, Du Bois also speaks to the paralyzing effects of prolonged stasis within a soul "torn asunder," and he goes on to catalog a range of crippling emotions that leave the psyche of what he calls "the black artisan" at war with itself:

> Here in America, in the few days since Emancipation, the black man's turning hither and thither in hesitant and doubtful striving has often made his very strength to lose effectiveness, to seem like absence of power, like

11. Du Bois, "Our Spiritual Strivings."

> weakness. And yet it is not weakness,—it is the contradiction of double aims. . . . This waste of double aims, this seeking to satisfy two unreconciled ideals, has wrought sad havoc with the courage and faith and deeds of ten thousand thousand people . . . and at times has even seemed about to make them ashamed of themselves.[12]

Du Bois's historicizing of the phenomenon of double consciousness is imperative in that it prioritizes the forms of mental and spiritual captivity that characterized the post-emancipation period through the nadir and beyond.[13] These were/are the forms of mental and spiritual terrorism that superseded physical bondage and that Chris has, to at least some degree, inherited. As a photographer, Chris also fits into the category of black artisan and exhibits many of the qualities that Du Bois describes. He is of course hesitant and doubtful in pursuit of double aims, specifically his desire to preserve the integrity of his blackness while at the same time hoping to gain the acceptance of Rose's family. And although Chris reveals his inner strength later during his ingenious escape, he demonstrates what appears like weakness in his first trip to the sunken place. Most significantly, he carries a profound sense of shame for not doing more to help his mother before she died. It is this shame that has made him passive throughout his life and that produces such anxiety for both him and the audience when the depths of the sunken place are revealed.

Peele stages Missy's possession of Chris as an exercise in how these DuBoisian terms—doubt and hesitation, seeming mental weakness, wasted energy, and shame—can be capitalized on by white desire. Missy first seizes upon Chris's fear of rejection by questioning his smoking habit and its potentially harmful effects on Rose; it is a bit of clever handling that further destabilizes Chris's equilibrium in the aftermath of Walter's bizarre charge at him in the backyard and Georgina's strange staring at her reflection in her bedroom window. Missy then uses the visual and aural focal point of a spoon scraping against a teacup to coerce Chris into revealing his deepest humiliation: that he sat watching television while his mother lay dying from a hit-and-run accident. The flashback to young Chris does not offer enough detail for us to discern whether his relationship with American popular culture, in this case television, has itself helped to facilitate an earlier break in his consciousness: we see only static on the screen. His inability to act in this crucial moment has nonetheless caused its own severe split in his mind.

12. Ibid.

13. My thinking here is indebted to Hartman, *Scenes of Subjection.*

Missy exploits this earlier trauma and assumes control over his gaze, forcing him to picture that which he has tried hardest to repress. This becomes readily apparent when, at one point during the hypnosis, Chris attempts to look away only to have Missy insist that he "look at [her]." From here, taking control seems just a matter of affirming his guilt-fueled paralysis:

> MISSY: You're so scared . . . you think it was your fault. How do you feel now?
> CHRIS: I can't move.
> MISSY: You can't move.
> CHRIS: Why can't I move?
> MISSY: You're paralyzed. Just like that day when you did nothing, you did nothing.

With all of Chris's primary defenses sufficiently immobilized and the rift in his consciousness fully exposed, Missy commands him to the sunken place.

Peele presents the sunken place as a formless void of black space where Chris floats in suspended animation. Missy's hypnosis has rendered him completely powerless, and, while staging such encounters with one's unmaking is one of the horror film's primary tropes, it takes on another more potent dimension when read in conjunction with Du Bois and through the film's own racialized terms. The sense of twoness that Du Bois ascribes to double consciousness and to which Peele gestures in the opening mirror sequence is elevated here through Peele's meticulously constructed *mise-en-scène.* Specifically, the use of long shots emphasizes the vastness of the abject, black space as well as the distance and isolation Chris feels within it, thus bolstering the salient point that the violent dissolution of black consciousness is a fundamentally traumatic, alienating, and isolating experience. These long shots work in a tight syntactic relationship with those taken from Chris's point of view, which makes it appear as though he is watching Missy on a small television from within the sunken place. Peele's strategic framing stresses Chris's physical distance from the screen and consequently how he has been, in the most horrific possible sense, separated from his own personhood. Du Bois himself could likely not have conceived of such a dynamic visual depiction of double consciousness. Moreover, this imagery points toward the deeper ideological and political ends of double consciousness, which has arguably always been the stripping of agency and volition, along with the advance of conquest through division.

Peele's visual rendering of double-consciousness does, though, shift Du Bois's ideas in some important ways. Instead of having Chris see himself through the eyes of others, the sunken place forces Chris to become his own *other* who looks outward from within the cage of his body. The result is a dialectical, identificatory relationship between Chris and the audience in which we all become passive spectators with no choice but to let the horror before us unfold as it is. While Du Bois described the peculiar sensation of double consciousness with considerable exactitude, Peele uses the film medium's unique capacity to have us take up Chris's point of view and experience this exaggerated form of subjection for ourselves. We witness Chris's terrified, panic-stricken expression, what Du Bois refers to as the "sad havoc" wrought by powerlessness, and we scream along with him in desperate yet ineffectual resistance as Missy shuts his eyes. The most frightening aspect of Chris's sunken place—Peele has suggested it would be different for each victim[14]—is therefore that he remains just conscious enough to see, hear, and feel, but is not "woke" enough to act. In this sense, the sunken place symbolizes the crippling immobility that stems from living with a divided sense of self as well as the psychological devastation that is the deeper legacy of chattel slavery, which was not simply a captivity of the body but also of the mind and soul.

Chris is not the only black character trapped in the sunken place, however, and the other moments in which we see those characters attempt to break free can also be elucidated by Du Bois's thinking. The "peculiar sensation" that Du Bois associates with double consciousness for example, accurately categorizes Chris's interactions with the film's other black captives. Their strange, affected posture, their anachronistic and stilted speech (which lacks any familiar qualities of African American Vernacular English), and their pained facial expressions all hint that Chris is talking with people who are not being and *cannot be* their true selves. This is especially true when Chris meets Walter for the first time. Realizing that he may have alienated the black *help* by not introducing himself, Chris reaches out to Walter for a face-to-face greeting. Walter provides no sense of a shared racial past or kinship, greeting him with an unnerving, almost clown-like smile and a disturbing description of Rose that makes her sound like a prize farm animal: "one of a kind, top of the line, a real doggone keeper." Everything about Walter's demeanor rings false, prompting a feeling of uncanny peculiarity for Chris as well as for the audience; we know that something is wrong with Walter, but the precise source of our unease remains elusive. Surely part of this feeling emanates from his stereotypically white dialect and his cryptic statement about "[minding his] own business," but Walter also gives off the

14. *Get Out.* See "Feature Commentary."

unmistakable impression that something more malicious lurks just beneath his well-mannered exterior, that he wears "the mask that grins and lies."[15] We later learn that his outward persona is in fact a lie and that patriarch Roman Armitage, the architect of the Coagula procedure who never recovered from his loss to Jesse Owens at the 1936 Berlin Olympics, has taken possession of Walter. Much of what makes this moment of the film so compelling then is that Peele ironically sets up a charged interaction between two black men in order to uncloak white fears that underneath the bearing of polite acquiescence lies black rage.

Chris's introduction to Walter also plays on Du Bois's veiling metaphor by revealing black fears about complete assimilation into white culture—of being so thoroughly immersed in the performative masquerade that one gets lost within it. The strangeness and tension of their dialogue relies upon Chris's having come into contact with another black man who appears to have been totally interpellated by his mask—or, as Du Bois would have it, someone with "no true self-consciousness." Walter, and later Logan (Andre), both offer Chris glimpses of the effects that Du Bois observed—men whose courage, faith, and deeds seem to have been forever robbed of their vitality. The pain and rage of being held hostage within his own body helps to explain Walter's decision to kill himself even after Chris frees him from the sunken place: Walter cannot seem to imagine freedom after having been held captive for so long and he can never be entirely himself again. At best, he would spend a lifetime struggling for control over his own body with Roman still trapped inside. Peele's treatment of Walter does a kind of *unveiling*, laying bare the long-term perils of a life spent within a fragmented consciousness.

Chris's interactions with Georgina are similarly punctuated by moments when her true self threatens to peek out from behind or perhaps more accurately from *beneath* the veil. One cannot walk away from the film or from Betty Gabriel's handling of the character without understanding the splitting of black consciousness as an act of subordination. The first of these scenes occurs when Chris joins Rose and her parents for iced tea. As Georgina pours tea into Chris's glass, she begins staring off into the distance with a disoriented and forlorn expression, which prompts her to spill some of it. Missy directs Georgina to "go lie down and rest," an instruction which suggests that a Georgina who is too *woke* threatens their elaborate illusion. Although the disruption only lasts for a brief moment, it divulges, as Brittany Willis has observed, that Georgina actively struggles to manumit her-

15. Dunbar, "We Wear the Mask."

self from the sunken place and, unlike Andre or Walter, she does not require the external trigger of the camera flash to do it. In her critical look at black women characters in the film, Willis argues that the resistance Georgina displays makes her character's presence a central rather than peripheral part of the story.[16] I would add that Georgina's role, and indeed the power and intricacy in Gabriel's performance, counters Du Bois's use of gendered pronouns when defining double consciousness. Even if Du Bois's language is more the product of grammatical consistency and the historical context in which he wrote than outright sexism, *Get Out* envisions double consciousness as a burden shared by black women in equal measure to men and perhaps even more so.

No moment of the film better illustrates Georgina's internal battle to free herself from the sunken place and reconcile her fractured self than her exchange with Chris during the garden party. Seeking a respite from the leering gaze of the white guests, Chris finds himself suddenly confronted by Georgina. As with Walter, nearly everything about Georgina's behavior feels somehow *wrong*. When Chris confides that he "gets nervous" around too many white people, Gabriel offers what is perhaps the film's most singularly iconic acting moment. In less than a minute, Georgina transitions from a look of intense but subdued anguish to a muffled cry and finally to a fraudulent smile paired with an ominous laugh, before she offers a troubling affirmation of how the Armitages treat her "like family." Here, Peele relies almost entirely on close-ups of Gabriel's face to convey the emotional torment of her break in subjectivity. By contrast, Chris's trip to the sunken place requires a carefully orchestrated series of twenty shots from different angles, only five of which are repeated. Gabriel's stunning work in this scene does much to transcend the limitations of Du Bois's masculine language and opens up space to consider how the "seventh daughter's" experience of duality differs from men's in ways that deserve closer attention. Georgina remains steadfast in her fight to liberate herself, and, despite the severity of the hold placed upon her, she still endeavors to give voice to her condition and tries to warn Chris. Unfortunately, he quickly dismisses her outburst, a gesture symptomatic of how black women's pleas for recognition so frequently go unheard even by black men.

Chris's introduction to Logan shares the same curious tonality as his encounters with Walter and Georgina, but, in other ways, adds a unique sexual component to Du Bois's image of the veil. Chris first spots Logan through his camera lens and is initially comforted by the sight of another

16. Willis, "Most Overlooked."

black face. Chris only briefly speaks one-on-one with Logan before his wife, a much older white woman interrupts them. Based on Chris's failed attempt at a fist bump and the way Logan is hurried away to parade for another white couple at the party, we can only assume that Logan has colonized Andre's body and hijacked his consciousness for the shared pleasure of himself and his wife. In addition to the already apparent horror of the sunken place, this revelation also makes Andre a rape victim, likely forced to undergo ongoing assaults every time the couple copulates. Andre's case differentiates itself from the others in that his immobilization while trapped behind the veil offers another sexual brand of painful subjection, albeit one still bound to the same fetishistic white desire. In this light, Rod's seemingly ridiculous conspiracy theory about the white demand for black sex slaves actually proves an accurate recognition of another way in which the paralysis prompted by double consciousness can be exploited.

Andre's temporary break from the sunken place shares more in common with Walter and Georgina's than it departs from them. It is, however, both more sudden and more violent, and because Chris himself initiates it, he cannot dismiss it as easily. After Chris passes off a party guest's absurd question about the "African American experience" to Logan, Chris attempts to take his picture and forgets to turn off the flash. (He thinks he recognizes him and plans to collect evidence.) Not unlike Georgina, Logan's face is suddenly overwhelmed with dread and his nose begins to bleed. He then charges at Chris, delivering the film's title and tagline: "Get Out!" Three aspects of this paroxysm stand out. First, Andre's response comes across as more visceral than Georgina's precisely because it is brought about externally rather than as a product of his own internal opposition. Second, his attempt to warn Chris transmits an extra level of urgency and resentment, perhaps because, while he was taken suddenly and had little chance to resist, Chris is granted multiple opportunities beforehand to recognize the jeopardy and still remains ignorant to the risks he faced. Finally, Andre's short escape from the sunken place reinforces the idea that extensive time spent in a separated state of consciousness may make it difficult to even find one's way toward reunification. Once released, he makes no pleas to save himself; he only implores Chris to escape while he still can.

Because we meet Walter, Georgina, and Logan after the Coagula procedure has already been completed, they in some ways provide even better examples of Du Bois's "two warring ideals in one dark body" than Chris does. With these characters, too, Peele literalizes Du Bois's more figurative construct and also points toward the need for more coherent, unified modes of black consciousness in the future. It seems probable that these characters suffered personal traumas that, as with Chris, made them more primed for attack and therefore for captivity. Peele's film proposes that the best defense against white supremacy is for black folks to heal the individual and collective wounds that have gone unacknowledged and untreated for too long. And while many of those wounds are themselves marks of white supremacy that have been seared onto the flesh and onto the soul, others are self-inflicted and could prove even more traumatic for all of their intimacy. Some manner of fractured consciousness may be impossible to avoid under the sway of neoliberal capitalism, but our journey out of the sunken places in our own lives will inevitably demand our willingness to pursue a richer, more authentic reckoning with the trauma that has been wrought by such systems. Du Bois could likely not have known how important the need for us to reconcile our strivings would still be more than a century after writing *The Souls of Black Folk,* but the task remains as important as any we face in the times ahead.

Bibliography

Allen, Ernest J. "Ever Feeling One's Twoness: 'Double Ideals' and 'Double Consciousness' in *The Souls of Black Folk.*" *Critique of Anthropology* 12, no. 3 (1992): 261–27.

Alston, Joshua. "First to Die: Evil Dead and Blackness in Horror." *Feminist Wire,* April 13, 2013. http://thefeministwire.com/2013/04/first-to-die-evil-dead-and-blackness-in-horror/.

Brooks, Kinitra D. *Searching for Sycorax: Black Women's Hauntings of Contemporary Horror.* New Brunswick, NJ: Rutgers University Press, 2017.

Childish Gambino. "Redbone." Donald Glover and Ludwig Göranson. Recorded November 2016. Track 6 on *Awaken My Love.* Glassnote. Compact disc.

Clover, Carol J. *Men, Women, and Chain Saws: Gender in the Modern Horror Film.* Princeton, NJ: Princeton University Press, 2015. First published 1992.

Dickson, Bruce. "W. E. B. Du Bois and the Idea of Double Consciousness." *American Literature* 64, no. 2 (1992): 299–309.

Du Bois, W. E. B. "Of Our Spiritual Strivings." In *The Souls of Black Folk.* Project Gutenberg, January 29, 2008. https://www.gutenberg.org/files/408/408-h/408-h.htm. First published 1903.

Dunbar, Paul Lawrence. "We Wear the Mask." In *The Complete Poems of Paul Lawrence Dunbar.* Project Gutenberg, May 7, 2006. https://www.gutenberg.org/files/18338/18338-h/18338-h.htm#Page_71. First published 1922.

Gaines, Mikal J. "The Black Gothic Imagination: Horror, Subjectivity, and Spectatorship from the Civil Rights Era to the New Millennium." Doctoral dissertation, College of William and Mary, 2015.

———. "Strange Enjoyments: The Marketing and Reception of Horror in the Civil-Rights Era Black Press." In *Merchants of Menace: The Business of Horror Cinema,* edited by Richard Nowell, 187–201. New York: Bloomsbury, 2014.

Get Out. Directed by Jordan Peele. USA: Universal Pictures, 2017. DVD.

Gilroy, Paul. *The Black Atlantic: Modernity and Double Consciousness*. Cambridge, MA: Harvard University Press, 1993.

Hartman, Saidiya. *Scenes of Subjection: Terror, Slavery, and Self-Making in Nineteenth Century America*. New York: Oxford University Press, 1997.

Holt, Thomas C. "Du Bois, W. E. B." *American National Biography*, February 2000. https://doi.org/10.1093/anb/9780198606697.article.1500191.

———. "The Political Uses of Alienation: W. E. B. Du Bois on Politics, Race, and Culture, 1903–1940." *American Quarterly* 42, no. 2 (1990): 301–23.

Itzigsohn, José, and Karida Brown. "Sociology and the Theory of Double Consciousness: W. E. B. Du Bois' Phenomenology of Racialized Subjectivity." *Du Bois Review: Social Science Research on Race* 12, no. 2 (2015): 231–48.

"Jordan Peele Get Out Keynote: 2017 Independent Film Forum." YouTube Video, 53:53. Posted by Film Independent, October 23, 1017. https://www.youtube.com/watch?v=YnpDiuE8HJU.

Lyubansky, Mikhail, and Roy J. Eidelson. "Revisiting Du Bois: The Relationship between African American Double Consciousness and Beliefs about Racial and National Group Experiences." *Journal of Black Psychology* 31, no. 1 (2005): 3–26.

Martinez, Theresa A. "The Double Consciousness of Du Bois and the Mestiza Consciousness of Anzaldúa." *Race, Gender, and Class in Psychology: A Critical Approach* 9, no. 4 (2002): 158–76.

Means Coleman, Robin R. *Horror Noire: Blacks in American Horror Films from the 1890s to the Present*. New York: Routledge, 2011.

Moore, Charles Pulliam. "The Hidden Swahili Message in 'Get Out' the Country Needs to Hear." *Splinter*, March 1, 2017. https://splinternews.com/the-hidden-swahili-message-in-get-out-the-country-needs-1793858917.

Moore, T. Owens. "A Fanonian Perspective on Double Consciousness." *Journal of Black Studies* 35, no. 6 (2005): 751–62.

Murphy, Bernice. *The Rural Gothic in American Popular Culture: Backwoods Horror and Terror in the Wilderness*. New York: Palgrave Macmillan, 2013.

Ross, Anne Warfield. "'Race' as an Interaction Order Phenomenon: W. E. B. Du Bois's Double Consciousness Thesis Revisited." *Sociological Theory* 18, no. 2 (2000): 241–74.

Smith, Zadie. "Getting In and Out: Who Owns Black Pain?" *Harper's*, July 2017. https://harpers.org/archive/2017/07/getting-in-and-out/.

Willis, Brittany. "The Most Overlooked and Underrated Characters in *Get Out* are Black Women." *Medium*, March 7, 2017. https://www.huffingtonpost.com/entry/the-most-overlooked-underrated-characters-in-get_us_58c3049de4b0a797c1d39c5.

CHAPTER 12

HOLDING ONTO HULK HOGAN

Contending with the Rape of the Black Male Psyche

ROBERT LARUE

THE TITLE of this chapter invokes the testimony given by Darren Wilson, a white Ferguson, Missouri, police officer, during his hearing for the shooting of black teenager, Michael Brown. Searching for the language that would most effectively allow him to characterize his perceived sense of self in relation to Brown's physical presence, Wilson analogizes himself to a helpless, if not hapless, opponent of the almost mythological figure of Hulk Hogan. Or, as Wilson describes the encounter, "When I grabbed him, the only way I can describe it is I felt like a five-year-old holding onto Hulk Hogan."[1] Wilson's decision to recast the black body of Brown as the white Hogan is no accident. Furthermore, the employment of this recasting during a hearing that was just as much about racial bias as it was the (mis)use of force is no insignificant matter. The analogy replaces the awe a child is expected to feel from meeting the comically exaggerated Hogan with the fright Wilson claims he felt in Brown's presence. Yet, this replacement never quite relinquishes either the fantasy of the contrast or the severity of the difference between the analogy's two figures. Hogan, a fictional persona created for the purposes of entertaining, and whose performance is intentionally exaggerated so as to incite both visceral and affective responses from his audience, could not be

1. *State of Missouri*, 212.

further from the reality of Brown's physical presence. Yet, Hogan's persona could not be closer to the truth of how Brown's physical presence was read in the context of a southern town that remains deeply entrenched in Jim Crow policies and opinions.

While much remains to be teased out of Wilson's statement, two points are most immediately relevant: First, Wilson's recoding of Brown's black body as the white body of Hogan points to a certain fluid fictitiousness of race in the white imagination, despite the harmful material consequences race brings to bear on certain racially marked bodies. Wilson's analogy makes visible how race always retains a certain malleability in its application, so that it becomes able to expand and contract as needed in order to perform various tasks. Or to put this differently, Wilson's analogy demonstrates that race is in excess of the body—even as it leads to physical consequences for the body. While an immediate reading of the analogy might suggest that Wilson was trying to divest himself of any racist leanings, I suggest that his recoding also effectively signals not only his conceptualization of Brown as he approached the teenager, but also, and perhaps most significantly, the very mechanisms by which acts of racialization come to be carried out. In order to make the body of Brown into something comprehensible, Wilson offers an image that effectively proves he never saw Brown to begin with, that he saw only a silhouette, into which he cast his own narrative. Second, in repositioning himself as the smaller, helpless opponent against the mountainous figure of Hogan, Wilson frames himself as the child figure forced to confront the untamable. By using the figure of the child, Wilson performs two tasks simultaneously: he appropriates for himself the child's innocence, offering himself as someone in need of saving, as well as casting Brown as a more-than-child, more-than-(hu)man figure; after all, it is only in Brown's presence that Wilson is made to "feel like a five-year-old."

I begin with this brief reading of Wilson's statement because it is part of a long history of misrepresenting the developmental stages of the black male in America. Not only do black men have a history of being referred to as "boy," but black boys are consistently being depicted as "men," as demonstrated by media representations of black youth such as Brown, Trayvon Martin, and Tamir Rice. While there has been much public outcry about the connections of these misrepresentations to the continued destruction of black bodies, little has been said of the psychological effects of this collapsing of developmental stages. Through an analysis of the infamous "tea cup" scene in Jordan Peele's recent film, *Get Out*, this chapter explores how the scene permits Peele to offer an extremely compelling visual representation of the psychological—and by extension, social and material—injury visited upon black males' sense of identity when they are constantly (mis-)interpellated as men/boys. By dramatizing the impact of a cultural discourse that continuously collapses the gap between black boyhood and black manhood, Peele's "tea cup" scene offers a useful means for visualizing the psychological damage such discourse inflicts on the black male sense of self.

Reframing the Tea Cup Scene

Reentering the house after a late-night smoke, Chris is surprised by Rose's mother, Missy, who is sitting in her dark office as he passes. She beckons him in, and Chris enters her office and sits on the couch, at which point Missy picks up a cup of tea sitting next to her. While she stirs it, Missy suggests that Chris seems interested in finding out how her hypnotism works, a suggestion that belies the fact that her process of hypnotizing him has already begun. With each statement, Missy probes Chris's mind with subliminal demands masquerading as questions. Beginning by interrogating him about his supposed interest in hypnotism, Missy pushes further by asking about his smoking habits before finally wedging her way into Chris's memories of the night his mother passed away.

> MISSY: Do you smoke in front of my daughter?
> CHRIS: I'm gonna quit, I promise.
> MISSY: That's my kid. That is my kid. Do you understand? What about your mother?
> CHRIS: What about her? Are we . . .
> MISSY: Where were you when she died?
> CHRIS: I don't wanna think about that . . . Home. Watching TV.
> MISSY: Do you hear the TV? What do you hear?
> CHRIS: Rain.
> MISSY: Rain. It was raining. Mmm. You hear the rain?
> CHRIS: Mm hmm.
> MISSY: You hear it? Find it. Tell me when you've found it.[2]

Underwriting each question is the clinking that results from Missy's stirring of her tea. This stirring is both soft, sensual, and yet terrifically insidious as it speaks beneath, around, and in between the pauses of Missy's statements. Chris attempts to resist each probing question until the clinking of Missy's

2. *Get Out.* All further references to the film are to this DVD.

spoon against her tea cup subconsciously overcomes his defenses. It is not long before Missy is able to move from Chris's smoking habits to his memories of sitting impotently while his mother died. The closer she pushes him toward rediscovering the child he "d[oesn't] wanna think about," the closer she pushes him toward the pain he has kept locked away, and the closer she brings him to tears and a sense of helplessness.

Although Missy refers to the process of hypnotism as ushering in a state of "heightened suggestibility," this description is misleading. Instead, Missy's hypnotism might be better understood as a variation of Wilson's analogy of Michael Brown to Hulk Hogan, since—as with Wilson's recasting of Brown—Missy's hypnotism replaces the reality of Chris's experience with his experience as *she* imagines it. Where Wilson's analogy displaces Brown's black body with the white body of Hulk Hogan, Missy's hypnotism displaces the assemblage that is Chris's self—developed as he has matured from the little boy sitting in front of the television screen to the man he is now—with the sense of self that most accurately reflects *her* conception of him. The self that Missy sees and endeavors to insert between Chris's consciousness and body is one predicated upon feelings of hopelessness and powerlessness. These characteristics do not reflect the Chris that first enters Missy's office after smoking his final cigarette. The Chris that enters the house, the film shows, is an individual who has found a way to "let [his] soul speak" through his photography and thus, as bell hooks suggests, "resist [the] dehumanization" that awaits the black man who is unable to heal from the emotional, social, historical, and interpersonal wounds inflicted upon him.[3]

As she forces her way into his memory and history, working to trap the adult Chris in his childhood trauma, not only does Missy dirty Chris's memories of himself and his mother's death, but she also enacts a form of molestation of both the grown man and the boy via this coerced act of re-membering. By claiming this as an act of re-membering, not only do I seek to foreground the entanglement of the act of recalling the past and the process of dis- and reassembling that past, but I also seek to call forth the notion of "rememory" as explored in Toni Morrison's novel, *Beloved* (1987). According to Caroline Rody, the use of the term "rememory" highlights "the problematics of the mind in time."[4] To put this in different terms, rememory blurs the lines between the past and present (and future) so that the past is carried not as memory but as reality. As the novel's protagonist, Sethe, explains, "If a house burns down, it's gone, but the place—the picture of it stays, and not

3. hooks, *We Real Cool*, 154–55.

4. Rody, "Toni Morrison's *Beloved*,"

just in my rememory, but out there, in the world. . . . The picture is still there and what's more, if you go there—you who never was there—if you go there and stand in the place where it was, it will happen again; it will be here for you, waiting for you."[5] In coercing Chris into a state of rememory, however, Missy corrupts the continuum envisioned in *Beloved.* In this way, Missy's molestation mirrors the molestation of black minds, memories, and psyches throughout this nation's history. The difference in this instance, however, is that we are asked to watch, to imagine this process as it unfolds. In imagining how this psycho-molestation disrupts both Chris's individual identity *and* his ability to function within his body and social environment, Peele returns to the present those who would seek to relegate the psychological warfare against black males to a distant past.

In that it calls him into a being apart from his own self-fashioning, Missy's molestation of Chris's psyche dramatizes a moment of interpellation that is similar to the moment of ontological denial described by Frantz Fanon.[6] Upon having been interpellated beyond his own self-identifications by a child, among other instances, Fanon declares that

> in the white world the man of color encounters difficulties in the development of his bodily schema. Consciousness of the body is solely a negating activity. It is a third-person consciousness. The body is surrounded by an atmosphere of certain uncertainty. I know that if I want to smoke, I shall have to reach out my right arm and take the pack of cigarettes lying at the other end of the table. The matches, however, are in the drawer on the left, and I shall have to lean back slightly. And all these movements are made not out of habit but out of implicit knowledge. A slow composition of my *self* as a body in the middle of a spatial and temporal world—such seems to be the schema. It does not impose itself on me; it is, rather, a definitive structuring of the self and of the world—definitive because it creates a real dialectic between my body and the world.[7]

Prior to having been interpellated as a Negro, Fanon imagined himself as inhabiting multiple categories. As he states, he "came into the world imbued with the will to find meaning in things."[8] Then he found himself to be a singular object: a black Negro. The moment of interpellation ignores the multiplicity of the black body and its various identities, despite Fanon's insistence

5. Morrison, *Beloved,* 36.
6. Fanon, *Black Skin,* 109.
7. Ibid., 110–11; emphasis in original.
8. Fanon, *Black Skin,* 109.

that the body of the black man is not only a physical presence but also a physicality fully entangled with its consciousness and experiences in the world. The black man's body, in other words, is more than a composite of organic material; it is an infinitely complex assemblage of organic, inorganic, linguistic, *and* psychological material that necessitates any one of them in order to activate and make active the others.

What is also important to note is that the moment of this disruption is inaugurated by a child. In a reversal of Wilson's invocation of Hulk Hogan as a way of heightening his own childish innocence, the child who interpellates Fanon as Negro repositions sites of power so that he and Fanon are on relatively similar levels. As the child draws Fanon from himself, the power between the two becomes equalized. Or, perhaps more precisely, in interpellating Fanon as "a Negro," the child demonstrates the ease with which he is able to displace the real experience(s) of Fanon's body through the substitution of an ideology of that body—an ideology constructed from understandings of the Negro as monstrous and nightmarish. While Fanon responds, seemingly anticipating Louis Althusser's claim that "ideology 'acts' or 'functions' in such a way that it 'recruits' subjects among . . . individuals," his response is not voluntary, but visceral.[9] Moreover, this moment of interpellation becomes possible precisely because the child does not see Fanon's grown body, a body that one would expect to come with a certain degree of protection from the child's questioning. In the public space of the street, the child dares to call out Fanon's body precisely because the child assumes that his own and Fanon's existences are the same. Or to put this differently, the child is able to so blatantly call out Fanon's body because, for him, Fanon's body is not too far removed from the level at which the child sees himself. This repositioning, as Fanon's reflection demonstrates, carries within it a certain undeniable violence against the individual's sense of self.

Missy's actions in the parlor illustrate a similarly violent repositioning. On the surface, Missy's hypnotism—deployed, as we come to find out, for the sole purpose of turning black bodies into vessels purchased and then inhabited, or colonized, by white lives—suggests a belief in the Cartesian dualism, mind vs. body. This reading of her immediate desires, however, misses an important point: Missy's hypnotism is not about evicting black consciousness from black bodies; it is about interpellating, dislodging, and then relocating black consciousness so that room can be made for white consciousness. This dislodging is akin to the dislodging of Fanon's self-identity instituted by the child's interpellation of him. That Missy Armitage is a

9. Althusser, "Ideology," 174.

psychiatrist is no accident. Her training imbues her with an understanding of precisely the connections between the consciousness and the body that Fanon, a fellow psychiatrist, discusses.[10] It is particularly interesting that Missy's understanding of Chris's body as vessel nonetheless recognizes that his body, without its present awareness, is never empty. This is nowhere more clearly evidenced than in the fact that, rather than completely removing or destroying Chris's consciousness, she relocates it to a *sunken place* that is simultaneously always present, but far removed. The moment Chris moves to protest Missy's assault on his consciousness, it is too late. "Wait," Chris pleads, "No!" He has already begun to sink.

In relocating Chris's psyche to the site of the *sunken place,* Missy's hypnotism works within the understanding of power as outlined by Judith Butler: "If conditions of power are to persist, they must be reiterated; the subject is precisely the site of such reiteration, a repetition that is never merely mechanical."[11] In the *sunken place,* Chris remains partially present and forced to constantly revisit the trauma suffered by the manipulation and rerouting of his childhood memories. This is evidenced as the film depicts the *sunken place* as a dark pit beneath a screen that displays Chris's view of the world. But unlike the equalization of power displayed in Fanon's moment of interpellation, the power dynamic in this scene sets Missy firmly as the parental authority, with Chris thrust into the role of the subjugated child (see figure 6). As Missy reminds Chris that he is smoking in front of "my child"—the possessive "my" serving to reinforce her role as both authority and parent—and thus interpellates him as the child he no longer is, she reiterates the very conditions of power Butler articulates. In subtle ways, the camera also indicates this dynamic as it reflects Chris's slide into Missy's grasp. As the conversation unfolds, Chris is situated in a medium shot, while the camera provides a tight close-up of Missy (alternating between her face and her hands as she stirs the cup of tea). As Chris falls deeper into the hypnotic trance, the camera zooms in on him until he too is captured within the frame of a tight, close-up. But at this point, it is not Chris we see; it is a hollowed version of his body as his consciousness begins sinking into the *sunken place.* In his eyes, we are able to see the pain, terror, helplessness he feels from sitting face-to-face with someone who seeks to molest and then cannibalize his consciousness.

Missy's hypnotism works by reconnecting the grown Chris with the young, boyish Chris. As with the camera's framing of him, the clean transi-

10. Fanon, *Black Skin,* 10–11.

11. Butler, *Psychic Life,* 16.

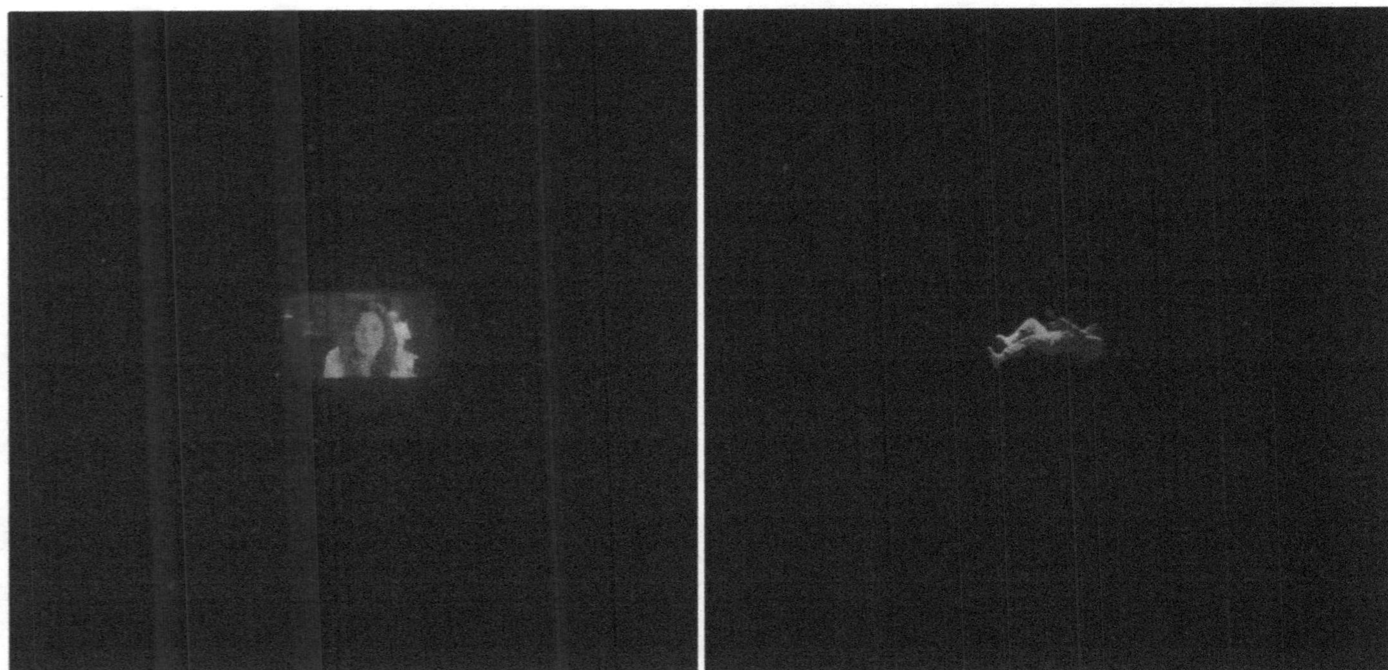

FIGURE 6. Chris in the black sunken place with Missy looming above him. *Get Out* (Jordan Peele, 2017).

tions from older Chris to younger Chris gesture toward a too-easily-made connection between the black man and boy. The ease with which Missy is able to ambush Chris and displace his consciousness to the site of the *sunken place* should be seen as an indicator of her continued reading of Chris as an object. It is easy for her to begin because, much like Wilson in his fictitious characterization of Brown's body, she never really sees the adult Chris to begin with. From the moment she meets Chris, she sees the boy he outgrew long ago. She uses a maternal tone in her interactions with him, for instance, and the tea cup scene is couched within moments of her scolding Chris for his smoking habits as if he were a child. With everyone else, there is a firmness to her soft voice that demands obedience; with Chris, however, that soft voice works to conceal its edges, making it all the more dangerous.

Spilling the "T" of the Tea Cup Scene

Few white characters within Peele's film can be said to be operating under a system of racism in which the categories boy and man become overtly interchanged, as might be expected of a racist culture or environment. In fact, many of the film's white characters work extremely hard to present themselves as model liberal citizens. Not only does Rose mock Chris's questioning of whether or not she has warned her parents that he is black—telling him that her mother "loves Idris Elba" and her father "would've legit voted for Obama a third time if he could've"—but Rose gets credit for "protecting [her] man" when she suspects Chris is being racially profiled.

The power of Peele's tea cup scene lies in its making painfully visible the racializations operating beneath polite interracial interactions—racializations that Peele keeps alive through the comic interjections of Chris's best friend, Rod. Rose's claim that her parents are unconcerned with race reflects a common articulation of racial color blindness, which "translates into the belief that racism no longer matters and those who continually point racism out are troublemakers 'playing the race card.'"[12] Color blindness, however, has simply taken the place of older, more overt forms of racism and stands as a manifestation of contemporary racial intolerance.[13] As Peele's formulation illustrates, this intolerance becomes apparent in the ease with which black males get caught in the discursive and sociopolitical space between boy and man.

---

12. Beeman, "Walk the Walk," 127.
13. See Neville et al., "Changes," 180–81.

When placed in the context of blackness, the exchangeability of the categories of boy and man points to what Calvin Warren describes, in the context of black queer sexuality, as a "problem space," or "the dissonance between humanism and fungibility."[14] This dissonance comes from the fact that while the human is permitted a range of categories and identities, this range is not granted to black bodies because their blackness risks cannibalizing all other categories. Working to address the impossibility of conceptualizing the violence enacted upon black individuals who are caught between humanist categories, Warren asserts that "since the black is *not* a human, it cannot claim 'difference' or 'particularity' as a feature of existence (because these belong to the human)."[15] What comes of this is that the blackness of the individual subsumes all other categories, resulting in her re-presentation as a monolith. Or, to put this differently, the black individual becomes *black* despite all of his other identities. This dissonance between the actual lived experience of multiple identities and the reduction to a singular identifier means that, when combined with blackness, labels such as "child"—or, in this instance, "boy" or "man"—create a space of rupture in which the individual under address becomes discursively slippery. So, when Missy calls up memories of Chris as a young boy, it is not the boy, but the man, she is after. In calling the boy, she does so with the recognition that the gap between Chris as a child and Chris as a man is easily collapsible and that this space is precisely what is needed for the sunken place to work effectively. In the film, the sunken place represents this space of rupture, in that it serves as the very means for reducing black lives to the blackness of their bodies.

In a way, then, it becomes possible to argue that Chris's hypnotism began long before he stepped into Missy's office the night of his last cigarette. As a black man in contemporary America, Chris has constantly been asked to negotiate systems that seek to interpellate him beyond his own consciousness. For instance, Chris does not protest when Officer Ryan demands to see his license the day he and Rose hit the deer. Nor does Chris protest when Dean parades him through his hall of black excellence, pointedly recounting both his pride in the triumph of (the body of) Jesse Owens and his admiration for Obama and his presidency. While these instances might be read as suggesting Chris's sense of respect for the authority figures that Dean, Missy, and Officer Ryan represent, it becomes clear throughout that their views deeply wound his sense of self and safety. In this way, Missy's hypnotism is just the latest iteration of what began during slavery.

---

14. Warren, "Onticide," 393.
15. Ibid., 394.

It is significant that the tea cup scene takes place on a plantation-like estate: this setting serves to situate Chris's molestation in its larger historical lineage, reconnecting it with the nation's history of slavery and thus bringing past and present enslaved bodies (and past and present enslavers) into dialogue with one another.[16] Furthermore, the commodification of black bodies, particularly through the process of Missy's hypnotism, challenges the notion that blacks have nothing to offer society. The very need to create systems of psychological erasure and repression—systems for breaking a person mentally—demonstrates a fracture within this logic of black worthlessness.

Through the hypnotism scene, Peele is able to repackage and redeploy the tensions within the commodification of the black body and the displacement of black consciousness, bringing both to the point of terrifying absurdity. Of course, Peele could not possibly be suggesting that white people are abducting black people in order to ride through life in their bodies. What makes this scene, and the film itself, so harrowing, however, is that this seems to be very close to what Peele is, in fact, suggesting: there has long been a system in place for the displacing of the consciousness of black bodies and the (re)filling of those bodies with a consciousness not of their own choosing. Accordingly, *Get Out* can be seen as concerned with the effects of a lack of representation in media and social images, in that it suggests that by being presented only with white lives, white ideas, and white values, black individuals are subtly made to internalize those lives, ideas, and values to the point that they displace any others. In fact, Ta-Nehisi Coates goes so far as to assert that the feeling of nakedness he felt while growing up was neither "an error, nor pathology," but "the correct and intended result of policy, the predictable upshot of people forced for centuries to live under fear. . . . However you call it, the result was our infirmity before the criminal forces of the world."[17] While Coates is expressly interested in the struggles of and for black bodies, like Peele, he is without a doubt also concerned by the ways in which the pressures of those struggles threaten to overtake the development of the black psyche.

By first figuring the *sunken place* as a blackness that serves to trap and dis-place Chris's black consciousness, and then allowing Chris to resist this negative depiction of blackness, Peele is able to offer an alternative relationship with blackness. Rather than succumb to the emptying of his black body, Chris fights to keep that body filled with his consciousness and his

16. See Sarah Juliet Lauro's chapter in this collection for an exploration of *Get Out* as slave revolt.

17. Coates, *Between the World,* 17–18.

constituent identities. It, then, becomes possible to see Peele's depiction of the *sunken place* as an extension of the notions of blackness worked through by James Baldwin. For Baldwin, it is never quite blackness itself that stands as the problematic; rather, it is the lies about that blackness—and an individual's susceptibility to falling victim to those lies—that stands as the problem. Once a black individual is able to resist "believing that you really are what the white world calls a *nigger*," he can begin finding the strength he will need to endure the onslaught of lies told about him.[18] In Baldwin's discourse, blackness is not the space of negativity, but the space of salvation—it is the space in which the love that can heal might be found.

Poet/Scholar Claudia Rankine offers the following reflection in her powerful work, *Citizen: An American Lyric*:

> "The subject of so many films is the protection of the victim, and I think, I don't give a damn about those things. It's not the job of films to nurse people. With what's happening in the chemistry of love, I don't want to be a nurse or a doctor, I just want to be an observer."[19]

Offered in her text in the form of a disembodied quote, complete with the included quotation marks, Rankine's passage resonates with Peele's film—particularly his tea cup scene. Almost as if embodying Morrison's final overtures in *Beloved*, Peele gives us a scene that is impossible to "pass on"—one that presents the power dynamics of American racism as a rememory that is carried into our present moment.[20] Peele's tea cup scene and the film in its entirety effectively rebut the findings that repeated exposure to racial diversity will help whites "gain greater awareness of race(ism)" and heal the racial divides within American society.[21] But the film is not about protecting any victims, at least, not in the traditional sense. Rather, this is a film about making visible the assault on black males within a society that claims to have given them all the space and tools they need to survive. As with Rankine, and Morrison, Peele is not interested in making clean the mess that has been made. The effects of the hypnotism and Chris's battle to free himself from the Armitages' control leave their effects on him in the end. In this, Peele's message becomes clear: In American society, the black man's growth and development still remains a phantasmagoric prestidigitation.

18. Baldwin, "My Dungeon," 291.
19. Rankine, *Citizen*, 155.
20. Morrison, *Beloved*, 324.
21. Neville et al., "Changes," 189.

At a time when Darren Wilson's recasting of the seventeen-year-old Michael Brown as a larger-than-life Hulk Hogan figure who threatened the safety of Wilson's own child-like, mid-thirties-aged body is enough to vindicate his actions, one of the most terrifying aspects of Jordan Peele's *Get Out* is its ability to so astutely foreground and to so persuasively re-present what scholars and activists alike have been saying for years: we live in a society in which slavery simply has changed names and taken up new tools.

Bibliography

Althusser, Louis. "Ideology and Ideological State Apparatus (Notes Towards an Investigation)." In *Lenin and Philosophy and Other Essays*, translated by Ben Brewster, 85–126. New York: Monthly Review Press, 2001. First published 1971.

Baldwin, James. "My Dungeon Shook: Letter to My Nephew on the One Hundredth Anniversary of the Emancipation." In *James Baldwin: Collected Essays*, 291–95. New York: Library of America, 1998. First published 1962.

Beeman, Angie. "Walk the Walk but Don't Talk the Talk: The Strategic Use of Color-Blind Ideology in an Interracial Social Movement Organization." *Sociological Forum* 30, no. 1 (2015):127–47.

Butler, Judith. *The Psychic Life of Power: Theories in Subjection*. Stanford, CA: Stanford University Press, 1997.

Coates, Ta-Nehisi. *Between the World and Me*. New York: Spiegel & Grau, 2015.

Fanon, Frantz. *Black Skin, White Masks*. New York: Grove Press, 1967.

Get Out. Directed by Jordan Peele. USA: Universal Pictures, 2017. DVD.

hooks, bell. *We Real Cool: Black Men and Masculinity*. New York: Routledge, 2004.

Morrison, Toni. *Beloved*. New York: Knopf, 1987.

Neville, Helen A., V. Paul Poteat, Jioni A. Lewis, and Lisa Spanierman. "Changes in White College Students' Color-Blind Racial Ideology Over 4 Years: Do Diversity Experiences Make a Difference?" *Journal of Counseling Psychology* 61, no. 2 (2014): 179–90.

Rankine, Claudia. *Citizen: An American Lyric*. Minneapolis, MN: Graywolf Press, 2014.

Rody, Caroline. "Toni Morrison's *Beloved*: History, 'Rememory,' and a 'Clamor for a Kiss.'" *American Literary History* 7, no. 1 (1995): 92–119.

State of Missouri v. Darren Wilson. Grand Jury—Transcript (2014).

Warren, Calvin. "Onticide: Afro-pessimism, Gay Nigger #1, and Surplus Violence." *GLQ: A Journal of Lesbian and Gay Studies* 23, no. 3 (2017): 391–418.

CHAPTER 13

THE HORROR OF THE PHOTOGRAPHIC EYE

KYLE BRETT

SAYING THAT Jordan Peele's breakout hit, *Get Out,* is obsessed with eyes and the gaze of both white and black characters is to say, ultimately, nothing new. The film presents us with uncomfortable close-ups of eyes as we follow Chris into the sunken place, and we are confronted with a wavy and distorted televised image of Jim Hudson as he reveals the object of his desire: Chris's photographic eye. Our skin crawls with the ever-present invasion of the gaze; we catch glimpses of lingering partygoers eyeing Chris, Rose's collection of Coagula victims posing in selfies, and Georgina looking into mirrors and dark windows. So it is no surprise that reviews of the film have been quick to comment on the importance of "seeing" in the narrative. Linking to the traditional horror film tropes of voyeurism and exploitation by means of the gaze, Lenika Cruz claims that Peele's insistence on sight and eyes throughout the film probes "the very real anxieties produced by racism," continuing that, "though the film is readily appreciated without deep analysis of its sight-related references, their effects are undeniably powerful."[1] Adopting a similar focus, Dianca London zeroes in on Peele's efforts to address and disrupt the power of the white gaze throughout the film, arguing that "by grounding his narrative within the tradition of the horror genre, the trauma that Peele's protagonist experiences" functions "as

1. Cruz, "In *Get Out.*"

a haunting metaphor for racism in America," as a "terror-inducing portrait" of a nation steeped in racial injustice.[2] As such, *Get Out* becomes a cinematic denial of the power of the white gaze by keeping Chris's experiences at the forefront of the film.[3]

Yet, to say that Peele's film is merely tapping into the horror tradition and that the first-time director employs cinematic history to amplify or decry racial terror misses the more radical nuance at play in the film. While we are presented with the teary-eyed gaze of Chris, the image-starved blind stare of Jim, and the dark eyes of a dying doe, we are also given mechanical eyes—namely Chris's cameras and the television that dominates the imagery of the sunken place. In this chapter, I expand Carol Clover's reading of the eyes of horror, specifically the reactive and assaultive gazes within horror films, by combining her reflexive reading of the genre with what Susan Sontag and Roland Barthes have described as the power dynamic at play between photographed and photographer. In doing so, I read Peele's film with an eye toward what I call *mechanical viewing* and *organic viewing*. Mechanical viewing denotes the traditional role of the photographer, gazing through a lens at a subject and artfully composing; organic viewing involves using a camera simply to record an event or a subject.

From the brief abstracted shots that adorn Chris's studio apartment to the not-so-covert snapping of a camera phone to expose bodily horror and racial possession, the cameras in *Get Out* disclose the paradox of privilege for a photographer—a passive nonpresence distorting the subject for artistic consumption, exercising immense power over who is and who is not photographed. With the initial positive reactions to Chris's documentation during the film and the current cultural climate of ongoing police brutality and the presence of snap-video-streams of violence at protests in mind, I argue that Peele does not draw a clear line between the artistic goals of Chris and Jim, nor between the professional camera and the Coagula; for Peele, the passive observation inherent in the traditional role of the photographer becomes an extension of the sunken place. Peele is advocating for something different at the conclusion of the film—for a more universal, organic, and unscripted photography: the instant documentation of a camera phone held in haste. Such organic viewing places the narrative of an image as secondary to the subject in the frame.

---

2. London, "*Get Out.*"

3. For more on the effect Chris's inaction against the white gaze, microaggressions, and suburban white supremacy has on the viewer, see Steele, "Horror." For the most comprehensive list of sources on the film and its intersection with race and gender, see Boson, "Horror Blackademics."

It is shocking to find that few critics direct their focus to the role of Chris's profession as a fine art photographer.[4] This lack of attention is especially problematic when we look at the history of the horror film genre and its ocular obsession. Films like *Rear Window* (1954), *Don't Look Now* (1973), *The Hills Have Eyes* (the original [1977] and the remake [2006]), *Halloween* (1978), and *Scanners* (1981), along with horror videogames like *Dead Space, Resident Evil 7, Amnesia: The Dark Descent,* and *Outlast* showcase the gaze of the viewer, victim, and villain. Clover's formulation of the "eye of horror" stems from the need to "pin down what horror movies themselves have to say about why people see them at all."[5] Grounding her division of the types of gazes that haunt horror films, Clover focuses on *Peeping Tom* (1960), a film that, like many horror narratives, offers a reflexive look at the genre. When the audience is given a point-of-view shot from the perspective of the victimizer, monster, or villain, we are seeing through a "predatory, assaultive gaze" that is also a "phallic gaze."[6] Likewise, when we inhabit the victim's perspective, we are an "eye on the defense [rather] than an eye on the offense."[7] In many cases, we are forced to inhabit both of these spaces, constantly having to reconcile the horror of a power dynamic that incorporates the violence of the assaultive gaze and the terror of the reactive gaze. While Clover's formulation about the metacommentary of the horror film and the perpetual anxiety surrounding the gaze is helpful, I believe Peele is responding to the artistic gaze in particular, highlighting not only the violence of a mechanical eye (as Clover did in *Peeping Tom*), but also working to disrupt the power dynamic that overshadows the art of both photography and cinematography.

Peele's film asks its viewers to resurrect the debate surrounding the photographed and the photographer. Hinting at both the possibility and limitations of photography, Susan Sontag reminds us that photographs are often "valued because they give information"; they record, help interpret, sell, and serve as tools to encounter and understand abject difference.[8] Images also lie, however, allowing us to assume the "world is more available than

4. See Jenkins, "Just What Kind." Jenkins tackles the role of Chris as an artist and how, contrary to the idea of a photographer as documentarian of social ills, Chris rarely uses his DSLR on the estate. Though somewhat simplistic, this is the only piece that tries to account for the disjunction between Chris's profession and his actions throughout the film, while also situating the film in conversation with films like *Rear Window.*

5. Clover, *Men, Women,* 168.

6. Ibid., 173.

7. Ibid., 191.

8. Sontag, *On Photography,* 22.

it really is."[9] Through the manipulation of the photographer, photography is an invading force that, according to Sontag, is "able to usurp reality" partly because the "photograph is not only an image (as a painting is an image), an interpretation of the real; it is also a trace, something directly stenciled off the real."[10] In this way, the photographer is able to wrest control from the subject, making the shadow become the object. Like Sontag, Roland Barthes also isolates the power of the mechanical eye: "What the Photograph reproduces to infinity has occurred only once: the Photograph mechanically repeats what could never be repeated existentially."[11] The allure and thus the inherent danger of the photographer is that he can own the image and thus, metonymically, own or control what that image displays, repeating or ignoring elements of the subject as she sees fit.[12]

And it is the image's ability to trump the reality of a situation that Peele foregrounds when Chris first enters the sunken place. During this six-minute scene, and before Chris's descent and Missy's command, Chris is left recounting his inability to act during his mother's death as we flash to Chris as an eleven-year-old in silhouette awash in the blue haze of a television set. Instead of responding to his mother's absence, young Chris sits in a dark room watching a blurry screen and picking at his bedpost, turning the fictional into a more concrete reality than the death of his mother.[13] In this way, Chris's personal sunken place becomes a space where he is forever trapped in the inaction that he experienced as a child. No longer given the agency to face the discomfort of making reality, Chris is left dislocated as a passenger in his own body.

It is no coincidence that, after waking up from his first entombment in the sunken place, Chris retreats behind his camera to snap a few pictures of the surrounding woods and, most importantly, to spy on Georgina as she examines her hairline. Yet, more than just a flâneur's voyeurism, this immediate turn to the mechanical eye links the camera to the sunken place. Awaking with a start, Chris attempts to reclaim his own control of reality

9. Ibid., 24.

10. Ibid., 154.

11. Barthes, *Camera Lucida*, 4.

12. Think of the famous photograph captured by Alfred Eisenstaedt, "V-J Day in Times Square." The seemingly loving embrace and kiss between a US sailor and a woman is, what many now realize, a kiss without consent between strangers. Because the trace of reality is merely that, a shadow, it does not convey the reality of the situation (assault between strangers), but rather a jubilant celebration of war-ending exuberance. What Sontag and Barthes would follow here is not the image itself, but the virality of the interpretation of the photographing trumping the reality of its subject.

13. *Get Out*. All further references to the film are to this streaming video.

by using the power of his telephoto lens—he is hunting for an image that captures his selective understanding of his environment. We follow Chris as he takes seemingly random shots of the wooded areas of the estate and then, returning to the house, hesitates before lifting his lens to focus on Georgina at a second-floor window. Shot from Chris's perspective, this scene forces our attention on the crosshairs of Chris's viewfinder, framing Georgina's behavior in front of a mirror; she is both photographed subject and target of investigation. With the inclusion of the crosshairs, we, like Chris, must limit our view of the scene: Chris is guiding our viewing through his camera to investigate the subjugated black (female) body. In a reversal of the previous scene in which Missy separates Chris from his body, we watch as Chris encloses Georgina in a different screen.[14] As photographer, Chris commits a similar form of violence to that which he experienced the night before, and he commits it through his mechanical eye.

Chris's camera also interrogates the experience of Logan King, linking the camera with the hidden horror of the exploitation of black bodies, repeating (again) the violence of the sunken place. By just "take[ing] some pictures," Chris is able to escape from the market of hungry white suburbanites as they touch and check his body. Yet, just as Chris mirrored the violence of the sunken place on Georgina's body, we are again presented with a moment in which Chris, using his camera, engages in a similar form of violent subjugation. We are again offered a point-of-view shot through Chris's camera as he scans the party, moving from Georgina and Missy (again immediately targeting the black body), to Dean and fellow partygoers, and finally to Logan, who is placed in the center of the crosshairs as he lazily shakes a cocktail from side to side. And it is immediately after this targeting that we are forced to watch as Chris begins to test Logan's blackness.

Feeling a sense of relief after setting his sights on Logan, Chris casually approaches his target, hoping to be able to connect with another person on the alienating Armitage estate. Chris moves quickly to the cocktail table and places a hand on Logan's shoulder, happily stating: "Good to see another brother 'round here." Logan slowly turns around and gasps hesitantly: "Ah, yes, of course it is." Five words and a suburban drawl is all it takes for Chris to feel uncomfortable. What was Chris expecting from Logan? With the help of his camera, Chris sees a target, a black body, and immediately constructs a reality from that image in his crosshairs: Logan is black and will respond

14. This seems to be an echo of the violence that Clover highlights in her examination of *Peeping Tom*. Here the camera is weaponized with the inclusion of the crosshairs. The crosshairs not only target and isolate but also foreshadow violence against those that are enclosed by the sights.

in a certain way in accordance with Chris's understanding of both blackness and social interaction. Logan will act like "another brother." When this reality is tested with Logan's accent and hesitant five words, Chris is left dumbfounded and suspicious. His mechanical eye failed to deliver the reality he desired. His disbelief is compounded when Logan confides to his wife that "Chris was just telling me how he felt much more comfortable with my being here." Not giving up completely, Chris attempts one last test of solidarity, the parting fist-bump, which ultimately fails as Logan grasps Chris's fist in his hand. On all fronts, Logan has failed to live up to the reality that Chris both hoped for and created through his lens; the photographer's camera is unable to understand the full picture of reality on the Armitage estate.

In both of these scenes in which we assume the viewpoint of the photographer, we are being forced to inhabit a type of cinematic sunken place, becoming, like Logan and Georgina, passengers to Chris's artful movements. We cannot resist following his eye, his framing of the scenes around him, and thus must take the images he presents as possible truth without resistance. Peele's reliance on these two point-of-view scenes threads the connection to the Coagula procedure in which black consciousness is placed behind a screen and rendered helpless. The viewer must enter their own sunken place following the photographer's gaze, seeing what he decides to show us through his lens. By assuming the viewpoint from behind the camera, we are also experiencing two embodied experiences in Peele's narrative: the soon-to-be victim and the displaced. We identify both with Chris as he commits this ocular targeting and with those trapped in a place of guided observation and mechanical viewing. Considering the timing of these scenes, both happening immediately after the first images of the sunken place, we must assume that Peele is linking not only the television to the Coagula but also the camera's viewfinder.

If the camera is a method of control, a focusing object that can displace subjects into objectivity, then by following who lays hands on the camera during the film, we can see how Peele offers yet another clue about the power of the camera. When first meeting Dean and Missy on the patio of the house, Chris's camera, which is usually slung around his shoulder, rests neatly on the table next to Dean. This is, ultimately, a strange detail, but one of vast importance to the connections that the film establishes between the mechanical eye of the camera and the racial horror that the Armitages and their order inflict on their victims. Considering that Dean and Missy are consistently masking their scheme of medical experimentation—distorting and hiding truth—it is no surprise that the instrument that can so easily make reality through artful composition and metonymy is adjacent to the hands of a black-clad Dean. This is also the first time we see the camera on the Armitage property, showcasing the transfer of power from Chris's hands to the family's. Before Chris slinks away to take some pictures, Dean has already placed his hands on both Chris's security and professional identity, and also his ability to document with that mechanical eye.

If Chris's use of his camera on the Armitage estate focuses on targeting black bodies to investigate or to confirm a distorted reality, and placing the viewers into their own form of the sunken place, then we should also examine the few images that we know Chris has produced as a professional fine art photographer. If, as Sontag, argues, photographs are a form of soft murder, then what do Chris's urban shots do to their subjects—and how do they relate to the habits he displays while on the Armitage estate?

After the film opens with the kidnapping of Andre and the title credits roll, we are immediately introduced to the street-photography that lines the walls of Chris's studio apartment. Before we see Chris, we see his images, evidence of his mechanical eye: these images are intrinsically linked to his character, his lifestyle, and, as we know from his behavior on the Armitage estate, his ability to direct and shape his own sense of reality. As we move from the quick shots of Chris's pictures, we immediately see Chris gazing at himself in the mirror, preparing to shave. Within no more than thirty seconds, we are given a look into Chris's image-heavy lifestyle—his pictures and the intense gaze into the mirror. Hounded by these images, we are asked to establish a sense of character from his shots (the pictures defining our sense of Chris's reality). What Peele privileges here is not Chris, but images and reflections of his character's life.

Chris's "striking urban photography" also links to the traditional assaultive "doing gaze" that Clover relates to the horror genre. Street-photographers like Chris are wanderers of city streets. They take images of landscape, of citizenry, and candid images of city life. Since many of the shots in Chris's apartment seem to be street photography, it is also then safe to infer another of Chris's traits: his ability to disappear and observe. Because of the demands of the candid shot, the street photographer lurks, deceives, and "shoots from the hip" to obtain that often-lauded decisive moment, becoming a photographic predator. Relying on smaller cameras, short lenses, and the hope of a quiet shutter, photographers walk the streets literally hunting for subjects, but that is not to say their power to craft a viral image is undercut by their nonpresence.[15] Bruce Barnbaum outlines

15. See Cole, "Joel Meyerowitz's Career" for more elaboration on the methods of street photography, especially his readings of the different types of street photography occurring in Meyerowitz's body of work. Particularly telling is his use of predatory lan-

more concretely the definition of street photography: it "differs greatly from formal portraits in that the subject matter is usually unrehearsed and often unexpected. This type of photography (which is certainly a form of documentary photography at its best) is geared to those who seek the unexpected and transitory."[16] Notice here the difference between formal portraits, where a subject is emphasized, and the conflation of spontaneously unrehearsed behavior with documentary photography. Here, Barnbaum falls for the trap of believing street photography is removed from the photographer's artful compositions—somehow made more real by the unrehearsed nature of the genre. But looking at Chris's body of work, which Peele foregrounds, we should be able to see how exactly Chris emphasizes his ability to shape and frame his photographs.

We see five main images as the apartment scene opens: all but two contain black bodies, and all are black and white shots, at times with heavy contrast. These images do not contain elements of standard or street portraiture but rather work to obscure or distract the viewer from seeing the human subject in frame. In two of the images it seems that a black subject is wrestling with a white object—balloons in the first image, making a grotesque monster-like shadow on the wall behind the subject, and, in the other image (see figure 7), a white dog fights against its owner's leash, rearing up on hind-legs trying to get at something off the left of the frame.

Banal on first glance, these images showcase Chris's ability to create a selective narrative from the environment that surrounds him. For example, the dog pulling on the leash runs in tandem with the struggle of the film: white subjects pulling and controlling displaced black bodies. By cropping the image to exclude the black subject, Chris brings focus only to the act of tension: the dog resisting its owner. Notice also how the dog is placed within the center of the frame—a technical misstep in composition. However, this centering emphasizes the movement already taking place by the retreating subject off to the right of the frame. In this way, Chris is foregrounding and distorting the struggle in the frame. By placing the dog in the center of the frame, the photographer compels us to give the dog's movement more agency, rejecting the half-subject. Indeed, our eyes follow the extension of the man's arm, to the leash, and then rest on the dog. Although our attention in reality would be more focused on the man pulling the dog away, Chris refocuses our gaze and builds a narrative around subjects in tension.

---

guage in describing the street photographer: "A great street photographer needs two distinct talents: the patience to lie in wait for unanticipated moments and the skill to catch them with the click of a shutter."

16. Barnbaum, *Art*, 5.

FIGURE 7. Chris's photograph of a dog on leash. *Get Out* (Jordan Peele, 2017).

The black subject in the image becomes just a vector for the emphasis on the dominant and centered white dog.

One image, however, resonates more for Chris: the image of a black pregnant woman (see figure 8). Dominating the left side of the picture's frame are the belly and breasts of the subject in the foreground, while walking off with his back to the camera is another subject moving toward the right. The movement of the image forces our eyes first to the woman's stomach and then backward to follow the second subject off the frame, ending on the slightly out of focus background of an apartment complex. I isolate this image because of how the composition of the shot links with Chris's own psychology revealed during Missy's hypnosis session. Visually, a mother is in focus but abandoned in the left of the frame. As with Chris's mother, we never see the entirety of the subject, only the bodily evidence of her maternity and her immediate environment. She is without face, place, or total subjectivity, and is filtered by Chris's composition, which emphasizes her imminent motherhood. The frame, then, is dominated by anonymous and frozen motherhood—the woman in the frame will always carry her child in expectation of birth. Like Chris's mother, this woman is caught between two realities: the world of the image and of the life that continued after the photographer left. She is at once in stasis, preserved in eternal pregnancy, and a subject outside of the frame of the camera's eye.

These urban shots catch the eye of Jim Hudson, a nature photographer turned art dealer after being rendered blind through an unnamed genetic disease. Like Chris, Hudson is another mechanical viewer, only he is not gifted with the "eye"—the mysterious artistic ability to compose powerful images. Jim tells Chris that, after attempting to make it as a photographer, he realized that he "didn't have 'the eye' for it." And that "No one took me seriously in the art world until I began dealing and then, of course, my

FIGURE 8. Chris's photograph of a pregnant woman. *Get Out* (Jordan Peele, 2017).

vision went to shit." This particular dialogue reveals the power of the artist over his viewer: the abstracted ability to have an "eye" for making images real to a public and also to profit from that career. Jim Hudson is not only physically but artistically blind. The only way he can promote and access the work of other artists is through a translation process: "My assistant describes work to me in great detail." Without sight, Hudson seems to be the perfect viewer of Chris's mechanical eye; unable to physically see and thus evaluate, Jim relies on a dual interpretation of the work. First Hudson must see the work through the eyes of his assistant (who is also interpreting the image), and then he must build the reality of that image in his mind, drawing from his experiences when he was sighted.

Not content with his subservience to the translation of others, Jim covets the very things that make Chris a successful photographer: his eyes. In essence, Jim wishes not only to inhabit Chris's body, but also in a way, to turn Chris's eyes into a biological camera. This reliance on the anatomical alludes to the photographic horror Peele embeds in the film: the hostile takeover of black bodies, consciousness, and identity, and the fashioning of those bodies into tools. It is not expression that Jim covets, but rather a biological camera through which to see and shape the world.

If Jim Hudson represents the extreme horror of mechanical viewing in which a living body can be made into not only a passive subject to be framed but also a living subject-less tool to convey the artist's narrative, then it is the universal camera phone's flash that shows the radical potential of organic viewing. In Peele's film, the only way the Coagula conditioning is momentarily broken is through the flash of Chris's camera phone. We see this occur two times: Logan's brief lapse into lucidity at the party and Walter's revenge/suicide at the conclusion of the film. In a narrative that works so very hard to establish the power dynamic of the professional photographer over his subject, Peele imbues a modern phone camera with liberatory power. In these moments in which both Logan and Walter are briefly rescued from their respective sunken places, Peele demonstrates the truth-making power of the photographer. Foregoing an expensive Canon 7D, lenses, theory, and artful composition, the camera phone's operator is merely snapping and sharing. There is no processing, no manipulation, and, in Chris's case, an inability to manage a flash, in the handling of the camera phone—just pointing and clicking. If mechanical viewing is that which is mediated not only by the presence of a camera but also artistic manipulation, then its opposite, organic viewing, is still mediated by a camera, but one without the desire or ability to distort the subject into a selective truth.

Focusing on Walter's awakening at the conclusion of the film, I want to underscore the reversal of Chris as professional photographer, as he becomes instead a person who merely records without the aid of an artistic eye. During the final minutes of the film, we follow Chris as he brutally escapes the Armitage estate, attempts to save an injured Georgina, and is quickly overtaken by the Jessie-Owens-obsessed Roman Armitage in Walter's body. As Walter and Chris are struggling on the road, Walter grasps Chris's face, covering his eyes. Left blinded, Chris operates his camera phone by instinct, taking a picture of Walter's eyes. Peele's screenplay emphasizes Chris's blindness in this moment: "Chris, blinded, raises his phone to Walter/Roman's face. He takes a picture, flashing straight into Walter/Roman's eyes."[17] No longer constructing reality with a camera, Chris is instead unseeingly reproducing reality. Unlike Chris's work on display in his apartment, moreover, this quick capture places the face of its subject in center frame. No longer abstracted like the pregnant mother, or the dog walker in Chris's street photography, Walter is allowed full representation in Chris's camera eye. As with Logan, the flash of a camera phone seems to echo behind the eyes of the possessed, allowing Walter a moment of power to take the rifle from Rose before turning it on her and then himself.

In this scene, Chris is no longer the photographer but rather a reporter, a documentarian without artistic motive. Blindly handling his camera without forethought, without deliberately composing the scene, Chris snaps a quick shot and, just as quickly, rescues Walter from the sunken place. It is hard not to see this ending scene, this rescue, as a moment that ties to the ongoing importance of street documentation of police violence against black bodies, or rallies and protests of white nationalist groups. In these cases, what is recorded on camera is not an image used to convey a message

17. Peele, "Get Out."

for profit or gain, but something that challenges other dominant images of order, justice, and effective policing. What these images and videos foreground is not a narrative, but rather a tangible subject. We must witness a body, a car striking a protester, an officer firing into the back of a fleeing man. We cannot retreat into narrative, asking why or how this happened, but must first be consumed by the overbearing reality of injustice committed against a subject; we must live with the bodies, the burning crosses, and the dying fathers. By constructing a narrative surrounding a professional photographer, Peele challenges us to wrestle with the power inherent in the images that assault and inform us. Like Sontag and Clover, Peele understands too well the violence the photographer inflicts on the subject—the ability to dodge and burn reality into an artistic vision, glorifying the beauty in violence, socioeconomic injustice, and urban sprawl. Chris's final turn to his camera phone presents a potential resistance to the artistic eye and, by extension, the power that Jim Hudson covets so dearly. Here Peele offers a revised position of a photographer and, potentially then, a filmmaker—one who sacrifices his own vision back to the reality of the subjects he frames. In this way, the photographer, professional or not, may be able to subvert the violence of capturing that perfect moment of reality on film. Like Chris riding away from the burning estate, the professional photographer must close their eyes and trust their subject to make the image.

Bibliography

Barnbaum, Bruce. *The Art of Photography: A Personal Approach to Artistic Expression.* 2nd ed. Santa Barbara, CA: Rocky Nook, 2017.

Barthes, Roland. *Camera Lucida: Reflections on Photography.* Trans. by Richard Howard. New York: Hill and Wang, 1981.

Boson, Crystal. "Horror Blackademics: The *Get Out* (2017) Syllabus." *Graveyard Shift Sisters,* June 15, 2017. http://www.graveyardshiftsisters.com/2017/06/horror-blackademics-get-out-2017.html.

Clover, Carol J. *Men, Women, and Chain Saws: Gender in the Modern Horror Film.* Princeton, NJ: Princeton University Press, 1992.

Cole, Teju. "Joel Meyerowitz's Career is a Minihistory of Photography." *New York Times Magazine,* January 18, 2018. https://www.nytimes.com/2018/01/18/magazine/joel-meyerowitzs-career-is-minihistory-of-photography.html.

Cruz, Lenika. "In *Get Out,* the Eyes Have It." *Atlantic,* March 3, 2017. https://www.theatlantic.com/entertainment/archive/2017/03/in-get-out-the-eyes-have-it/518370/.

Get Out. Directed by Jordan Peele. USA: Universal Pictures, 2017. Streaming video.

Jenkins, Rupert. "Just what Kind of Photographer is *Get Out*'s Chris Washington?" *One Good Eye,* May 17, 2017. http://onegoodeyeonline.com/2017/05/17/get-out-chris-washington/.

London, Dianca. "*Get Out* and the Revolutionary Act of Subverting the White Gaze." *Establishment,* March 9, 2017. https://theestablishment.co/get-out-and-the-revolutionary-act-of-subverting-the-white-gaze-c769cb620496.

Peele, Jordan. "Get Out." Unpublished screenplay.

Sontag, Susan. *On Photography.* New York: Picador, 2001. First published 1977.

Steele, Taylor. "The Horror and the Work: What *Get Out* Teaches Us." *Black Nerd Problems,* May 24, 2017. http://blacknerdproblems.com/the-horror-and-the-work-what-get-out-teaches-us/.

CHAPTER 14

THE FANTASY OF WHITE IMMORTALITY AND BLACK MALE CORPOREALITY IN JAMES BALDWIN'S "GOING TO MEET THE MAN" AND *GET OUT*

LAURA THORP

REVIEWERS AND online commentators have celebrated Jordan Peele's *Get Out* for both its subversion of contemporary racial discourse (our purportedly "postracial" age) and its engagement with the history of horror movies. There is, however, a set of intertexts and a particular context that commentators have generally passed over: the largely contemporaneous, renewal of interest in James Baldwin as a figure with things to teach us about our current racial moment. This interest is evident in a number of places, from the outpouring of scholarly books to the film *I Am Not Your Negro* (Raoul Peck, 2016) and Ta-Nahesi Coates's 2015 book *Between the World and Me*, which models itself on Baldwin's *The Fire Next Time* (1963). *Get Out* is both a part of this renewed interest while serving as a devastatingly Baldwinian indictment of "whiteness" in the fantasy construction of American race and gender identities.

Placing *Get Out* into dialogue with Baldwin's 1965 short story "Going to Meet the Man," this chapter first examines the longstanding construction of blackness in the United States as an abjected object of desire and repulsion, especially as this enables a white fantasy of immunity from finitude; this fantasy performs specific work, I suggest, in the historical moment of the short story and the film. Finally, I argue that both Baldwin's story and Peele's film contest this fantasy of white immortality through the abjection of the black body in specific, historically shaped, and politically fruitful ways.[1]

James Baldwin's "Going to Meet the Man" opens with Jesse, a white Southern sheriff, lying in bed with his wife and recounting an earlier violent altercation with a young black man who had been participating in a protest outside of the town's courthouse. Jesse then recalls the first lynching he attended as young boy (ten or eleven years old), and this memory serves as the focus of the story's action. The story establishes this memory as a crucial moment in Jesse's life and a critical component in shaping his identity as an adult white man.

My theoretical model for approaching the conversation between Baldwin's indictment of whiteness, central to "Going to Meet the Man," and Peele's *Get Out* centers on the issue of the body's finitude and derives ultimately from Baldwin's literary theorization of racial identity as an effect of a sociohistorical version of Freud's primal scene. I argue, that is, that the lynching scene in "Going to Meet the Man" initiates Jesse into white manhood by staging the production of whiteness in and as a denial of mortality that is propped upon the black man's ravaged body.[2] In *Get Out*, this scene is translated and transformed into the hyperbolic realization of the ultimate fantasy of whiteness in the scene(s) of experimentation and of white consciousness rendered immortal through its placement in black bodies. Thus, I believe that these scenes are connected as a series of intensifying reprisals that trace and expose the path from desire for power over the body to violent fetishizing and ultimate colonization of the other's body as a way of defending a fantasy of white immortality that is rooted in a radical dependency on black male corporeality.

The Baldwinan theory of whiteness, which culminates in a scathing indictment, is where my reading begins, and this theory develops, primar-

1. The structure of my argument has its roots in the body of work that, following Baldwin, grafts psychoanalysis onto an historically sensitive critical race theory. In particular, the work of Jean Walton provides crucial groundwork by asking questions about "what kind of knowledge might be produced if articulations of gendered subjectivity were considered in terms of their being dependent on or imbricated with implicit assumptions about 'whiteness' and 'blackness,' insofar as perceptions of fantasies of racial difference might shape a significant axis of identity formation." Walton, *Fair Sex*, 5; see also Bergner, *Taboo Subjects*. I seek to expand upon work by Walton and Bergner by looking to the work done on race by Dyer, *White;* Scott, *Extravagant Abjection;* and Brim, "Papas' Baby."

2. A wealth of work has been done on Baldwin's story, and many have attempted to grapple with the complicated intertwining of race and sexuality. See especially Brim, "Papas' Baby," and Griffith, "James Baldwin's."

ily, out of *The Fire Next Time* and "Going to Meet the Man." It is with Jesse's memory of the lynching scene in "Going to Meet the Man" that Baldwin most clearly establishes what I am identifying as the sociohistorical primal scene of whiteness—specifically white manhood. This "sociohistorical" primal scene does not involve Jesse observing his parents having sex, as in the Freudian primal scene. It does, however, involve a crucial moment (perhaps *the* crucial moment) in Jesse's social history that weaves in obvious elements of sexuality and pleasure culminating in the darkly blissful "orgasmic" simultaneous release of the crowd.[3] Tracing the levels of identification and desiring in this moment allows us to see the primal scene unfolding within the lynching scene. Jesse first describes his mother as "more beautiful than he had ever seen her, and more strange," so she is depicted as the object of desire but also as being far away and fully "othered."[4] In her strangeness, she is both the mother and not the mother, so she becomes the true object of oedipal desire—an object that must be replaced due to the incest taboo.

It is important to note that from the very beginning race is always already present in this primal scene and oedipal process. Jesse's mother looks so beautiful and strange due to her eroticization of and desire for the black male body displayed before her. In desiring his mother because of this strange new beauty, Jesse observes her desiring the black male body. Jesse himself then sees the black body as "the most beautiful and terrible object he had ever seen," so he sees the desire of the black body through his mother's eyes, thus identifying with his mother's own desire.

Crucially tied up in this dynamic is another side of Jesse's desire for the black male body: feelings of inadequacy, inferiority, and a desire to physically become *like* the black body. As he watches his father's friend "cradle" the black man's "privates," Jesse feels his own "scrotum tighten" as he observes the sheer size and weight of them, claiming that the black man's penis is "the largest thing he had ever seen."[5] At the same time, Jesse immediately compares his father's penis to that of the black man, stating that it is "much bigger than his father's," thus referencing a white paternal legacy of fears of physical inadequacy in comparison to the black male body. This legacy of the "sexual prowess" attached to the black male body and the attendant feelings of fear and inadequacy in the white male imagination has a long and well-documented history that has essentially cemented the black

3. Griffith, "James Baldwin's," 520.
4. Baldwin, "Going," 247.
5. Ibid., 248.

man as a "walking phallic symbol."[6] In his comparison of the black man's penis with his father's smaller penis—a comparison that comes in the same moment as Jesse's own obvious desire for the black male body—Jesse is demonstrating his own movement into this legacy of fears regarding physical and sexual inferiority.

The moment of desire for the black male body is subsequently translated into a repudiation of that same body and completes the oedipal process by pushing Jesse fully into white manhood. This comes in the moment when Jesse makes eye contact with the beaten and tortured black man just seconds before his castration: Jesse recognizes the reality of castration and realizes that he can either *be* the knife or become its victim. To be like the black man, to give into the desire to be the black man, is to become the knife's victim. On the other hand, to enter into white manhood is to wield the knife, to become the knife itself, and thus eliminate the threat of becoming the object under the knife. This is a primary component of the "great secret" that becomes "the key" to Jesse's life.[7] To be white is to repudiate and deny the identification with and desire of the black body; it is to wield the knife and exact power and dominance over the black body.

This scene depicts Baldwin's theory of the construction of whiteness (specifically white manhood): the movement into a white subjectivity *is* the simultaneous desire for and violent repudiation of the black male body. Less obvious in this particular scene is the connection between Baldwin's primal scene and the white fantasy of immunity from the body's finitude, but this crucial component of Baldwin's theorization of race (hyperbolically realized in *Get Out*) can be found in *The Fire Next Time.* This text explores how the fear serving as the undercurrent of white racial violence against black bodies is inherent to whiteness: it is a fear of the body's *finitude*—specifically, fear of mortality and death. In *The Fire Next Time,* Baldwin states, "Perhaps the whole root of our trouble, the human trouble, is that we will sacrifice all the beauty of our lives, will imprison ourselves in . . . races, armies, flags, nations in order to deny the fact of death, which is the only fact we have."[8] Baldwin complicates this claim by pushing it further and stating that "white Americans do not *believe* in death, and this is why the darkness of my skin so intimidates them."[9] Not only do white Americans fear death, they completely deny the fact of death by refusing to believe in it as a reality *for them-*

6. Brim, "Papas' Baby," 186; Taylor, "Denigration," 46; and Harris, *Exorcising Blackness,* 20.

7. Baldwin, "Going," 248.

8. Baldwin, *Fire,* 91.

9. Ibid., 92; emphasis added.

selves. And this denial of the reality of death is, according to Baldwin, the very root of racial violence; the violence enacted on black bodies by white bodies is the pathway and process through which whiteness denies its own finitude and the fact of death. For if the "darkness" of the black body intimidates whiteness because it is a constant reminder of death and the finitude of the body, then violently abjecting the black body allows whiteness to create a fantasy of "controlling" death in order to ultimately deny it.

This violent refusal of the body's finitude is part and parcel of white identity formation. Combining Baldwin's own theory with a brief examination of Richard Dyer's theory of whiteness helps to illuminate this white fantasy of immortality and freedom from bodily finitude. As Dyer claims, a necessity of "whiteness" is a kind of disembodiment, a transcendence and mastery of the body wherein the "white spirit" rises above and overcomes the darkness of the body and its weaknesses.[10] Dyer grounds this idea of the weakness or darkness of the body in the act of sex and sexual desire; however, this connection is better illuminated by Lacan's theory of desire for the Other. This desire refers not only to sexual desire but to desire in general—which entails the desire of the Other and the desire to know the Other.[11] This desire is an inherent and necessary part of being in a body and thus is beyond individual control. It is seen as a bodily weakness not only because it manifests as sexual (physical) desire but because the very presence of this desire is a recognition that the individual is not complete within his own body and mind. That this desire is beyond our control and cannot be mastered or transcended makes it dark and "other"—an element of otherness within our own bodies.

The problem with the darkness of sexuality and its revelation of the weakness of the body is that it is inescapably tied up with the reproduction of whiteness. As Dyer claims, "To ensure the survival of the race, they have to have sex—but having sex, and sexual desire, are not very white: the means of reproducing whiteness are not themselves pure white."[12] Thus it is that whiteness is always haunted and threatened by the darkness of sex and the vulnerability of the body because whiteness cannot be reproduced without sex, and this notion of sex cannot exist without an element of darkness and weakness. In order to protect itself from this truth, whiteness projects the inherent weakness and darkness of the body onto the bodies of "dark[er] races"; this allows whiteness to distance and protect itself by pointing to the darkness on the surface of the skin as evidence of the darkness within

10. Dyer, *White,* 23.
11. Lacan, *Four,* 38.
12. Dyer, *White,* 26.

certain bodies.[13] This allows for the (troubled) conclusion that an absence of the visual evidence of darkness must signal an absence of inherent darkness within certain other bodies.

Whiteness seeks to be eternal, universal, and all-encompassing; this is impossible if whiteness is shackled to the finite and fallible body, so whiteness is located in the "white spirit," which can transcend and master the body—thereby mastering its finitude and mastering death. But the fact of the body and the *darkness* of its weakness and mortality can never be fully denied. The desire for the Other and the element of otherness inherent within all bodies is a reminder that the borders of the body cannot be fully shored up. It is always susceptible to that which is rejected, forced out, abjected. Julia Kristeva points out that this inescapable permeability of the body (and thus the permeability of the self or "spirit") is intimately connected with the fact of death: death is the "utmost of Abjection" because it is the ultimate permeation and destruction of the body and the self.[14] Whiteness, in its construction as a denial of the body and death, forces others to live this inescapable reality in the place of "white" people. Thus desire, the inescapable weakness of the body, and the fact of death are projected onto the skin of "dark[er] races" as an abjected blackness that allows white people to deny their own embodiedness and finitude.[15] However, this denial is threatened by the very presence of darker or black bodies, as Baldwin points out, because the idea of "the Negro" as it is constructed by whiteness/white Americans, serves as a constant reminder of the fact of death.[16] Hence the only way whiteness can persist is by dominating and destroying the black body.

With this in mind, we can begin to see how *Get Out* engages with the Baldwinian primal scene and notions of the construction of whiteness while rendering hyperbolically real the white fantasy of freedom from finitude and the violent denial of death. Dean Armitage and his son Jeremy are immediately implicated in a chain of transference of identification, desire, and denial in relation to the black male body, and this is made explicit in Jeremy's obsession with Chris's athleticism and physical strength. At the Armitages' dinner table, Jeremy grills Chris about getting "into street fights as a kid" and being interested in mixed martial arts, claiming that with Chris's "genetic makeup," he could "be a fucking beast" if he trained hard enough.[17] Jeremy's comments echo a legacy of the white male ego's obsession with and fear of

13. Ibid., 28.

14. Kristeva, *Powers*, 3–4.

15. Dyer, *White*, 28.

16. Baldwin, *Fire*, 92.

17. *Get Out*. All further references to the film are to this DVD.

the power and potential superiority of the black male body that played into and supported an affective economy of white supremacy.

It is important to note that this conversation begins with Dean asking Chris what his "sport" is, a hint that the obsession Jeremy displays is shared and transferred from his father. This implication is made more explicit by some of Dean's comments during Chris's tour of the house. In discussing Jeremy, Dean states that "[he] went through a couple dark spots but came out on the other side just fine. He's studying medicine now. He wants to be just like his old man." At this early point in the film, this particular comment seems innocuous, but it becomes increasingly insidious as it is revealed that being "just like his old man" involves Jeremy kidnapping black men (and likely black women as well) and training to be a neurosurgeon so he can forcibly transfer white consciousness into stolen black bodies.

The role of the mother (and white women in general) is slightly rewritten in the movement from Freud to *Get Out*. The sexualization and eroticization of Chris's body is mediated through Rose—the sister/daughter as opposed to the pleasure of the mother. It is Rose and her romantic/sexual relationship with Chris that brings him into her family's clutches in the first place. It is also this relationship that prompts one of the white female partygoers to ask Rose (in front of Chris) "So, is it true? The love-making. Is it better?" In an explicit connection to the affective economy of white supremacy during the Jim Crow era, the relationship between Chris and Rose, and Rose's prominent and active role in "procuring" black victims for her family's experiments, brings in issues of miscegenation and the fear of black men violating white women. Jeremy's (and Dean's) focus on Chris's physical superiority, then, coupled with Rose's relationship with Chris, gives the film an undercurrent that echoes the prelude to a black man's lynching.

The role of the actual mother in the film, Missy, is a bit more complex because, as Rizvana Bradley brings up—and as Jordan Peele alludes to in the screenplay for *Get Out*—Missy has the potential, for the briefest moment, to serve as a mother figure for Chris.[18] But it is Missy who forces Chris (and presumably all of the Armitages' victims) into the violent abjection of the "sunken place." Through hypnosis, she forces black consciousness out of (or much deeper into) the black body in order to make room for white consciousness to enter that same body. As Bradley states, "Peele's device of the 'sunken place' visually conveys the force of the submerged black body as a graphic metaphor for subjection, which Saidiya Hartman theorized as "the

18. Peele, screenplay for *Get Out*, 24, and Bradley, "Vestiges," 46.

singular imposition of violence upon blackness."[19] Missy is positioned as allowing her husband and son (and the Armitages' friends) to both desire and violently repudiate the abjected black male body. It is also Missy who allows for the violence of the lobotomy—a moment that most closely echoes the horror of castration in the Freudian primal scene. The lobotomies performed by Dean (with assistance from Jeremy) involve literally cutting open and cutting out—or cutting off—part of a black body for the benefit of white consciousness. The black body—particularly the black male body—serves as a symbol of power that whiteness seeks to control by cutting it apart. Further, Dean's scalpel is a phallic symbol used to violently control (and destroy) the power of the black body, and Jeremy desires and expects to become the one holding the scalpel (as opposed to its victim).

But *Get Out* does not merely function within the Baldwinian framework as a simple retelling of the racial primal scene; it takes this framework and pushes it to its logical conclusion by literally acting out the fantasy of whiteness and forcing whiteness to face its own impossibility by exhibiting the undeniable agency of the black body. In the final climactic scenes of the film, Chris literally destroys the fantasy of white immortality by using the very tools the Armitage family wielded to suppress his agency—the very tools necessary to the fantasy construction of whiteness—to force them to contend with their own mortality and the finitude of their bodies by killing them. He uses his physical strength and intelligence to outsmart and overpower Jeremy (who fetishized and stereotyped Chris's physicality while invalidating his intelligence). He kills Missy in the office where Missy hypnotized Chris and forced him into the sunken place. He stops short of killing Rose and instead walks away, allowing her (presumably) to die from the injuries she had already sustained. This is a crucial moment because as we can see from Rose's maniacal smile and screaming when she thinks a cop car has pulled up, she wants Chris to hurt her because this plays into the narrative of black men posing a threat to white women—a narrative that is used to support the fantasy of white immortality by simultaneously "displaying" the purported purity of white women and permitting the violent destruction of black men. Because Chris does not play into this narrative, he doesn't give Rose what she wants, which doesn't necessarily mean that the narrative is completely broken or destroyed, but it is fractured.

Dean's death is potentially the most important death in the film. Chris uses the buck's head to impale Dean, thus taking a term that denigrates young black men and using it to destroy the person who initially wielded

19. Bradley, "Vestiges," 46.

it to suppress Chris's agency. Chris is clearly connected to the film's deer imagery, and Dean's statement of—"one down, a couple hundred thousand to go. . . . I do not like the deer. I'm sick of it, they're taking over"—is a not-so-subtle nod to this connection and to Dean's true feelings toward Chris and all of the Armitages' victims. Further, and even more importantly, Dean's death is also the clearest and most visceral depiction of the fantasy of whiteness being confronted with the impossibility of its immortality because Dean's death represents the realization of the fear at the heart of the Baldwinian primal scene: Dean is impaled by the phallic symbol of the deer's antlers and becomes the victim of "the knife," even in the same moment that he is wielding the "knife" (scalpel) meant for Chris.

It is important to note the lack of bloodshed and overt violence that actually takes place on-screen during *Get Out*'s run time. The majority of the violence is implied or hinted at but never actually shown. The film shows some of the Armitages' deaths (notably Dean's and Jeremy's), but we don't see the actual moments when Missy and Rose die. We see the aftermath of the completed (and purportedly "successful") experiments on Georgina, Walter, and Logan (Andre); we see Andre being kidnapped in the opening of the film; we see Chris falling into the "sunken place" and narrowly escaping the same fate as the three characters listed above. The violence remains just out of sight, not because it doesn't exist or isn't as severe as that of the Jim Crow era, but because white supremacy and white violence has attempted to disguise itself, to hide behind the mask of white neoliberalism in an effort to claim that twenty-first-century America is a postracial society where institutionalized racism no longer exists—and, in fact, being black has more advantages than being white. And it is the very penetration of the institutions and structures of society by racism that has allowed for this disguising in the first place, to the point that even the average white American progressive (as the film points out) genuinely does not believe him- or herself to be part of these racist structures and systems. As Lenika Cruz points out, Jim Hudson (the man who purchases Chris's body), is representative of the danger of "well-meaning white liberals and those who believe in a postracial America. . . . He comes across as the kind of person who'd say he doesn't 'see race' while caring very little about the well-being of black Americans."[20]

Beyond this, and perhaps more importantly, this lack of on-screen violence is a literal depiction of whiteness's continued repudiation of its own finitude and mortality. Taking this into account, the film offers a complex

20. Cruz, "In *Get Out*."

conclusion regarding the relationship between whiteness and the black body. Through the reprisal of the Baldwinian primal scene, *Get Out* reveals that this relationship is necessary to the very construction and existence of whiteness itself. The Armitages and those like them don't simply want to colonize black bodies purely as a result of jealousy or an inferiority complex (though this dynamic is certainly present in both the story and the film). They want to harness and control a certain kind of power that they believe to be inherent within the domination of the abjected black body—power over finitude and death. Beyond this, and more importantly, is the revelation that whiteness *necessarily* entails the denial of finitude through the colonization of black bodies. In the case of *Get Out*, this is effected through the possession of the black body by white consciousness via the violent abjection of black consciousness. The Armitages and their comrades thus align themselves with the crowd of lynchers by "holding death . . . on a leash," thus controlling the black body in order to deny finitude—a denial that is the very root of whiteness. Crucially, however, this is a denial that cannot persist, that must fail *because* "death is the only fact we have."[21] Even in colonizing black bodies, the Armitages (and whiteness in general) must still confront the fact of death because they are inhabiting the very corporeality they seek to destroy in bodies that will still eventually die. It is this failure of the fantasy that keeps the violence of whiteness going: it must control more and more black bodies—in new and evolving ways—in order to continue the fantasy of denial.

If *Get Out* reprises Baldwin and traces a progression of the production and reproduction of whiteness, then it seems that the film offers the conclusion that if this is the nature of whiteness (wherein the body of the racialized other must be violently colonized), then whiteness as it is constructed not only must be destroyed, but ultimately will be destroyed. As Dan Sinyinkin points out in his review of the film via James Baldwin's "apocalyptic vision" of the future of race in America, *Get Out*'s answer to the notion of "Can't we all just get along?" is a resounding "No."[22]

Arguably, Baldwin presents this same conclusion. In *The Fire Next Time*, Baldwin argues that instead of fearing or denying death, all people should find joy in the fact of death.[23] But whiteness as it is constructed does not allow for this joy and instead creates the insidious joy of destroying the black body. To accept the fact of finitude and the reality of death is to annihilate whiteness itself. The character of Chris acts this out in the final show-

21. Baldwin, *Fire*, 91.
22. Sinykin, "Apocalyptic Baldwin," 15.
23. Baldwin, *Fire*, 91.

down of the film: he destroys whiteness by destroying the bodies of his white captors. In the moment of death, they experience the ultimate confrontation with their absolute finitude, and Chris is able to survive.

The inevitable conclusion seems to be that, as Kevin Lawrence Henry claims, there is "no redemption for whiteness. Whiteness' reproductive terroristic power is secured by its appetite for blackness."[24] The only way to destroy this "reproductive terroristic power" is to destroy whiteness itself. Indeed, the film displays black bodies forcing whiteness to contend with its own finitude and come to the realization that there is nothing whiteness can do to prevent its own destruction—up to and including the violent, literal colonization of black bodies. The destruction of whiteness is inherent in the structure of the very fantasy by which it is constructed. This conclusion is present in Baldwin's racial framework, but *Get Out* makes it explicitly and undeniably clear: whiteness—as it is constructed—cannot exist as fully disembodied consciousness free from the reality of finitude, and this impossible fantasy of immortality is at the very root of whiteness' inevitable demise.

Bibliography

Baldwin, James. *The Fire Next Time.* New York: Vintage Books, 1993. First published 1963.

———. "Going to Meet the Man." *Going to Meet the Man.* New York: Vintage Books. 1993. First published 1965.

Bergner, Gwen. *Taboo Subjects: Race, Sex, and Psychoanalysis.* Minneapolis: University of Minnesota Press, 2005.

Bradley, Rizvana. "Vestiges of Motherhood: The Maternal Function in Recent Black Cinema." *Film Quarterly* 71, no. 2 (2017): 46–52.

Brim, Matt. "Papas' Baby: Impossible Paternity in 'Going to Meet the Man.'" *Journal of Modern Literature* 30, no. 1 (2006): 173–98.

Cruz, Lenika. "In *Get Out,* the Eyes Have It." *Atlantic,* March 3, 2017. https://www.theatlantic.com/entertainment/archive/2017/03/in-get-out-the-eyes-have-it/518370/.

Dyer, Richard. *White: Essays on Race and Culture.* New York: Routledge, 1997.

Get Out. Directed by Jordan Peele. USA: Universal Pictures, 2017. DVD.

Griffith, Paul. "James Baldwin's Confrontation with Racist Terror in the American South: Sexual Mythology and Psychoneurosis in 'Going to Meet the Man.'" *Journal of Black Studies* 32, no. 5 (2002): 506–27.

Harris, Trudier. *Exorcising Blackness: Historical and Literary Lynching and Burning Rituals.* Bloomington: Indiana University Press, 1984.

---

24. Henry, "Review," 334.

Henry, Kevin Lawrence, Jr. "A Review of *Get Out*: On White Terror and the Black Body." *Equity & Excellence in Education* 50, no. 3 (2017): 333–35.

Kristeva, Julia. *Powers of Horror: An Essay on Abjection*. Translated by Leon S. Roudiez. New York: Columbia University Press, 1982.

Lacan, Jacques. *The Four Fundamental Concepts of Psychoanalysis*. Edited by Jacques-Alain Miller. Translated by Alan Sheridan. New York: Norton, 1998.

Peele, Jordan. Screenplay for *Get Out*. Distributed by Blumhouse Productions. 2017.

Scott, Darieck. *Extravagant Abjection: Blackness, Power, and Sexuality in the African American Literary Imagination*. New York: New York University Press, 2010.

Sinykin, Dan. "The Apocalyptic Baldwin." *Dissent* 64, no. 3 (2017): 15–19.

Taylor, Sara. "Denigration, Dependence, and Deviation: Black and White Masculinities in James Baldwin's 'Going to Meet the Man.'" *Obsidian* 9, no. 2 (2008): 43–61.

Walton, Jean. *Fair Sex, Savage Dreams: Race, Psychoanalysis, Sexual Difference*. Durham, NC: Duke University Press, 2001.

CHAPTER 15

SCIENTIFIC RACISM AND THE POLITICS OF LOOKING

CAYLA McNALLY

IN A quietly chilling scene in Jordan Peele's *Get Out*, protagonist Chris finds a box in his girlfriend Rose Armitage's closet that contains photos of everyone she had previously brought home as sacrifices to her family. As he flips through the photos, Chris is forced to confront his partner's betrayal of him over and over again. Her complicity is clear. We know, as does Chris, that the keys will not be found, and that he and Rose will not be driving away from the oppressive atmosphere of the house. In that moment, the immense danger of Chris's situation becomes part of a long legacy of white violence toward black men.

The violence portrayed in the film is also part of another legacy: scientific racism, part of a longstanding process to portray racial difference as biological in order to uphold uneven power structures. It frequently includes the supposition that whiteness is evolutionarily superior to nonwhiteness and that races are genetically predisposed to have different strengths. Usually, the predispositions are that white people have mental acumen, while black people have physical prowess. It is opinion issued under the cover of fact. As Rutledge Dennis points out, "[Scientists] seek in the present day to overwhelm us with what they claim is the beauty and purity of their data, but their pronouncements are just as ideologically driven and racially and politically inspired as those of their predecessors."[1] The dispassionate prejudice of scientific racism, given the appearance of unbiased legitimacy, has been a mainstay of white supremacy since the founding of the United States. Peele's film both criticizes and complicates modern understanding of scientific racism by subverting the audience's expectations regarding what racism looks like and how it is combatted.

By setting his film in a northern state, Peele plays with the audience's own prejudices about liberalism's relation to race. The concept of "good" and "progressive" whiteness plays into the churning evil within the film and the distress viewers feel while watching. Iris Marion Young criticizes the type of colorblindness exhibited by the Armitages, noting, "Liberal sentiments sometimes prompt us to assert that grouping by race, sex, religion, ethnicity, region, and so on, ought to carry no more significance than grouping by hair color, height, or the make of car we drive. Such an invocation calls for groups to be considered as mere aggregates, a classification of persons according to some attribute they share."[2] Seeing race as anything other than a political structure is to decontextualize the oppression perpetuated by that structure. The result is a maintaining of the status quo with regard to social framework. Whiteness, in the hands of the Armitage family, becomes a tool as effective and as malicious as Dean's scalpel and Missy's tea cup.

The Coagula serves as a modern iteration of scientific racism in that both have the same goal: the control of black bodies. I think there is value in laying bare the ways scientific racism by and large encompasses an attitude that feeds into the concept of race itself, as well as the way it pervades how race is represented in *Get Out*. Everyone—with one exception—in the Coagula is white, and all their documented victims are black. This points toward a pathology within the Coagula. They don't need to verbalize their racist intent, because it speaks for itself. Similarly, the discourse surrounding modern scientific racism is about abilities, metrics, and environments, not about race. The lack of discussion of race, both in the film and in real life, allows plausible deniability when it comes to malicious racial intent. It is a conversation defined as much by what is not mentioned.

It is somewhat difficult to pin down the role race plays within the film and in scientific bias because race is rarely discussed in either the film or in scientific texts pertaining to racial difference. Instead, these discourses often rely on linguistic signifiers like "physical advantages" and "your genetic

1. Dennis, "Darwinism," 250.
2. Young, "Five Faces," 177.

makeup." The malice of the Coagula hides behind a blithe colorblindness. We could even argue that the Armitages don't hate black people (though, I'm not going to make that case here). But perhaps this is because we as viewers have problematic expectations of what racism looks like. The Armitages might not personally hate Chris, but they think his life is worth less than theirs, that his body is available for invasion, and that his mind is negligible. Always, for there to be an act, there first needs to be an attitude. The attitude of the Armitages regarding black people—that they are inferior and disposable—engenders their violence toward Chris.

Scientific racism requires that its subject—in this case, black people—is rendered object. While scientific racism can be quite subtle in its oppression, it is at its core a process of dehumanization. *Get Out* is predicated on the very danger of subjectivity presented as objectivity. The Armitage family attempts to silence Chris permanently by dehumanizing him. Chris challenges them with an oppositional gaze, unravelling the structure the Armitage family works so hard to maintain. Chris reclaims the gaze and asserts his personhood against the assumptions of the Coagula. Scientific racism is combatted within the framework of the film, then, by the act of looking.

Scientific Racism and the Coagula

The use of science to justify the girding of whiteness through race is as old as race itself. However, the concept of race is remarkably unstable and has gone through marked changes between the late nineteenth and mid-twentieth centuries. Those of different races were first seen by Western scientists and philosophers as different species, then as a single species consisting of subgroups with immutable dispositions. Racial categories usually also included moral components: the *red* race was arrogant and the *black* race was lazy, while the *white* race was high-minded. As generations shifted, race was seen as evolutionary, then geography-based. Testing surrounding these claims has also changed, from physical (phrenology) to mental (intelligence tests).[3] These changes are not necessarily the result of expanding research, but are rather a justification for changing situations surrounding race in America and Europe. That is to say, while my genes remain the same, I am often read differently with regard to race depending on where I am in both location and time.

3. Roberts, *Fatal Invention*, 39.

Precisely because of this mutability, Dorothy Roberts argues, race cannot be biological: "We know race is a political grouping because it has political roots in slavery and colonialism, it has served a political function over the last four hundred years since its inception, and its boundary lines—how many races there are and who belongs to each one—have shifted over time and across nations to suit those political purposes."[4] Changes in racial groupings were motivated by both racism and nativism; in essence, there was gatekeeping surrounding how people were categorized and which categories properly belonged in America, with the goalposts continually moving either to admit or reject different races and ethnicities. As a structure, racism facilitated the creation of race as a way to segregate and centralize social, legal, and political power. Surprising no one, the categories served to further legitimize those who were already benefitting from their place in the social hierarchy, namely white men. The social power wielded by insiders who maintained the barriers to citizenship and personhood is the same power wielded by the Armitages and members of the Coagula in the film. While we don't know the socioeconomic history of the Armitage family, they are clearly culturally entrenched Americans with financial privilege. Chris stands in sharp contrast to them culturally and financially, and spends much of the film being Othered for reasons outside of his control.

Like all racism, scientific racism involves a certain level of obsession with blackness. In a letter, Jean Louis Agassiz, who is seen as the father of scientific racism, once described a dinner party he attended where he was captivated by the black servers: "It is impossible for me to repress the feeling that they are not of the same blood as us. . . . I could not take my eyes off their faces in order to tell them to stay far away."[5] Blackness is abject, at the same time attracting and repulsing Agassiz, as it also does for Dean Armitage in the film. Fairly early on, Dean laments to Chris, "I hate the way it looks."[6] While Chris understands this to be about a wealthy white family with black employees, Dean's statement can also be understood as his distaste for the aesthetics of the Coagula. To thrive, his family members must exist in black bodies, and he hates it. In order to hold onto his father's legacy of whiteness, Dean must cling to blackness. It becomes his "vessel" for whiteness.

The Armitage family's experiments are predicated on the idea that they are biologically different from the black people they hollow out. They are overtaking young black bodies to shore up their own sociopolitical capi-

4. Ibid., 5.

5. "Father," 38.

6. *Get Out.* All further references to the film are to this DVD.

tal. Jean Belkhir suggests, "Scientific work on intelligence is not value-free because it originates in a society that has problems with the idea of social equality between and among race, sex, and class."[7] When speaking on issues at the intersection of race, gender, and personhood, science does not equal objective truth because scientists are still influenced by the messy subjective realities of the social, cultural, and political structures they inhabit. Those in *logical* fields—medicine, science, data analysis—still grow up exposed to racism and sexism, and those predispositions play out in their work. Dean and Missy are doctor and analyst, respectively, yet their fact-based jobs do not make them immune to subjective views regarding racial hierarchy. On the contrary, one could infer that their beliefs compel their interests in their fields. Similar to the way in which racism conceptually created race, the Armitages' racism molded the finer details of their lives. They cannot separate their careers from their proclivities because it is those very proclivities, and the belief system behind them, that solidified their life path.

It is especially telling that Roman, the Armitage patriarch and creator of the Coagula, is still stinging from a loss to Jesse Owens a lifetime previously. His loss is personal—he is bested by another athlete—but it also represents larger mindsets regarding race; Owens's victory "proves" the existence of black excellence. Roman's body is inferior to Owens's, but in his death, he seeks to obtain the ultimate payback, a way to turn his loss into a victory. His body has failed him, but he secures the legacy of his mind and the minds of his family members. As he tells all of his victims, "You have been chosen because of the physical advantages you have enjoyed your entire lifetime. With your natural gifts and our determination, we could both be part of something greater. Something perfect." There is a physical hyperawareness that the Armitages indulge when looking at Chris. Surrounded by the detritus of dinner, Jeremy muses, "With your frame, and your genetic makeup, if you really pushed your body . . . you'd be a fucking beast." Chris is only an exterior to them—that's why it's important that he doesn't smoke, that he is muscular. All of the Armitages assume they will outsmart their victims because they are genetically more intelligent. Chris eventually defeats them physically and mentally by playing against these expectations. He does this not only by physically overpowering almost every Armitage but also by anticipating how they will act. Taking the long view Jeremy boasts of the night before, Chris stuffs his ears with cotton and Jujitsu maneuvers Jeremy

7. Belkhir, "Sex, Class," 53.

into leg-stabbing range. Using their overconfidence in their own superior intelligence as his leverage, Chris is able to obtain his freedom.

Dean and Missy are able to lure their victims in because they appear to be a very *of the times* family. They are upper-class, East Coast liberals and use that guise to subvert expectations about what they morally prioritize. But in reality, they *are* a very *of the times* family, because the white supremacy that undergirds their power is both established and current. To Dorothy Roberts, white liberals are as guilty as white supremacists when it comes to perpetuating the idea of biologically determined race. Peele certainly plays with this idea as well, pulling back the layers of a liberal East Coast elite family until only the ugly pulsing kernel remains. The Armitages don't see their success as their wealth or their education but rather as their whiteness. Wealth and education are extrinsic factors of success, while their race implies that they are intrinsically better; their superiority stems from the moment of birth, just as Chris's inferiority does. The Armitages aren't taking the bodies of uneducated people or poor people, they are taking bodies exclusively from black people. And while it is difficult to extrapolate evidence of the lives of Chris's predecessors, Chris stands as a shining example. He is a promising artist who lives in a nice apartment in a major city, well on his way to becoming successful. He seems to be well-educated, of moderate financial means, and has a skill that could become even more lucrative in the near future. Socially, he is gaining on Dean and Missy, just like Jesse Owens physically gained on—and then overtook—Dean's father. Chris proves that all the Armitages have left to feel superior about is their whiteness.

Gazes in Opposition

Dean's speech at the party, present in the screenplay but not in the film itself, serves to demonstrate the Armitage attitude with regard to race and the implications of scientific racism:

> You know, if Dad were alive, I know he would remind us of how the knights of old would gather in honor of a new crusade. He'd ask us to remember that though they massed great fortunes, the Templar lived lives of humility. So as we gather here today in celebration, let us not forget that our mission is far from over. In fact it's just beginning. And in the years to come let us not forget the sacrifices that have been made so long ago so that we might enjoy this wine, and these games. So for now let us drink to the

> dawn of a new era. One that has been given to us by the generations before us. Thank you. Cheers.[8]

To Dean, as it clearly was to his father before him, the Coagula's mission is a divine one. His speech, while perhaps too on-the-nose, demonstrates that the Coagula is a crusade, a life of dedication and sacrifice that will have tangible positive effects, both in their individual lives and in broader society. It attempts to make their racist, transhumanist nonsense appear noble. Dean thinks he is a god, telling Chris: "Even the Sun will die someday, Chris. It is us who are the divine ones. We are the gods who are trapped in cocoons."[9] The cocoons are their aging white bodies. The black bodies they consume are their liberation, achieved by prematurely ending the lives of young, healthy black people. They want their everlasting family to be the vanguard of an everlasting white race. In order to preserve their own legacy and bloodline, the Coagula is willing to destroy countless other bloodlines. Peele's lead-in to the screenplay quotes Romans 12:1–2: "I appeal to you therefore, brothers, by the mercies of God, to present your bodies as a living sacrifice, holy and acceptable to God, which is your spiritual worship. Do not be conformed to this world, but be transformed by the renewal of your mind, that by testing you may discern what is the will of God, what is good and acceptable and perfect."[10] But rather than present themselves as sacrifices, members of the Coagula assume a divine superiority that gives them the right to claim sacrifice from others. And their minds are never renewed; instead, they remain stalwart in their harmful ways of thinking as the boundaries of their bodies are blurred. It is the bodies of their victims that are offered up as sacrifice to those who fancy themselves gods. The minds of their victims are transformed, but their own minds are not.

The Armitages are enacting what Young refers to as cultural imperialism, "the experience of existing in a society whose dominant meanings render the particular perspectives and point of view of one's own group invisible at the same time as they stereotype one's group and mark it out as 'other.'"[11] The victims of cultural imperialism are faced with a loss of subjectivity, a theory reified by Frantz Fanon's assertion that "the black man has no ontological resistance in the eyes of the white man,"[12] meaning that the distinctness of self is lost under the gaze of a co-opting eye. Under that gaze, one is

8. Peele, "Get Out," 52.
9. Ibid., 75. This line is in the film.
10. Ibid., 1.
11. Young, "Five Faces," 191.
12. Fanon, *Black Skin*, 90.

simultaneously consumed and rendered Other. Chris is constantly pushing against Fanon's assertion, consistently demonstrating his resistance against the gazes leveled at him in ways that are both diffusing and confrontational. He diffuses the gaze through his camera, placing its lens between himself and the members of the Coagula, able to see without being seen. An example of this occurs at the party as Chris observes unseen through his camera; when caught by Dean and a large group of guests, he simply shifts his focus slightly to the side and drifts away. At other moments, Chris simply looks his adversaries—namely Jeremy and Georgina—squarely in the eyes.

Looking is a way for Chris to challenge the imperialism being directed at his body, a way to reclaim his interiority and assert his personhood. The sunken place is where subjectivity goes to die, the person aware but unseen, trapped in his own existence. Missy paralyzes Chris in his own trauma, his own inaction. This is the last time in the film that he is inactive, living out Fanon's lament that "I crawl along. The white gaze, the only valid one, is already dissecting me. I am *fixed.*"[13] Chris's existence within the warped reality of the Armitage household is mirrored by the deer that bracket his experience. They are bound by helplessness; Chris watches as one dies on the side of the road; one watches as he comes to terms with his mortality in the basement. In a screenplay-exclusive scene from the sunken place, Chris even coexists with a deer-like creature:

> Chris tries to light his lighter again. . . . Each flash illuminates a large face beside his. He doesn't see it. The amorphous antlered thing emerges from the shadow. Its eyes glow and flicker faint blue in its sockets. He finally lights the flame and feels the beast's presence he turns, but the creature is gone. He turns back and there it is. Very close. Its head is the skull of a deer and it has dim blue glowing eyes. It MOANS A WRONG SOUNDING MOAN OF HATEFUL ANGUISH.[14]

For the first time since stepping into Rose's world, Chris shares an experience and gaze with something. He sees and is seen in return. Chris is constantly trying to find the shared experience with other black characters, and is consistently disappointed and alienated because they do not share his perspective on the Armitages and the party. But as Chris helplessly stares, tied to a chair in the Armitage basement, toward the television positioned in front of him, the deer impassively stares back. Chris is reflected in its eyes.

---

13. Ibid., 95.
14. Peele, "Get Out," 78.

If the Armitages would get their way, Chris would, like the deer, be used up piecemeal. He too would stare impassively back, watching another co-opt his gaze.

As a result of the morbid fascination the Coagula members direct toward him, Chris is left existing in two bodies: his body as he experiences it and the body the white characters perceive. His interiority is erased. The Armitages and their friends are allowed to hide in their whiteness, while Chris stands out in his blackness. To his credit, Chris is always watching, unflinchingly, as he is sized up by everyone at the gathering; he is not simply viewed, he is also viewer. As demonstrated in real life tragedies like the death of Emmett Till, the act of simply looking while black is dangerous because it subverts white supremacist frameworks. When the structure burns to the ground, Chris can finally avert his gaze. The screenplay ends in this vein, as "Chris in the passenger's seat watches Rose get smaller in the rear view mirror. He takes a breath and shuts his eyes."[15]

Members of the Coagula project their realities onto Chris's body. His form is one of possibility to them: strength, virility, talent. Their desires can run wild when presented with his body, supporting bell hooks's theory, "Whereas mournful imperialist nostalgia constitutes the betrayed and abandoned world of the Other as an accumulation of lack and loss, contemporary longing for the 'primitive' is expressed by the projection onto the Other of a sense of plenty, bounty, a field of dreams."[16] Chris's internal workings are immaterial to them, because they only have use for the *primitive* vessel. Jim Hudson literally wants to steal Chris's gaze, telling him, "Some people wanna be stronger, faster, cooler. . . . What I want is deeper: Your eye, man. I want those things you see through." Even when he is desired, he is desired in pieces. His eyes and body are valuable, but never his mind. Chris is simultaneously erased and essentialized. Perhaps the clearest example of this occurs when, in the throes of the Armitage *family reunion,* he escapes upstairs to catch his breath. Everyone at the party downstairs falls silent, tracking Chris's steps as he walks overhead. He is absent but startlingly present. On a deeper level, the Coagula hopes to eradicate him while keeping his form intact. They need his body yet do not want his interiority.

Through their actions, the Armitage family upholds an oppressive system that directly benefits them. Chris's rapt presence, his watchful eye, begins to unravel their system. When he tries to take a covert photo of Logan during the party, for example, Logan—momentarily freed from his inner sunken

15. Ibid., 98.

16. hooks, *Black Looks,* 25.

place—lunges at Chris, wild-eyed, shouting at him to "Get out!" over and over until he is dragged away to be rehypnotized. In that moment, every party guest sees the potential cracks in their system. They are reminded that their new homes are never fully theirs. They, like Chris at certain points, are stuck as spectators, watching events outside of their control unfold around them. When Logan returns to apologize, his presence really acts to reassure everyone that their system has stabilized. Missy tells him, "We're just very happy that you're yourself again," to which he replies, "Yes, I am. And I thank God for you calming me down. I know I must have frightened you all quite a bit." The guests can then leave with the false sense that their system will persevere. But Chris, by watching and waiting and fighting for his life, is able to disempower the system with his own two hands.

Chris's experience with the Armitages is of course absurd, a work of pure fiction. But it indicates a common anxiety—entering an all-white space as a person of color—with the tension ratcheted up as far as it can go. Chris and his unraveling of the Armitage household can perhaps be read as a microcosm of our current cultural nightmare. It may feel like a leftover of an old world, but scientific racism remains painfully current, especially in this collective moment of extreme resistance. It is plastered over our newsfeeds; we have normalized it, often without recognizing its role in the discourse around race and ability. When we as a culture tell prominent athletes like LeBron James, Colin Kaepernick, and Serena Williams to shut up and stick to playing sports, we perpetuate the racist belief that their bodies are the only valuable part of them. When we attribute disproportionate strength to black children as justification for their state-sanctioned murders, we uphold far-reaching systems of oppression. Peele's film is a warning, both to those who cannibalize culture and those who are consumed. And, perhaps, it is an invocation to burn the house down from the inside.

Bibliography

Belkhir, Jean. "Sex, Class & 'Intelligence': Scientific Racism, Sexism & Classism." *Race, Sex & Class* 1, no. 2 (1994): 53–83.

Dennis, Rutledge M. "Darwinism, Scientific Racism, and the Metaphysics of Race." *Journal of Negro Education* 64, no. 3 (1995): 243–52.

Fanon, Frantz. *Black Skin, White Masks.* New York: Grove Press, 2008. First published 1952.

"The Father of Scientific Racism." *Journal of Blacks in Higher Education*, no. 8 (Summer 1995): 38.

Get Out. Directed by Jordan Peele. USA: Universal Pictures, 2017. DVD.

hooks, bell. *Black Looks: Race and Representation.* Boston: Sound End Press, 1992.

Peele, Jordan. "Get Out." Unpublished screenplay.

Roberts, Dorothy. *Fatal Invention: How Science, Politics, and Big Business Re-create Race in the Twenty-first Century.* New York: New Press, 2011.

Young, Iris Marion. "Five Faces of Oppression." In *Rethinking Power,* edited by Thomas E. Wartenberg, 174–95. Albany: State University of New York Press, 1992.

CHAPTER 16

"DO YOU BELONG IN THIS NEIGHBORHOOD?"

Get Out's Paratexts

ALEX SVENSSON

THE HORRORS of Jordan Peele's *Get Out* are not just rooted in the film itself but within and across its varied paratexts. Running the spectrum from the official marketing campaign (trailers, outdoor advertisements, press releases, and experiential events)[1] to quasi-official and homemade works (social media hype, parodies, memes, fan art), these paratexts are more than marketing gimmicks or ancillary works. They ultimately reveal *Get Out* to be an intricate textual network of jarring, surreal, darkly humorous, and often confrontational images that work to construct, maintain, and spread a richly mediated world beyond the narrative of the film. Following the idea that media paratexts are never "simply add-ons, spinoffs, and also-rans,"[2] I argue that they are in fact as meaningful as the film itself. More than mere echoes of *Get Out*, these texts also share in, complicate, and extend the film's dread, tension, and biting sociopolitical commentary. Their function is not only to sell *Get Out* to the movie-going public but also to anticipate, reference, and rearticulate Peele's vision in new configurations. Indeed, the film becomes an even more complex work when we consider the multiple and

1. The official marketing campaign consists of both outside work by marketing firm LA & Associates and in-house initiatives by Universal Pictures, Blumhouse Productions, and Jordan Peele himself, primarily through public speaking engagements, press releases, and his Twitter account, @JordanPeele.

2. Gray, *Show*, 6.

varied media forms utilized to express its nightmarish, subversive take on racial politics and the black American experience.

My interest in this paratextual world is based to a great extent on the way I understand *Get Out* to be predicated on material contingency and vulnerability. As works informed by the tropes of horror, the film and its paratexts are given to the genre's penchant for shock and the exploration of corporeal volatility and excess. The affective thrust of horror can function as a "disruptive intensity," forcing us to reconsider any "previously held notions of ideological (and biological) cohesion."[3] Horror works to reveal that meaning is inherently unpredictable and wildly diverse, especially in the context of how we understand our bodies and the bodies of those around us. Indeed, the film and its promotional paratexts—many of which include key art featuring photos of the cast divided and marred by broken glass—are also very much interested in the shattering of facades and the exposure of ugly realities such as fake offerings of romantic and familial love, deceitful impressions of racial tolerance, the masked racism of white progressives, or the falsehood that the Obama era somehow ushered in a postracial society.

While vulnerability in terms of horror might lead us at first to think of transgressed borders and broken-down bodies, *Get Out* and its paratexts also remind us that there is horror to be found in the assertion of boundaries—a process that, despite its aim of stability, can nonetheless carve up space and distribute power in uneven ways, leaving bodies susceptible to Othering and exploitation. One particular text found across *Get Out*'s promotional campaign most clearly works with this idea of aggressively established boundaries by asking its viewers a blunt and ominous question: "Do You Belong in This Neighborhood?" (see figure 9). Eerily appearing to come from an anonymous source (the question is not attributed to anyone, and the title of the film is positioned more as a declaration than a piece of promotional information), the ad and this question in particular bring to mind the nightmares of segregation, Trumpism, immigration reform, urban housing crises, conflicted municipalities, encroaching corporate and state powers, and entrenched community distrust. These real-world sociopolitical issues were made especially visible during the "Do You Belong?" campaign's run in Los Angeles, where the billboards became associated with an ongoing community debate about housing development in minority neighborhoods.

---

3. McRoy, "'Parts,'" 192.

FIGURE 9. Advertisement for *Get Out*. Reprinted with permission of Daily Billboard Blog.

Ultimately, a focus on *Get Out*'s paratextual fluidity, in concert with horror's own potentially unbounded, fragmentary, and defamiliarizing nature, can lead to a better understanding of the ways *Get Out* and its promotional materials want both to unsettle our previously held understandings about a "postracial" America and shock us by exposing the horrors of racism, inequality, and border establishment that permeate everyday life. Looking toward the specificity of Los Angeles and the "Do You Belong?" campaign as but one example, I argue that issues of textual malleability force us to consider where paratextual, horror-tinged experiences situate themselves and spill out into public life, and how the public and the local impact the reception, usage, and even resistance of such texts. *Get Out*'s focus on vulnerability and its varied paratextual existence across hypermediated and deeply contested public spaces do more than foster a dialogue (between people, places, and other outdoor media) and point to and unearth already present fears and unease. They also complicate the very terms of *vulnerability*, using notions of instability and boundlessness not just to emphasize the devaluing and destruction of black bodies but also to consider bodies and spaces in more positive, energizing ways—as always unfixed, engaged in negotiation, and resistant to forces that seek to dominate, divide, and displace.

The Sunken Place in Paratextual Form

Jay McRoy argues that horror often engenders fear "by exploiting the all-too-human trepidation over the potential loss of physiological integrity."[4] Indeed, bodily breakdown and excess is on full display in promotional materials that utilize Chris's crying eyes and tear-stained face, a now iconic image prominently found across trailers, billboards, promotional stills, movie reviews, home video packaging, film magazine covers, and memes. Showing his mouth agape and eyes shockingly wide, bloodshot, and overflowing with tears, the image and its minor variations (some showing a more intense scream) are taken from a pivotal moment in the film in which Chris is hypnotized by his girlfriend's mother, Missy. This launches him into a surreal and frightening state known as the sunken place, where control over his own body vanishes. Acting as a metaphor for slavery and other insidious forms of corporeal regulation and dehumanization, the moment as rendered into a promotional still traps Chris in this state; the sunken place exists wherever the image does—a never-ending nightmare mapped onto a myriad of public and private spaces. Additionally, the isolated, frozen image locks viewers into his gaze, forcing a confrontation with not only his vulnerability but also our own potential culpability in the cultural and political systems that offered his body to be consumed by such horrors in the first place.

Artistic renderings of the sunken place are not just central to official marketing materials but to other professional and fan-made works that embrace, interpret, and ultimately contribute to the worldview and world-building of *Get Out*. In March 2017, select works (many of them culled from Instagram) were featured in an online gallery hosted by Universal;[5] this gallery later expanded and moved into physical space when in November 2017 Peele, Universal, and Blumhouse hosted an exhibition and screening event at the Lombardi House in Hollywood (a victory lap of sorts for the creative team, as awards season buzz had started to grow more intense).[6] Featuring print, paintings, and multimedia installations, many works used the sunken place and images of Chris's face as jumping-off points to think critically about broad issues of racial tension and political division in America. One striking video installation featured a digital rendering of Chris's terrified visage, slowly bursting apart into fragments of text taken from popular press praise

4. Ibid., 196.
5. Frank, "Bunch of Artists."
6. Ellwood, "Jordan Peele."

of and commentary on the film; words like *racism, together, lies, lampoon, frightening, framed, American,* and *thieves* collided with and drifted away from one another and, in doing so, seemed more like a patchwork of current news headlines than film reviews.

Interviewed at the Lombardi House event for the *Get Out*-inspired work, Peele commented on the way that "Daniel's face seems to be resonating" with people, perhaps because "the image of a black man being vulnerable, being scared, we don't get to see that. Black men don't get to be vulnerable things. We're either the tough drug dealer or we're the president of the United States."[7] As a specific portrait of black male vulnerability, the image as widespread promotional work inserts itself in a hypervisible way into public life and forcefully calls upon its audience to *feel something*—whether that be shock, discomfort, empathy, or a rush of all three. While such affective experiences can of course be mobilized and rerouted into further systems of promotion and consumption, the intent of the ads extends beyond mere marketing buzz. Rather, the use of Chris's face in promotional materials unsettles what it means to engage with and consume the black body as pop cultural image, exploding spectatorial assumptions of either extreme black strength or deviance to show black male experience as far richer and more emotional. The public display of the image (from DVD cases to the sides of massive office buildings) creates sites where everyday experience can be shaken up and where the image of black male vulnerability can potentially (hopefully) resonate in confrontational and deeply moving ways.

Echoing Peele, author Daren W. Jackson explains that there has long existed a historically transmitted set of rules and regulations that "both govern and exalt black manhood."[8] In his memoir *Invisible Man, Got the Whole World Watching: A Young Black Man's Education,* Mychal Denzel Smith details these unwritten rules: "Teach him to suppress, teach him to be unfeeling, teach him to lead without asking, teach him solitude, teach him not to cope, teach him to explode. All in the name of maintaining the myth."[9] While of course Chris's affective response in this image is one derived from horrific coercion, not some profound personal challenge to the myths of black manhood, there is still something about it that, in isolation from the film proper, accrues new representational powers. Taken as an image featured across the paratextual network, it morphs into a symbol of horrors and repressed feelings suddenly unbound from social norms. The more the image gets repeated and circulated across mediated space, the more it seems not only

7. Washington and Porreca, "Jordan Peele."
8. Jackson, "Black Vulnerability."
9. Ibid.

to want to confront us with such vulnerability but also to ask of its viewers: why are you not weeping as well? Indeed, Peele seems to support this type of shared experience; as he mentioned at the 2017 Film Independent Forum, "By the middle—or even earlier in the film—everyone is Chris," he writes. "Everyone is looking through the same set of eyes."[10] Extending this idea, the online art gallery was accompanied by this quote from Peele: "Art is the one tool we have against the true horrors of the world. I hope that *Get Out* is an inclusive experience that inspires people to just talk."[11] The paratextual materials for the film seem invested in participating in such conversations, confronting us out in the real world with subversions of myths of postracial harmony that, in turn, provide us with a different visual language for thinking and talking about both black male vulnerability and how the horrors of racism and intolerance in America get insidiously woven into banal, everyday practices.

Belonging, Borders, and Political Horrors

While promotional materials drawing from the sunken place are quite explicit in their references to the world of the film, the aforementioned "Do You Belong in This Neighborhood?" ad campaign is far more vague, relying solely on bold white text and a slightly blurred, cracked image of a quaint row of suburban homes. In this way, the image opens itself up for interpretation, functioning as a site for different and potentially clashing approaches to and conversations about precarity. Though not totally abandoning the specificity of the black male experience so central to the film and its paratexts, the ambiguity of the question at the heart of the ad (which appears intent on making the potential respondent—or in this case, the *accused*, the *suspect*—doubt their belonging within what seems like a supposedly shared space) allows room for themes of Trumpism, immigration, housing reform, and broader racial tension.[12] In many ways, this is not simply the "Do You Belong?" campaign's doing; connections to political matters have been a defining feature of *Get Out*'s paratextual world. Peele has frequently

10. Ramos, "*Get Out*."

11. Frank, "Bunch of Artists."

12. *The Collins English Dictionary* defines Trumpism as either "the policies advocated by Donald Trump, especially those involving a rejection of the current political establishment and the vigorous pursuit of American national interests," or "a controversial or outrageous statement attributed to Donald Trump," https://www.collinsdictionary.com/us/dictionary/english/trumpism.

tweeted out images from news reports of Donald Trump speaking with or whispering to black celebrities and politicians, most notably Tiger Woods[13] and the US Department of Housing and Urban Development (HUD) Secretary Ben Carson,[14] with the same caption: "Now You're in the Sunken Place." Extending the same joke, comedy website Funny or Die released a politically charged parody trailer for the film, titled "Get Out (of the White House),"[15] which re-edits the original trailer to replace Chris's girlfriend Rose with news footage of Ivanka Trump, imagining their relationship as a front for the Trump family's nefarious, racist motives—most specifically his plan for a border wall between the US and Mexico.

The idea and image of the border wall in fact heavily permeated discourse about the "Do You Belong?" campaign. In February 2017, horror genre and pop culture blogger Hunter Bush (@Dr_H_Bus) tweeted out a photograph of two movie posters he saw sharing a wall inside a Philadelphia subway station.[16] On the left was the "Do You Belong?" poster. Directly to its right was an ad for Zhang Yimou's *The Great Wall*, a CGI-filled action spectacle that finds star Matt Damon battling ancient monsters in tenth-century China. Whereas *Get Out* was being discussed as a work of brutal racial honesty, sensitivity, and inclusivity that could break down barriers within both the horror genre and the film industry writ large, *The Great Wall* was looked at as yet another tired and insensitive case of Hollywood whitewashing.[17] Taken together, the disparities between both the posters and the films they represented seemed to capture not only the racial barriers that actively structure the media industries but also the concepts of borders and human illegality, so prevalent across our political landscape. To be clear, Hunter's tweet of the photograph didn't make mention of any of this. There is no elucidation of the political implications of the posters, either on their own or in collision with one another. Instead, he winkingly captioned the photo in brief: "Matt Damon starring in *The Great Wall* juxtaposed with 'Do you belong in this neighborhood?' *Get Out* posters. It's too perfect."[18] Clearly, he sees this juxtaposition as meaningful and quite obvious; the vagueness and joking tone of the tweet seems to indicate that anyone reading it and

13. Rogo, "Jordan Peele."

14. Butler, "*Get Out.*"

15. Funny or Die, "Get Out."

16. Hunter Bush (@Dr_H_Bus), Twitter post, February 16, 2017, https://twitter.com/Dr_H_ Bus/status/832288277973626881.

17. Sims, "What Is."

18. Hunter Bush (@Dr_H_Bus), Twitter post, February 16, 2017, https://twitter.com/Dr_H_ Bus/status/832288277973626881.

seeing the images in question would automatically get how both ads seem to overtly link to (and, perhaps indirectly, speak to each other about) Trump's proposed border wall.

In this particular case, the "Do You Belong?" art for *Get Out* became textually intertwined with another form of Hollywood promotional media, with both texts being used in tandem to point to the horrors of Trumpism's approach to border security. Significantly, the billboard campaign was able to do this without such overt pop cultural juxtapositions; as one contributor to an online media and gaming forum put it, after encountering the ad as an outdoor billboard,

> I was driving around Eagle Rock, LA yesterday when I saw this. Even knowing about Jordan Peele's new film, "Get Out," it took me a second to realize it was an ad for this. It nails the crux of what the film seems to be about (race relations, inclusion, the "other," etc.) and definitely made me uneasy for the couple of seconds it took me to realize it was an ad.[19]

The first response to this post on the forum was blunt in linking the promotional signage to the concurrent political moment: "Could've been a Trump Campaign slogan." The textual world of *Get Out* here becomes a part of the political and cultural lexicon, a collection of images, sounds, and catchphrases to draw from when searching for ways to express a range of political feelings, from discomfort in the face of everyday intolerance to radical opposition in the face of institutionalized racism—often with a dose of dark humor that allows memes, parodies, and social media posts to become more palatable, relatable, and digitally spreadable.

The "Do You Belong?" billboard becomes perhaps an even more fascinating object when considered in terms of more local spatial contexts, where the *neighborhood* in question actually gets defined. Specifically, its presence in Los Angeles quickly fostered connections to ongoing battles over gentrification, housing reform, and building development. In this case, the billboard's question of belonging became mapped onto similar questions being asked within LA about who gets to belong in and shape certain neighborhoods across the city. As Anne M. Cronin has argued, "Advertising texts and structures are woven into the fabric of the city—and indeed into the very history of cities. And histories get re-inscribed and re-spatialized in regenerated urban areas where history is offered back to the public as images (now

19. starchild excalibur, "Can We Stop."

FIGURE 10. Advertisement for *Get Out* adjacent to political billboard in Los Angeles. Reprinted with permission of photographer Robin Bennett Stein.

detached from the original invitation to buy a product)."[20] In 2017, the "Do You Belong?" billboard found itself overlapping with such local histories and concerns in Los Angeles, as it was prominently displayed next to another billboard, a piece of political signage asking residents to vote "Yes on S: Save Our Neighborhoods March 7th" (see figure 10). Initially introduced in 2016 as the Neighborhood Integrity Initiative, Measure S was the product of a concerted effort of Los Angeles residents, activists, and politicians to place a two-year moratorium on the development and construction of new building projects throughout the city. While those against Measure S touted proposed developments as essential to solving LA's housing needs and aiding its growth as a "smart," technologically advanced city, those in support of Measure S saw such developments as "deleterious to the local quality of life, increasing traffic, blocking views and, in addition, crushing existing affordable and rent-controlled dwellings to make way for new market-rate or luxury apartments."[21] For those advocating for "Yes on S," "smart devel-

20. Cronin, "Publics," 272.
21. Anderton and Artsy, "Measure S."

opment" was a dirty phrase, a sly code for the displacement of vulnerable populations and the erasure of local communities and architecture.

In this particular case, questions of *belonging* relate to being given or denied access to a particular place—from the white familial spaces of privilege at the heart of *Get Out* to the space of the nation supposedly safeguarded by Trumpism from immigrant and refugee populations. The discourse surrounding Measure S also points to how local populations suddenly feel unstable and expendable within the very communities they have helped to build. Beyond the fact of access, the juxtaposition of the two billboards brings to mind a denial of the ability of people to have a say in how their communities both maintain themselves and continue to grow. This juxtaposition was not lost on those creating media for and about the debates surrounding Measure S. Photographs of the billboards quickly found themselves attached to articles, campaign sites, and politically inclined blogs commenting on the Yes on S movement, including the site of BLAction365, a self-described "Network of Black Nationalists, Pan Africanists & Revolutionary Nationalists committed to the L!beration & Advancement of the Oppressed Peoples of the World!"[22] In part, the group seems dedicated to addressing, battling, and ultimately ending the vulnerability that seems to define much of the black experience in cities like Los Angeles, where daily life is marked by the exploitation, surveillance, mistreatment, and execution of black and brown bodies. Used in a blog post about putting an end to gentrification in Los Angeles, a low-resolution image of the "Do You Belong?" billboard is accompanied by the following text, reproduced here in the fully capitalized form seen on the BLAction365 site:

> WE HAVE BEEN DENIED & CONNED OUT OF OUR RIGHTFUL SHARE OF LAND & RESOURCES FOR TOO LONG [. . .] WE DO NOT OWE ANYTHING FOR THE LAND & RESOURCES WHICH ARE NECESSARY TO SURVIVE [. . .] THE SOURCE OF OUR PHYSICAL MENTAL EMOTIONAL & SPIRITUAL INSTABILITY IS WE HAVE CONSISTENTLY BEEN DENIED & DISPLACED [. . .] LAND & RESOURCES ARE PAST DUE & OUTSTANDING DEBTS OWED TO US [. . .] WE MUST ABSTAIN FROM ANY FURTHER PARTICIPATION IN THE MONTHLY ROBBIN OF OUR FINANCIAL WEALTH BY MEANS OF RENT LEASES MORTGAGES BILLS FINES FEES INTERESTS ETC [. . .] #GentrifierBAN[23]

22. "About Us," BLAction365.
23. "Tuesdays," BLAction365.

It is difficult to tell if the image of the billboard (which is presented without any information regarding the film) is being understood in connection with the above text as a piece of promotional work that aligns with BLAction365's mission or as a piece of antagonistic political signage intended to do more harm to minority communities. Indeed, as a billboard placed high above buildings and complicated by other surrounding media and architecture, the fine print that marks it as a film—mention of Jordan Peele as director and a February 24 release date—might be difficult for passersby to make out. In a way, such confusion seems to be an unavoidable (if not overtly intentional) byproduct of the ad campaign, as the above blog post once again points to instability as a key organizing principle and political concern that can be linked to *Get Out*'s paratextual world. A billboard like the one for the film's "Do You Belong?" campaign works to highlight the vulnerabilities (of spaces, of bodies) already in place within society writ large. In so doing, it becomes a text ripe for usage by individuals and groups looking to articulate the problems they experience in everyday life (from economic inequality to police brutality), problems that *Get Out* weaves and condenses into its fictive horror narrative.

While the billboard was clearly able both to attach itself to and put into relief already existing tensions across Los Angeles, its immediate political powers only extended so far. In March 2017, Measure S failed at the ballot. According to the *LA Times*, opponents of Measure S—"including labor unions, business groups and Mayor Eric Garcetti—warned it could eliminate jobs and exacerbate the housing crisis, throwing the city into economic turmoil."[24] Ultimately, such perspectives and warnings convinced two-thirds of Los Angeles residents to vote against the measure. For some, the "Do You Belong?" billboard even helped their case; as the aforementioned KCRW piece detailed, the billboard's question of belonging and declaration to "get out" appeared to "stand in for the perceived NIMBYism [Not in My Backyard] of the Yes on S movement, the sense that Angelenos who owned their homes and had lived here a while did not want to let in newcomers."[25] In this way, the message of the *Get Out* ad campaign was perversely reworked, its question of belonging understood as applicable to fears of property developers, capitalist expansion, and urban reinvention as much as it was to fears of bodies and communities of color. Arguably, it seems somewhat of a stretch to view either Measure S or the "Do You Belong?" billboard as symbols *for* isolation and intolerance. Measure S was, among many causes,

24. Reyes, Poston, and Zahniser, "Measure S."
25. Anderton and Artsy, "Measure S."

an attempt to rally against the eviction of Koreatown residents from their homes, whose owners wanted to transform them into luxury hotels and massive residential towers[26]—the "newcomers" those against the measure seemed so eager to protect. However, as much as it can be cited as enabling more politically liberal or radical interpretations and usages, the "Do You Belong?" campaign's ambiguity also lends itself to interpretations that clash with *Get Out*'s own understandings of instability and vulnerability, allowing—for better or worse—specific fears, aversions, and misunderstandings to bubble to the surface.

In the case of the "Do You Belong in This Neighborhood?" billboard's contested presence in Los Angeles, a text intended to advertise *Get Out* got detached from its intended purpose and woven into locally specific political discourse—even if some of that discourse seems to be in contrast to everything the film, its creators, and its supporters stand for. Such tensions in meaning-making make sense, however. As Cronin points out, if "outdoor advertising attempts a kind of 'call and response' engagement with people, it is a dialogue that is often resisted, ignored or reworked. The grammar of desire and ownership marked on spaces by advertising is one which is fractured by the everyday messiness of people's visual and material encounters."[27] In many ways, this seems like the point of the "Do You Belong?" key art. Its vague and yet blunt message seems intentionally designed to fit all too neatly into a host of sociopolitical negotiations and clashes across physical and virtual space. The fact that it might even be mistaken for an *actual* political attack ad—from a Trump campaign slogan to a Los Angeles–specific ad advocating for the forceful dismantling of neighborhoods and devaluing of nonwhite bodies—is perhaps *more horrific* than any fictions the horror genre or Hollywood more generally can muster. After all, the billboard critiques prevailing power structures by fashioning itself in the form of the very rhetoric and visual iconography often associated with such forms of power, be they at the national or local level. It is a risky move; confusion over the political intentions of the billboard could lead to more anxiety for local residents, not to mention negative marketing for the film, which could complicate its political and cultural objectives.

Despite examples like the defeat of Measure S, however, it seems that *Get Out*'s promotional paratexts, as experienced in person and as captured, spread, commented on, and parodied in physical and digital contexts, have offered the possibility for marginalized groups to find in them a continuously renewable and circulating source of political support and solidarity.

26. Anderton, "Does Luxury Housing."

27. Cronin, "Publics," 275.

This might not mean immediate change—*Get Out*, like the Obama presidency Peele used as inspiration for the film, has not magically created a postracial America. Yet, like the film itself, the paratexts of *Get Out*—from images of billboards to political blogs and social media memes about the sunken place—can still function as tools able to unearth, understand, and systematically eradicate the racist ideologies and practices that so persistently haunt, destabilize, and terrorize.

Bibliography

"About Us." *BLAction365*, http://www.blaction365.com/.

Anderton, Frances. "Does Luxury Housing Trickle Down to Affordable Apartments?" *Design and Architecture*. Podcast MP3 audio, March 8, 2016. https://www.kcrw.com/news-culture/shows/design-and-architecture /does-luxury-housing-trickle-down-to-affordable-apartments.

Anderton, Frances, and Avishay Artsy. "Measure S was Defeated. Now What?" *KCRW*, March 8, 2017. http://blogs.kcrw.com/dna/measure-s-defeated-now.

Butler, Bethonie. "*Get Out* Is Inspiring Some Pretty Great Memes." *Washington Post*, March 10, 2017. https://www.washingtonpost.com/news/arts-and-entertainment/wp/ 2017/03/10/get-out-is-inspiring-some-pretty-great-memes/?utm_term=.85e8098ca27d.

Cronin, Anne M. "Publics and Publicity: Outdoor Advertising and Urban Space." In *Public Space, Media Space*, edited by Chris Berry, Janet Harbord, and Rachel Moore, 265–76. New York: Palgrave, 2013.

Ellwood, Gregory. "Jordan Peele and Universal Celebrate Art of *Get Out* as Oscar Awaits." *Playlist*, November 18, 2017. https://theplaylist.net/jordan-peele-universal-celebrate-art-get-oscar-awaits-20171118/.

Frank, Priscilla. "A Bunch of Artists Made Absolutely Chilling Images Inspired by *Get Out*." *Huffington Post*, March 14, 2017. https://www.huffingtonpost.com/entry/get-out-movie-fan-art_us_58c81ef7e4b0598c669a1605.

Funny or Die. "Get Out (Of the White House)." YouTube Video, March 6, 2017. https://www.youtube.com/watch?v=TllKdcjgJCI.

Gray, Jonathan. *Show Sold Separately*. New York: New York University Press, 2010.

Jackson, Daren W. "Black Vulnerability." *Chicago Tribune*, July 10, 2016. http://digitaledition.chicagotribune.com/tribune/article_popover.aspx?guid=08730a87-284f-4de7-88f4-ab6ede8ab038.

McRoy, Jay. "'Parts is Parts': Pornography, Splatter Films and the Politics of Corporeal Disintegration." In *Horror Zone: The Cultural Experience of Contemporary Horror Cinema*, edited by Ian Conrich, 191–204. New York: I. B. Tauris, 2010.

Ramos, Dino-Ray. "*Get Out* Director Jordan Peele on Divisiveness, Black Identity & the 'White Savior.'" *Deadline*, October 22, 2017. http://deadline.com/2017/10/jordan-peele-get-out-film-independent-forum-keynote-speaker-diversity-inclusion-1202192699/.

Reyes, Emily Alpert, Ben Poston, and David Zahniser. "Measure S Defeated after a Heated, Costly Battle." *LA Times*, March 8, 2017. http://www.latimes.com/local/lanow/la-me-ln-measure-s-20170307-story.html.

Rogo, Paula. "Jordan Peele Calls Out Tiger Woods for Playing Golf with Trump: 'Now You're in the Sunken Place.'" *Essence*, November 27, 2017. https://www.essence.com/celebrity/jordan-peele-tiger-woods-golf-trump-sunken-place/.

Sims, David. "What Is Matt Damon Doing on Top of *The Great Wall*?" *Atlantic*, August 2, 2016. https://www.theatlantic.com/entertainment/archive/2016/08/what-is-matt-damon-doing-on-top-of-the-great-wall/494090/.

starchild excalibur. "Can We Stop to Appreciate the *Get Out* Billboard?" Off-Topic Discussion Forum, *NeoGAF*, February 16, 2017. https://www.neogaf.com/threads/can-we-stop-to-appreciate-the-get-out-billboard.1344754/.

"Tuesdays—End Gentrification 3–28–17." *BLAction365*, March 28, 2017. http://www.blaction365.com/bpa2017-daily-reports/tuesdays-end-gentrification-3-28-17/.

Washington, Arlene, and Brian Porreca. "Jordan Peele and *Get Out* Team Celebrate Fan-Inspired Art." *Hollywood Reporter*, November 18, 2017. https://www.hollywoodreporter.com/news/jordan-peele-get-team-celebrate-fan-inspired-art-1059794.

CAST

CHARACTER	ACTOR
Chris Washington	Daniel Kaluuya
Rod Williams	Lil Rel Howery
Rose Armitage	Allison Williams
Missy Armitage	Catherine Keener
Dean Armitage	Bradley Whitford
Jeremy Armitage	Caleb Landry Jones
Walter	Marcus Henderson
Georgina	Betty Gabriel
Andre / Logan King	LaKeith Stanfield
Jim Hudson	Stephen Root
Hiroki Tanaka	Yasuhiko Oyama
Roman Armitage	Richard Herd
Philomena King	Geraldine Singer
Detective Latoya	Erika Alexander
Detective Drake	Jeronimo Spinx
Officer Ryan	Trey Burvant

CONTRIBUTORS

LINNIE BLAKE is head of the Manchester Centre for Gothic Studies at Manchester Metropolitan University, UK, where she is reader in Gothic film and literature and Pathway Leader for the MA English Studies: The Gothic. She is a member of the editorial boards of the journals *Gothic Studies* and *Horror Studies* and the University of Wales's Horror Studies Series. She has published widely on film, televisual, and literary texts of a dark persuasion, focusing on the political dimensions of such texts. She is author of *The Wounds of Nations: Horror Cinema, Historical Trauma and National Identity* (Manchester University Press, 2008). Her most recent book, coedited with Agnieszka Soltysik-Monnet, is *Neoliberal Gothic: International Gothic in the Neoliberal Age* (Manchester University Press, 2017).

KYLE BRETT is a PhD candidate at Lehigh University, studying nineteenth-century American literature and Transatlantic Romanticism. His dissertation focuses on sentimental writers' engagement in the nineteenth-century literary market. His other critical interests are predominately centered on American horror in relationship to traditional Gothic conventions and Lovecraftian mythos.

DAVID L. BRUNSMA is professor of Sociology at Virginia Tech. He is founding coeditor of *Sociology of Race and Ethnicity*, the official journal of the Section of Racial and Ethnic Minorities of the American Sociological Association, and coeditor of numerous books on social institutions, race, and human rights, among them *Movements for Human Rights: Locally and Globally* (Routledge, 2016), *Institutions Unbound: The Role of Social Institutions in Human Rights* (Routledge, 2015), and *The Sociology of Katrina: Perspectives on a Modern Catastrophe* (Rowman and Littlefield, 2007). His research currently centers on racial identity, white opportunity hoarding, and race and cultural consumption.

JONATHAN BYRON has taught English and American literature for the last twelve years at Oakdale High School in California, where he was a 2015–2016 nominee for Stanislaus County Teacher of the Year. In his ever-present quest to engage the minds of high school students, he has developed his own course in film form and critical theory, focusing on literary conventions present in classic and modern cinema. He has recently completed his graduate studies in English at California State University, Stanislaus, where he was awarded a Graduate Equity Fellowship. Most recently, his research on the use of poison in Christopher Marlowe's Renaissance dramas advanced him to the state finals of the California State University Student Research Competition.

ERIN CASEY-WILLIAMS is assistant professor of English and chair of the Humanities and Gender and Diversity Studies programs at Nichols College, a small business college in Dudley, Massachusetts. Her scholarly interests include zombies, superheroes, and popular culture, as well as early modern literature. She is currently working on a manuscript focused on seventeenth-century women's writing, specifically how such marginalized figures discuss sovereignty; her project examines what these texts can elucidate about modern theories of bodily control, gender, and biopolitics.

ROBYN CITIZEN, PhD, is the international programmer for the Short Cuts program at the Toronto International Film Festival and a programmer for the Human Rights Film Festival. She was a lecturer in the departments of Asian Studies and Theatre and Film at the University of British Columbia from 2012 to 2017. Her primary research interests involve the circulation of representations of race, ethnicity and national identity, and the horror/science fiction genres. She has published "Are Black Women the Future of Man?" in *The Liverpool Companion to World Science Fiction Film* (Liverpool University Press, 2014) as well as other essays in edited collections and online and print film journals, and she has presented her research at numerous conferences.

MIKAL J. GAINES, PhD, is assistant professor of English at Massachusetts College of Pharmacy and Health Sciences University in Boston, MA. He is the author of "Strange Enjoyments: The Marketing and Reception of Horror in the Civil Rights Era Black Press" in *Merchants of Menace: The Business of Horror Cinema* (Bloomsbury Academic, 2014) and "Spike's Blues: Re-imagining Blues Ideology for the Cinema," in *Fight the Power: The Spike Lee Reader* (Peter Lang, 2008). His article, "They Are Still Here: Possession and Dispossession in the 21st Century Haunted House Film" will appear in *The Spaces and Places of Horror* (Vernon, 2020). His research areas include Africana Studies, American Film, Literature, Popular Culture, Horror and Gothic Studies, and Critical Theory.

SARAH ILOTT is senior lecturer in English and Film at Manchester Metropolitan University, UK. Her main research and teaching interests are in postcolonial literature and genre fiction, particularly comedy and the gothic. Her publications include *New Postcolonial British Genres: Shifting the Boundaries* (Palgrave, 2015), *Telling it Slant: Critical Approaches to Helen Oyeyemi* (coedited with Chloe Buckley; Sussex Academic Press, 2017), *New Directions in Diaspora Studies* (coedited with Ana Cristina Mendes and Lucinda Newns; Rowman and Littlefield, 2018), and *Comedy and the Politics of Representation: Mocking the Weak* (coedited with Helen Davies; Palgrave, 2018). She has published multiple journal articles, including in *The Journal of Commonwealth Literature, The Journal of Postcolonial Writing,* and *Postcolonial Text,* as well as book chapters on subjects ranging from "Gothic Immigrations" to "Subcultural Fiction and the Market for Multiculturalism." Her current research project focuses on the shifting representations of British multiculturalism in screen comedy from the 1960s to the present.

DAWN KEETLEY is professor of English, teaching horror/gothic literature, film, and television at Lehigh University in Bethlehem, PA. She has most recently published in *Journal of Popular Culture, Horror Studies, Journal of the Fantastic in the Arts, Journal of Popular Television, Journal of Film and Video,* and *Gothic Studies.* She is editor of *We're All Infected: Essays on AMC's* The Walking Dead *and the Fate of the Human* (McFarland, 2014) and coeditor (with Elizabeth Erwin) of *The Politics of Race, Gender and Sexuality in* The Walking Dead (McFarland, 2018). She has also coedited (with Angela Tenga) *Plant Horror: Approaches to the Monstrous Vegetal in Fiction and Film* (Palgrave, 2016) and (with Matthew Wynn Sivils) *The Ecogothic in Nineteenth-century American Literature* (Routledge, 2017). Her monograph, *Making a Monster: Jesse Pomeroy, the Boy Murderer of 1870s Boston,* was published by the University of Massachusetts Press in 2017. Keetley is working on essays on ecohorror and on the contemporary horror film as well as a monograph on folk horror. She writes regularly for a horror website she cocreated, www.HorrorHomeroom.com.

ROBERT LARUE is assistant professor of English at Moravian College. His work addresses the intersections of sexual, racial, gendered, and (inter) national difference, with a particular interest in articulating the need for these various differences and their various manifestations to have spaces of their own, and on their own terms. His most recent writing projects take up Martin Luther King Jr., Monica Arac de Nyeko's "Jambula Tree," and the television show *Empire.*

SARAH JULIET LAURO is assistant professor of Hemispheric Literature at the University of Tampa. She is the author and editor of many works that address the figure of the living dead zombie in literature and film, including the article "A Zombie Manifesto" in *boundary 2* (2008), the book *The Transatlantic Zombie: Slavery, Rebellion, and Living Death* (Rutgers University Press, 2015), and the collection *Zombie Theory: A Reader* (University of Minnesota Press, 2017). Her next book project turns from zombies as a figuration of slavery and slave revolt, which is her central interest in the monster, to commemorations of slave rebellion in literature, art, film, and digital culture.

NOVOTNY LAWRENCE earned his PhD from the University of Kansas in Theater and Film (now the Department of Cinema and Media Studies). He is currently an Associate Professor at Iowa State University where he is on a joint appointment between the Greenlee School of Journalism and Communication and the English Department. Dr. Lawrence teaches classes such as Media and Society, History of African American Images in Film, and Qualitative Research Methods. His research primarily centers on African American film and mediated experiences and popular culture. Dr. Lawrence is the author of *Blaxploitation Films of the 1970s: Blackness and Genre* (Routledge, 2007), the editor of *Documenting the Black Experience* (McFarland, 2014), and the coeditor of *Beyond Blaxploitation* (Wayne State University Press, 2016). He has also published journal articles/book chapters on *Black Dynamite,* the comedy of Dave Chappelle, *C.S.A.: The Confederate States of America,* and *The Jeffersons.*

ADAM LOWENSTEIN is professor of English and Film/Media Studies at the University of Pittsburgh. He is the author of *Dreaming of Cinema: Spectatorship, Surrealism, and the Age of Digital Media* (Columbia University Press, 2015) and *Shocking Representation: Historical Trauma, National Cinema, and the Modern Horror Film* (Columbia University Press, 2005). His essays on topics including Alfred Hitchcock, Japanese cinema, the art film, David Cronenberg, and Ben Wheatley have appeared in *Cinema Journal, Representations, Film Quarterly, Critical Quarterly, boundary 2, Discourse,* and numerous anthologies. He has been interviewed on issues of cinema and culture in the *New York Times,* the *Village Voice,* and in Adam Simon's documentary *The American Nightmare.* He is also a board member of the George A. Romero Foundation.

CAYLA McNALLY is a Philadelphia-based writer examining the intersection of academia, social justice, and pop culture. A graduate of Bryn Mawr College and Lehigh University, she is particularly interested in Otherness, contamination, and monstrosity. Her website is caylamcnally.com.

ROBIN R. MEANS COLEMAN is Vice President and Associate Provost for Diversity and a professor in the Department of Communication at Texas A&M University. A nationally prominent and award-winning professor of communication and African American studies, Dr. Coleman's scholarship focuses on media studies and the cultural politics of Blackness. Dr. Coleman is the author of *Horror Noire: Blacks in American Horror Films from the*

1890s to Present (Routledge, 2011) and *African-American Viewers and the Black Situation Comedy: Situating Racial Humor* (Routledge, 2000). She is coauthor of *Intercultural Communication for Everyday Life* (Wiley-Blackwell, 2014), the editor of *Say It Loud! African American Audiences, Media, and Identity* (Routledge, 2002), and coeditor of *Fight the Power! The Spike Lee Reader* (Peter Lang, 2008). She has also written a number of other academic and popular publications. Her research and commentary have been featured in a variety of international and national media outlets, including the critically acclaimed documentary film *Horror Noire* (2019). Her current research focuses on the NAACP's participation in media activism.

BERNICE M. MURPHY is lecturer in Popular Literature in the School of English, Trinity College, Dublin. She has published extensively on topics related to horror fiction and film. Her books include *The Suburban Gothic in American Popular Culture* (Palgrave, 2009), *The Rural Gothic: Backwoods Horror and Terror in the Wilderness* (Palgrave, 2013), *The Highway Horror Film* (Palgrave Pivot, 2014), and (edited with Elizabeth McCarthy) *Lost Souls of Horror and the Gothic* (McFarland, 2017). She is the cofounder of the online *Irish Journal of Gothic and Horror Studies* and is a founding member of the Irish Network for Gothic Studies (INGS). Her current work-in-progress is a monograph entitled *California Gothic*. She was made a Fellow of TCD in 2017.

TONY PERRELLO is professor of English at California State University, Stanislaus. He has taught Renaissance and medieval literature for over twenty years. He regularly teaches a seminar, Horror in Literature and Film, and has published several essays on issues related to the medieval and early modern periods, including his own discovery of a previously unnoticed macaronic riddle hidden in the margins of a medieval manuscript and an argument for a new historical source for the Gloucester subplot in Shakespeare's *King Lear*. He has also published in the fields of horror and film studies, authoring a chapter in Steffen Hantke's *American Horror Film: The Genre at the Turn of the Millennium* (University Press of Mississippi, 2010) and a chapter for the *Handbook to Horror Literature*, a collection of essays published by Palgrave Macmillan. He has delivered twenty-five conference presentations and has organized and chaired more than ten sessions of his own design.

TODD K. PLATTS is associate professor of Sociology at Piedmont Virginia Community College. He has published multiple journal articles and book chapters on the subjects of horror films and zombie films, including "The New Horror Film" in *Baby Boomers and Popular Culture* (Praeger, 2015) and the coauthored "Scary Business: Horror at the North American Box Office, 2006–2016" in *Frames Cinema Journal*. His current research focuses on slasher films and horror films of the 2010s.

ALEXANDER SVENSSON (formerly Swanson) earned his PhD in Indiana University Bloomington's Media School/Department of Communication and Culture. His research explores the intersections between horror and promotional culture, and examines contemporary experiential marketing gimmicks for horror content—often linked to digital networks—that configure shock as affective capital. His recent work can be found in *Participations: Journal of Audience & Reception Studies* and *Transformative Works and Cultures.*

LAURA THORP holds an MFA in Poetry from North Carolina State University and is currently a PhD candidate in the Department of English at the University of South Carolina. Her research focuses on American and African American Literature of the twentieth and twenty-first centuries with a particular emphasis on horror studies, psychoanalytic theory, affect theory, and their connections with race and gender in literature and film. Some of her recent work focuses on the intersection of psychoanalysis and affect theory in relation to horror and the function of time and Black temporality in horror films as well as the function of time and Otherness in Postcolonial literature. She works as an administrator at USC and as an adjunct instructor at Columbia College.

INDEX

NEW SUNS: RACE, GENDER, AND SEXUALITY IN THE SPECULATIVE

Susana M. Morris and Kinitra D. Brooks, Series Editors

Scholarly examinations of speculative fiction have been a burgeoning academic field for more than twenty-five years, but there has been a distinct lack of attention to how attending to nonhegemonic positionalities transforms our understanding of the speculative. New Suns: Race, Gender, and Sexuality in the Speculative addresses this oversight and promotes scholarship at the intersections of race, gender, sexuality, and the speculative, engaging interdisciplinary fields of research across literary, film, and cultural studies that examine multiple pasts, presents, and futures. Of particular interest are studies that offer new avenues into thinking about popular genre fictions and fan communities, including but not limited to the study of Afrofuturism, comics, ethnogothicism, ethnosurrealism, fantasy, film, futurity studies, gaming, horror, literature, science fiction, and visual studies. New Suns particularly encourages submissions that are written in a clear, accessible style that will be read both by scholars in the field as well as by nonspecialists.

Jordan Peele's Get Out: *Political Horror*
EDITED BY DAWN KEETLEY

Unstable Masks: Whiteness and American Superhero Comics
EDITED BY SEAN GUYNES AND MARTIN LUND

Afrofuturism Rising: The Literary Prehistory of a Movement
ISIAH LAVENDER III

The Paradox of Blackness in African American Vampire Fiction
JERRY RAFIKI JENKINS

CPSIA information can be obtained
at www.ICGtesting.com
Printed in the USA
LVHW090211130421
684247LV00001B/10

9 780814 214275